Praise for *America Against the World*

"A shrewd character analysis of the planet's remaining superpower"

—Bloomberg News

"A fascinating—and troubling—look at how the rest of the world views us."
—Booklist (starred review)

"If you've been wondering why the rest of the world often misunderstands, dislikes, and even fears the United States, this book offers compelling answers. Andrew Kohut, Bruce Stokes, and their colleagues have done impressive original research and produced truly arresting insights."
—Doyle McManus, Washington Bureau Chief, Los Angeles Times

"Provocative reading. . . . Americans like to think of themselves as the city on the hill. Could it be that others see just another suburb in the smog?"
—The Washington Times

"By holding up two mirrors—how we Americans look to ourselves and how we look to others—Andrew Kohut and Bruce Stokes hit us with a reality full of surprises, comforting and unsettling insights, and a full meal for policymakers and the rest of us to digest or pay the consequences. Very carefully and fairly analyzed, this is a truly important book."
—Leslie H. Gelb, president emeritus, Council on Foreign Relations

AMERICA AGAINST THE WORLD

AMERICA AGAINST THE WORLD

HOW WE ARE DIFFERENT
AND WHY WE ARE DISLIKED

ANDREW KOHUT

AND BRUCE STOKES

AN OWL BOOK

HENRY HOLT AND COMPANY | NEW YORK

Owl Books
Henry Holt and Company, LLC
Publishers since 1866
175 Fifth Avenue
New York, New York 10010
www.henryholt.com

Distributed in Canada by H. B. Fenn and Company Ltd.

Library of Congress Cataloging-in-Publication Data
Kohut, Andrew.
    America against the world : how we are different and why we are disliked /
Andrew Kohut and Bruce Stokes.—1st ed.
       p.   cm.
  ISBN-13: 978-0-8050-8305-7
  ISBN-10: 0-8050-8305-7
    1. National characteristics, American.   2. Values—United States.
3. Individualism—Political aspects—United States.   4. Anti-Americanism.
5. United States—Foreign public opinion.   6. United States—Foreign
relations—2001–   7. Great powers.   I. Stokes, Bruce.   II. Title.
E169.12.K59 2006
973.931—dc22   2005055979

Originally published in hardcover in 2006 by Times Books

First Owl Books Edition 2007

Designed by Victoria Hartman

Printed in the United States of America
1   3   5   7   9   10   8   6   4   2

CONTENTS

FOREWORD

TO A GIRL growing up when and where I did in Europe, America shimmered. It was both the embodiment of freedom and its most powerful defender. Americans in uniform had crossed two oceans to help save Europe and Asia from Fascism and imperialism. When Communists seized power in my native Czechoslovakia, I crossed the ocean myself, but in the opposite direction, steaming past the Statue of Liberty at the age of eleven with no other ambition than to become a true American.

I could not have imagined then or even a few years ago that I would one day write a foreword to a volume entitled *America Against the World: How We Are Different and Why We Are Disliked*. To me, and I think to many Americans, it seems as if the world has come loose from its moorings. The gap between how we see ourselves and how others see us has become a chasm, dangerously so. U.S. military and economic power notwithstanding, we cannot be secure without the respect, support, and yes, the affection, of people in other lands. We are losing that; indeed, we may have lost it—and not just here and there, but in many places, even among longtime friends. Why? And what can we do about it?

One approach is to see the problem as a giant misunderstanding. If only people knew that we are generally religious, love our children, are generous, and have high-minded goals, surely they would like us again.

A second approach is to blame the global media for distorting our intentions and misreporting our actions, creating a grotesque image of our country as imperialistic, uncaring, and violent. If only people knew the truth, they would see how good we are; but how do we ensure that?

A third strategy, more likely to succeed, begins with a serious analysis of what has caused people overseas to form the opinions they have, to probe deeply into the nature of those judgments and ask what it might take to soften them. The exhaustive and unprecedented surveys cited and analyzed in this invaluable book provide a platform for just such a strategy. Although the study can make for sometimes unpleasant reading, it is the starting point for an all-important job—restoring America's image and leadership around the globe.

One might ask: What can we really learn from polls? In my experience, the answer is quite a lot. From 1989 until 1991, I participated in an extensive survey sponsored by the Times Mirror Center for the People & the Press on attitudes toward democracy in the Soviet Union, then on the verge of its historic collapse. To summarize a vast work in a single sentence, we found enormous enthusiasm for democracy in the abstract and enormous ignorance about what that system of government would actually entail. In the subsequent decade, I drew on this information repeatedly as U.S. ambassador to the United Nations and secretary of state. The validity of the survey results was borne out in the struggles that the former Soviet republics experienced in trying to make a successful democratic transition.

Beyond the significance of its insights at the time, the project had two additional effects. First, the polling established benchmark measures of social, economic, and political values not only in Eastern and

Central Europe but also in many parts of the West. Second, it brought me into a close working relationship with the survey's director, Andrew Kohut. When I left government service in 2001, Andy and I teamed up again on an international poll, this time to study the emerging impact and likely consequences of globalization. That survey, which evolved into a multiyear project and broadened in scope in the wake of September 11, 2001, provides much of the data that inform this volume.

Looking to the future, it is hard to think of a more important topic than the relationship between the world's most powerful nation and its global neighbors. If that relationship is not understood properly, our leaders are unlikely to take the actions and pursue the policies that will garner international support. If America is unable to lead, a vacuum will be created that others will surely fill with consequences it is impossible to foresee. This book does not include a road map for restoring America's reputation or lifting it to new heights of international popularity. It does, however, include significant signposts that could, if heeded, begin to move us in the right direction. That is a big "if," just as this book is a large contribution to our understanding of America's place in the world.

—*Madeleine K. Albright*

INTRODUCTION: AMERICA'S IMAGE

IT IS FAIR to say that the Pew Research Center's Global Attitudes Project is the first and foremost chronicler of the rise of anti-Americanism around the world in the first decade of the twenty-first century. The findings of Pew's surveys have brought home to Americans and their leaders the challenge the United States faces in restoring America's image and its influence overseas. Much of the discontent that we have documented can be attributed to criticisms of U.S. policies, especially the war in Iraq. In addition, there is strong resentment and suspicion of America's unrivaled power in the post–Cold War world, as well as concerns that globalization is unduly strengthening U.S. cultural and economic influence.

We originally intended to write a book that would provide readers with in-depth insights into America's image problem, which we gained conducting 91,000 interviews in fifty nations and the Palestinian Authority from 2002 through 2005. But in the course of considering the roots and rise of anti-Americanism, we were struck by how little attention had been paid to the American public and whether it contributes to the problems people around the world have with the United States.

How different are American values and attitudes from those held by people in other countries? Is there an American way of thinking about things? In particular, are American values different in significant ways from those of Europeans, with whom many Americans share ancestry and who live at a comparable level of economic development? Where are the biggest attitudinal gaps between Americans and the rest of the world? Are these differences growing? How could that be in this age of globalization that some say is molding a common culture? Are some groups and regions of America—the Democratic-voting "blue states"—really closer to Europe in outlook and attitude than the rest of the country, that is, the Republican-voting "red states"?

And, most important, to the extent that these differences between Americans and other people exist, in what ways are they shaping the United States' image in the new century? Are the values and attitudes of the American public fueling much of the anti-Americanism in the world?

These questions became even more relevant after George W. Bush's reelection in 2004. Prior to that, overseas critics of the president found it easy to say their problem with America was really President Bush, not a considered judgment of the American people. But the results of the 2004 U.S. presidential election made that rationalization untenable. The November 4, 2004, page-one headline of the British tabloid *Daily Mirror* put it this way: "How can 59,054,087 people be so DUMB?"

A second question about the American character evolves out of the worldwide impact of American customs, products, and popular culture. There is so much America almost everywhere in the world: from a Starbucks inside Beijing's Forbidden City to rap beats in the popular music of every continent on the globe, the ubiquitous popularity of the cartoon character Bart Simpson, the global notoriety of Michael Jackson, and the infiltration of American idioms and expressions into every major language in the world. What is it about American culture and products that make them so attractive, yet at the same time raise such alarm about Americanization and the spread of American power?

So this is a book about Americans—how their attitudes and values differ from those of other publics and the way those differences affect the world's views of the United States. This is not a work of speculation, opinion, or theory. It relies principally on international survey data to address the issues. With international attitudes polarized on so many important matters today, such a book is timely and long overdue. But it is only now that it can be written. It is now that sufficient in-depth, multinational public opinion data has become available to approach the issues properly. The surveys are in part a beneficial by-product of globalization, which has created the capacity to do professional market research in many countries of the world.

At the same time, as a result of the spread of democracy, public opinion in all nations has come to play an increasingly salient role in shaping foreign policies. It is therefore of significant interest, if not concern, for the entire international community.

Unlike in many other parts of the world, polls and public opinion have been an integral part of American politics for decades. But it is only since the American defeat in Vietnam, which owed as much to the lack of public support at home as to events on the battlefields of Southeast Asia, that public opinion has been accorded a strong seat in foreign-policy decision-making councils. In the twenty-first century, this pattern is being extended throughout much of the world.

THE PEW GLOBAL ATTITUDES PROJECT

For this book, we rely heavily, though not exclusively, on survey data collected by the Pew Global Attitudes Project with which we have been associated from its beginnings. The project had its origins in the work of its predecessor organization, the Times Mirror Center for the People & the Press. In the summer of 1989, under the direction of Donald S. Kellermann, the newly formed center was preparing to study European public opinion in the run-up to the formation of the single European market. Within a few short months, however, the world was transformed by near cataclysmic events: the fall of the Berlin Wall, the ensuing collapse of the Soviet Union as a military power, and the demise of communism as an ideology. The Times Mirror Center survey was quickly reoriented to examine how the publics of the former Soviet empire as well as the people of Western Europe and the United States were coping with these extraordinary events.

Over the next two years, the Times Mirror team, including then-Professor Madeleine K. Albright, who served as an adviser on Soviet affairs, and Andrew Kohut, the survey director, conducted opinion polls and focus group interviews in seventeen nations across the breadth of Europe. The results uncovered the existing attitudes and values of the Russian, Ukrainian, and other peoples of Eastern and Central Europe. The findings anticipated difficulties in the coming transformation of their political and economic lives from communism to democracy and free-market capitalism. Released in September 1991, the results exposed the reemergence of ethnic hostilities that led to the subsequent breakup of Czechoslovakia, the huge adjustment gap between younger urban dwellers and the older and rural segments of former Soviet bloc societies, and the extent to which Russians would lag behind other peoples of the former Soviet empire in accepting democratic reforms and free-market principles.

Beyond the significance of its insights at the time, the project had two additional effects. First, the polling established benchmark measures of social, economic, and political values and attitudes across Europe and the United States. Second, by her own accounts, the survey's results importantly influenced and informed the thinking of Ms. Albright, first as ambassador to the United Nations and later as secretary of state. At the end of the Clinton administration, she and Kohut agreed to team up again on an international poll, this time to study the emerging impact and likely consequences of globalization. In the summer of 2001, the Pew Charitable Trusts gave the Pew Research Center a grant to conduct the largest international public opinion survey ever undertaken, one whose principal focus was on the ways that the peoples of the world's nations were coping with an increasingly interconnected planet where ideas, information, and products circulate and interact with extraordinary speed and ease.

On September 10, 2001, a Pew Global Attitudes study group, including the authors, met with Mark Malloch Brown, then administrator of the United Nations Development Program, to discuss in detail the objectives of the new survey. From an office overlooking U.N. headquarters with the New York skyline as a backdrop, we wondered aloud whether any conceivable event might radically change the world political landscape as had the fall of the Berlin Wall in 1989. Could anything supplant globalization as the top international issue in the foreseeable future? We agreed, after brief reflection, that no such cataclysmic change was on the horizon. Of course, we could not have been more wrong.

Literally overnight, on September 11, the terrorist attacks on the towers of the World Trade Center and the Pentagon changed the world as dramatically as it was changed on the eve of our first international polling when the Iron Curtain rose unexpectedly. The Global Attitudes Project team immediately began to examine how to reconsider its objectives. In conjunction with the *International Herald Tribune,* we conducted a survey of politicians, journalists, religious leaders, scientists, and world opinion leaders. That poll helped inform the redesign of the questionnaire used in the first two years of surveys in the Pew Global Attitudes Project. It also foretold the mounting storm of concern about American power and its use in the post–September 11 war on terrorism. The opinion leaders we interviewed described the publics of their countries as sympathetic to the United States for its losses in the Al Qaeda attacks, but they also, to our surprise, signaled hidden resentments toward America. Large majorities of these individuals, for example, agreed that "it was a good thing that the Americans knew what it is like to be vulnerable."[1]

From this, the Pew Research Center report concluded that while opinion leaders around the world saw the events of September 11 as opening a new chapter in history, many of their views about the United States and its fight against terrorism reflected a long-standing "love-hate" relationship with America. The report pointed to huge differences between U.S. opinion leaders and those in other parts of the world regarding the causes of terrorism, with influentials in most regions expressing the belief that U.S. policies were a principal cause of the September 11 attacks. And though the report found popular support for the war on terror in most regions, many thought that the United States was overreacting to the attacks.

While our polls of opinion leaders was prescient in many respects, a phrase in the report—"a more familiar love-hate relationship with America"—underestimated the degree of change in global public opinion that would soon develop. That relationship would not be the same "familiar" one, at least for some time into the future. Pew polls one year later, in 2002, described the slipping image of America in the world. And in 2003, following the start of the war in Iraq, Pew's polling found even more marked deterioration in attitudes toward America in nearly every country where trend measures were available. Not only had the war inflamed the Muslim world and enlarged the rift between Americans and Western Europeans, it had intensified fears about U.S. unilateralism and, as Pew's 2003 report observed, "significantly weakened global public support for the pillars of the post–World War II era—the U.N. and the North Atlantic alliance."[2]

Subsequent rounds of polling in 2004 and 2005 showed little improvement in America's image. Anti-Americanism runs deeper and is qualitatively different than in the past, when it was largely attributable to opposition to unpopular U.S. policies, such as the Vietnam War. Several factors led to this conclusion. First, America's image had declined around the globe, not merely in Europe and among Muslim publics, where opposition to the invasion of Iraq and criticism of the Bush administration were the strongest. Second, attitudes toward the American people, in addition to the U.S. government, were adversely affected. Third, the United States was being criticized for its ideals as well as its policies. Fourth, citizens around the world feared America's unrivaled power and opposed not only what Washington did, but also what it was capable of doing. And, possibly most troubling, this new-found anti-Americanism was proving itself to be quite robust and long-lived.

This book has as its principal objective to consider the difference between U.S. opinion and world opinion so as to understand global anti-Americanism. We will look deeply into how Americans and people all around the world—but especially our long-standing allies in Europe—look at democracy, the role of the individual in society, the role of government, and beliefs about business, social attitudes, and religion. In so doing, we will first revisit Alexis de Tocqueville's observations and concerns about American exceptionalism in its earliest manifestations. We will also compare and contrast the views of Americans with those of other publics on contemporary world issues, such as globalization, unilateralism, and the use of military force, which estrange the United States and Americans from other countries and peoples.

Finally, it is not our purpose to indict or exonerate public opinion. Our purpose is to clarify the extent to which Americans are different and consider how much that really matters. While the Pew Global Attitudes Project is not the first attempt to use survey research to test the premises of American exceptionalism, it is the largest in scope among efforts that provide statistical comparisons between the United States and the rest of the world. *America Against the World* describes what we found, along with what we have learned from our colleagues at the World Values Project, the Gallup Organization, the German Marshall Fund, and others.

AMERICA AGAINST THE WORLD

1

AMERICA UNDER THE MICROSCOPE

AMERICA HAS BEEN subject to minute inspection in recent years. A dazzling array of analyses both in the United States and abroad have attempted to deconstruct the country's many problems with its former allies: How did the rift emerge? What are its causes? Who is to blame? How deep is the divide? What are the prospects for a revival of Atlantic solidarity? And why, even before the Iraq war, had America become enemy number one for Islamic fanatics?

With the advent of globalization, the focus on America now encompasses not only U.S. military and foreign policy actions abroad, but also global discontent with those American values that affect the daily lives of people around the world. The decade of the 1990s had been, for the most part, a quiet time: history had "ended," and foreigners marveled at America's achievements—its technological feats, soaring prosperity, and commercial products. The first hints that the world was becoming troubled by America came soon after the election of George W. Bush. An international survey by the Pew Research Center for the People & the Press and the *International Herald Tribune* in August 2001 found that the new U.S. president was poorly regarded compared to his predecessor, Bill Clinton. His early policy decisions—such as backing away from the Kyoto global warming protocol—were unpopular abroad and he was viewed personally as neither interested in nor understanding of Europe and its concerns. Nonetheless, our survey concluded that despite misgivings about the new president, solid majorities of Europeans did not see a widening rift between the United States and Europe. This view was most prevalent in Italy and Germany, but even in Great Britain and France fewer than a quarter of those polled felt that differences between the United States and Europe had increased.[1]

That was before the September 11 attacks, before the war on terrorism, and before the divisive war in Iraq. While critics of the United States have long complained of a values gap between America and Europe, after the terrorist strikes on New York and Washington, some scholars hoped that transatlantic differences would narrow. Professor Francis Fukuyama of Johns Hopkins University, for example, suggested, "America may become a more ordinary country in the sense of having concrete interests and real vulnerabilities, rather than thinking itself unilaterally able to define the nature of the world it lives in."[2]

Rather the reverse appears to be the case, at least to some observers. Two years after the attacks, the editors of the British newsweekly *The Economist* declared, "America has not become 'a more ordinary country,' either in foreign policy or in the domestic arena. Instead, the attacks of 2001 have increased 'American exceptionalism'—a phrase coined by Alexis de Tocqueville in the mid-nineteenth century to describe America's profound differences from other nations."[3]

Pew's reporting since then has documented the growing depth of disenchantment and discontent with the United States and the widening rift with old allies. Our polls contained many indicators of America's newly sullied global image, but none more disturbing than the reversal of attitudes toward the American people. Previously America's policies might have been unpopular, but opinions of Americans themselves remained high. In the years since 2001, these favorable views deteriorated. In our 2003 polling, which was conducted after the conquest of Baghdad, we found that, compared to the year earlier, favorable opinions of the United States had declined in nearly every country for which trend data were available. Moreover, opinions of the American people, though still largely positive, began to slip and fell further in subsequent surveys. As *The Economist*'s editors observed, "The features that the attacks brought to the surface were already there, but the Bush administration has amplified them. As a result, in the past two years the differences between America and other countries have become more pronounced."[4]

The reelection of George W. Bush in 2004 provided new fodder for foreign critics who interpreted the election result as an endorsement of U.S. unilateralism, of the war in Iraq, and of other administration policies unpopular around the world. The indictment went far beyond criticism of the Bush administration and its policies to include America and the American people. Tony Judt, writing in the *New York Review of Books*, summarized the view of "a growing number of Europeans" that "the American pursuit of wealth, size, and abundance—as material surrogates for happiness—is aesthetically unpleasing and ecologically catastrophic. . . . Contemporary mass culture in the U.S. is squalid and meretricious. No wonder so many Americans turn to the church for solace."[5]

Our purpose in this book is not to confirm or refute such criticisms. Nor is it to psychoanalyze Americans or their president, condemn or bolster U.S. foreign policy, or pass judgment on America for being at odds with its traditional allies and their peoples. Rather, we intend to take advantage of the comparative opinion surveys conducted by the Pew Research Center and other international polling groups to look at the American people in contrast to the rest of the world, particularly compared to publics of other advanced nations. We will show the manner in which American values and attitudes differ from others, the degree to which these differences are central to U.S. foreign policy formulation and execution, and the degree of global discontent about the way the United States plays its role in the world. The objective is not to hold Americans accountable for the way people around the world see them and their country, but to describe in detail how Americans stand out in this crowded world and how and why this matters in a world with fewer warm friends and more deadly enemies than perhaps ever before.

THE NEW POWER OF PUBLIC OPINION

Even as the image of America changes, the role of public opinion itself is also changing, in the United States and elsewhere. As never before, the views and attitudes of ordinary people, as reflected in opinion polls, are being heard in debates about international policy around the world. On the eve of the Iraq war, Ronald Brownstein noted in the *Los Angeles Times* that diplomatic maneuvering was being shaped, more so than in previous international crises, by "the spread of public opinion polling and the continued growth of global media networks that transmit such findings almost instantly." Brownstein quotes the director of the London-based think tank Demos, Tom Bentley, who states, "We are seeing something absolutely different. Citizen preferences, and public opinion more generally, have become a real-time factor in diplomatic decision making in a way it never has before." Other analysts, according to Brownstein, speculate that "worldwide public opinion may be emerging as such a force because the Iraq controversy is crystallizing a broader anxiety about the way the United States is exercising its power as the world's sole remaining superpower." The United States, its power and its policies, have engaged global public opinion.[6]

In some respects, opinions about America in the twenty-first century could serve as the first case study in how the people of the planet reach consensus or become more divided on mega-international issues. There is simply no precedent for systematically assessing the differences in public perceptions of the United States and their ramifications. But unlike in the past, the survey mechanisms and media are now in place to tell the story—and have it heard.

The opportunities for global public opinion to be heard, and heard in time to affect policy and action, are, of course, a consequence of the communications revolution. Marshall McLuhan's aphorism—"The medium is the message"—has materialized dramatically, as satellite television and the Internet have stitched the peoples of the world together to observe and share common experiences in real time. As Newton Minnow, former chairman of the Federal Communications Commission, said, "Satellites have no respect for political boundaries."[7]

The first television satellite, Telstar I, was launched in 1962, but it was only with the creation in 1980 of Ted Turner's news channel, Cable News Network, that information began to be delivered into homes nearly instantaneously, consistently, and around the clock. By the mid-1990s, CNN International was being broadcast in six languages, including English, to more than 130 million people worldwide. Other international news channels followed, including BBC and Reuters TV. State-controlled or subsidized local television networks within individual countries, such as Zee TV in India and Phoenix TV in China, began picking up more international programming. Satellite television stations such as Al Jazeera have multiplied in the Middle East.

The effect is that news now travels incredibly swiftly. A Gallup International Association poll taken days after the September 11 attacks found that most of the people of the world learned of the events within three hours of their happening. Word of potential health epidemics travels only somewhat more slowly. In 2003, awareness of the SARS outbreak reached the vast majority of the publics of twenty nations who were being polled at the time by the Pew Global Attitudes Project, within seven weeks of the first case.[8]

The spread of news across borders is not neutral: it has consequences. It stimulates thought that produces opinion. Today, the views of ordinary people abroad—especially those in Western democracies—play an increased role in shaping the political reactions in their countries to international events, and in particular, to American conduct. Allied nations feel able to act independently of U.S. wishes now that they no longer require American military deterrence of a Soviet menace on their borders. Germany illustrated just how much things had changed when the U.S. attack on Iraq was imminent. Unlike two decades earlier, when the German government accepted intermediate-range U.S. missiles on its territory despite widespread public opposition, in 2002 Social Democratic Chancellor Gerhard Schröder trumpeted his opposition to the war in defiance of Washington to win a closely contested reelection. Two years later, after terrorists bombed Madrid commuter trains killing nearly two hundred people, a conservative Spanish government, which had sent troops to aid American forces in Iraq, was defeated by Socialists proclaiming their opposition to the war that the Spanish public had overwhelmingly opposed from the start.

Public opposition to the war was not limited to Europe by any means. It was also strong in Muslim nations like Pakistan and Turkey, and though it did not produce spectacular policy reversals by their governments, the opposition engendered deep and potentially long-lasting resentment, if not outright hatred, of the United States. Global public opinion constrained the Bush administration's policy options and complicated American leadership efforts in the world, and the administration has attempted to reshape America's public image. In the years since September 11, millions of dollars have been appropriated, new foreign broadcast propaganda outlets have been created, and three different public diplomacy czars have been appointed in an effort to ameliorate the anti-Americanism in the world.

It is a historic coincidence that the policies and actions of the United States, the world's oldest democracy, should be the first to come under strong global scrutiny rather than those of authoritarian countries. Imperial Britain in the nineteenth century and the European powers of the early and mid-twentieth century were little if at all constrained by global public opinion as they shaped events and redrew maps around the world. To be sure, public views on international issues were not wholly irrelevant. Opposition to slavery led Britain to use its navy to enforce an international ban on the slave trade. Publics were manipulated by the press and by governments to create war fever, as in the Spanish-American War, and to endure the battlefield slaughter of World War I. But there is little evidence that public opinion in those decades arose as an independent force to influence policy decisions. The American public did not react to the atrocities perpetrated in Hitler's Germany prior to World War II; Franklin Roosevelt's struggle to win support for helping the Allies failed until the United States was attacked directly. Not until Vietnam did public opinion rise to challenge the decisions of men in power. Since then, largely because of international television, public revulsion has, for better or worse, demanded that governments act to halt ethnic cleansing in the Balkans or to withdraw U.S. forces from Somalia when the costs in blood became too gruesome.

If the emergence of global media can shape and spread global public opinions, the emergence of frequent multinational polling—by Pew, the Gallup Organization, and the German Marshall Fund—has given voice and clout to the views of ordinary people. As he did with so many developments regarding public opinion, George H. Gallup saw the possibilities first. With a very limited budget, he organized the first global survey in 1974 whose results, he claimed, represented the views of two-thirds of the world's population and more than 90 percent of the people of those nations that permitted opinion surveys at that time. ("Communist nations, Arab countries and a few military dictatorships do not now permit [independent] public opinion surveys," he noted.) The 1974 survey was focused almost entirely on social and economic rather than geopolitical issues. Gallup wrote that he "sought to gain greater insight into people around the world with respect to their lives and self-image," including their sense of well-being and the quality of their lives. With his sponsor, the Kettering Foundation, Gallup hoped to establish a prototype for subsequent periodic global surveys. That he did.

As polling spread globally, it also delved more deeply into the personal attitudes and values of individuals. Most notable in this respect is the groundbreaking World Values Survey, built on the European Values Survey of 1981 and conducted by academic scholars, which compiles and analyzes data relating to sociocultural and political change. The project has carried out four sets of representative national surveys, the latest 1999 to 2002, of the basic values and beliefs of publics in sixty-one societies on all six inhabited continents, covering almost 80 percent of the world's population. From 2002 through 2005, the Pew Research Center's Global Attitudes Project has conducted more than 91,000 interviews in fifty countries and the Palestinian Authority. (The appendix contains further information on the Pew Global Attitudes Project's polling.) All of these surveys and others have been the basis for our effort to raise and answer questions about how Americans compare to people in other parts of the world and to contrast the views of Americans with those of other publics.[9]

Our analysis has honed in on a recurring theme of American life: the premise, and effects, of American exceptionalism. At the outset, we need to make a basic acknowledgment. As we are using it, the word *exceptionalism* is a "term of art," not a value judgment. By exceptionalism, we refer to the distinctiveness of the American public, with no implication of superiority. Historically, this has not always been the case. Many authors have used and continue to use *exceptionalism* to imply American superiority. Note the definition provided in 2005 by the populist encyclopedia, Wikipedia:

> **American exceptionalism** is the idea that the United States and the American people hold a special place in the world, by offering opportunity and hope for humanity, derived from a unique balance of public and private interests governed by constitutional ideals that are focused on personal and economic freedom.
>
> Some interpret the term to indicate a moral superiority of Americans, while others use it to refer to the American concept as itself an exceptional ideal, which may or may not always be upheld by the actual people and government of the nation.[10]

Moreover, it goes without saying that America is exceptional in any number of positive ways. The United States has unparalleled wealth, unrivaled military power, a unique immigrant heritage, and is blessed with land and natural resources that few other nations can claim. Seymour Martin Lipset, the most influential modern scholar on the subject, views exceptionalism as fundamental to American history and the American identity: "Born out of revolution, the United States is a country organized around an ideology which includes a set of dogmas about the nature of a good society. The revolutionary ideology which became the American Creed is liberalism in its eighteenth- and nineteenth-century meanings." In a similar vein, G. K. Chesterton wrote: "America is the only nation in the world that is founded on a creed. That creed is set forth with dogmatic and even theological lucidity in the Declaration of Independence." Of course, the question of whether the special qualities of American attitudes and values have encouraged these and other qualities of American superiority is a central question in our inquiry.[11]

We have stuck with *exceptionalism* not because of this question surrounding American superiority but because the term is so widely used in the ongoing public debate about American hegemony in the twenty-first century. Our inquiry relates more broadly to understanding the values and attitudes of the American people—whether superior or not. Our approach, too, is different from nineteenth-century and other early considerations of American exceptionalism. None were based on empirical data, whether opinion surveys or other quantitative methods of observation. In *America Against the World,* we step back from the largely anecdotal portrayals of Americans to examine such characterizations in the light of the data.

AN EXCEPTIONAL POWER

Concerns about the United States' use of its power and wealth have made American exceptionalism fashionable shorthand for American nationalism and, in turn, an intellectual basis for claims that the nation has embarked, intentionally or not, on the creation of an American empire. As a result, "American exceptionalism" has been batted around in the popular press in recent years. A content analysis

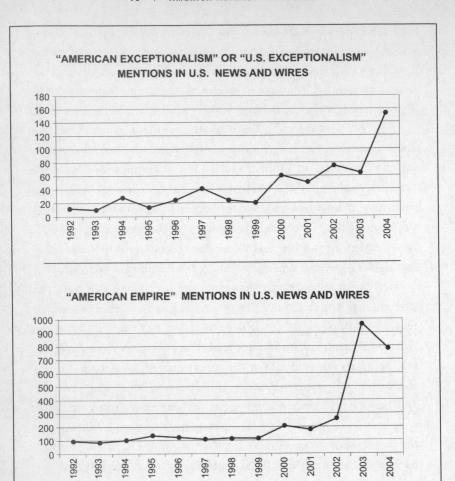

"AMERICAN EXCEPTIONALISM" OR "U.S. EXCEPTIONALISM" MENTIONS IN U.S. NEWS AND WIRES

"AMERICAN EMPIRE" MENTIONS IN U.S. NEWS AND WIRES

Source: Lexis-Nexis

of leading U.S. papers found that while the phrase was mentioned in merely twelve news stories in 1992, by 2002 it was cited seventy-five times and more than twice that frequently in 2004.[12]

Similarly, there was little reference to U.S. empire building in public discourse throughout the 1990s, although America was already recognized as the world's sole superpower. The same content analysis of news stories found relatively few mentions of "American Empire" until 1999, after which the number doubled, and then in 2003, after the U.S.-led invasion of Iraq, reached a level tenfold greater than that in 1993.[13]

The Bush administration's aggressive new directions in American foreign policy, moreover, coincided with a hastening of the free flow of American ideas and consumer products. The confluence of American foreign policy and globalization gave rise to a new complaint: America was intent on "cultural imperialism" through its export of television, music, films, and videos—resentments detailed by Professor Joseph Nye of Harvard University in his book, *Soft Power*.[14]

Modern critics view American exceptionalism as an ideology intent on creating an "imperial America" by converting the world to its ideas. In his book *Rogue Nation*, Clyde Prestowitz writes: "America is the only country with an 'ism' attached to its name," which intentionally or not calls up the specter of odious ideologies such as Fascism and Communism. Prestowitz argues that "America was founded on a set of ideas and one becomes an American by converting to those propositions," listing these founding ideals as liberty, equality, individualism, populism, and limited government. But, he insists, that does not imply that Americans think themselves better than others or view their creed as exclusive. Instead, Prestowitz writes, "the nice thing about this religion is that it is a kind of super church that anyone can join regardless of other beliefs or associations. Indeed the chief reason Americans are blind to their own empires is their implicit belief that every human being is a potential American, and that his or her present national or cultural affiliations are an unfortunate but reversible accident."[15]

America is also exceptional in its brand of nationalism. In an article in the journal *Foreign Policy*, Carnegie Endowment scholar Minxin Pei takes a mostly upbeat view of American nationalism, though he contends it includes an unacknowledged desire to impose American ideology on others:

> American nationalism is hidden in plain sight. But even if Americans saw it, they wouldn't recognize it as nationalism. That's because

American nationalism is a different breed from its foreign cousins and exhibits three unique characteristics:

First, American nationalism is based on political ideals, not those of cultural or ethnic superiority. . . . That conception is entirely fitting for a society that still sees itself as a cultural and ethnic melting pot.

American nationalism is triumphant rather than aggrieved. In most societies, nationalism is fueled by past grievances caused by external powers. Countries once subjected to colonial rule, such as India and Egypt, are among the most nationalistic societies.

But American nationalism is the polar opposite of such aggrieved nationalism. American nationalism derives its meaning from victories in peace and war since the country's founding.

Triumphant nationalists celebrate the positive and have little empathy for the whining of aggrieved nationalists whose formative experience consisted of a succession of national humiliations and defeats.

Finally, American nationalism is forward looking, while nationalism in most other countries is the reverse. Those who believe in the superiority of American values and institutions do not dwell on their historical glories (though such glories constitute the core of American national identity). Instead, they look forward to even better times ahead, not just at home but also abroad. This dynamism imbues American nationalism with a missionary spirit and a short collective memory.[16]

Most critics see American nationalism as far less benign. Anatol Lieven, a British journalist, claims there is a "wounded and vengeful nationalism" in America today, a nationalism that is the antithesis of the American creed. It is far more virulent, he argues, because it is encouraged by conservative evangelical religious forces who, unlike the Founding Fathers, are anti-Enlightenment in their attitude toward modern science, particularly biology and evolutionary theory.

Jeremy Rifkin, in his article "The European Dream," is still harsher: "America is no longer a great country. To be a great country, it is necessary to be a good country. It is true that people everywhere enjoy American cultural forms and consumer goods. [But] our way of life no longer inspires; rather, it is now looked on as outmoded and, worse yet, as something to fear, or abhor." To Rifkin, the American Dream is an anachronism, with a third of Americans no longer even believing in its essential elements of economic growth, personal wealth, and independence. Rifkin argues that "the American Dream is largely a European creation transported to American soil and frozen in time. . . . While much of Europe eventually tempered its religious fervor, its scientific zeal, and its enthusiasm for unbridled market capitalism, preferring a compromise in the form of democratic socialism, America did not. Instead, successive generations chose to live out those older traditions in their purest forms, making us the most devoutly Protestant people on earth and the most committed to scientific pursuits, private property, capitalism, and the nation-state."[17]

Still, many continue to admire America's creed. They point to the country's egalitarian society, in which common men can rise to head major corporations or become president—indeed, where an immigrant Austrian body builder can become a movie star and governor of California—and where progress and achievement are both celebrated and demonstrated. Moreover, in a recent book, *They Made America: From the Steam Engine to the Search Engine—Two Centuries of Innovators,* the noted British journalist and editor Harold Evans argues that America has not only advanced faster than other nations but has also pushed the world forward, thanks to, among other things, the American economic structure, its political and educational systems, and even its psychological attitude. Examining what he considers to be the exceptional character of Americans whose innovations became huge commercial successes, Evans writes, "When they disembarked, blinking in the bright light of the New World, they had no idea what their destinies would be. The magic was in the way they found fulfillment for themselves—and others—in the freedom and raw competitive excitements of the republic. Innovation, the concept and activity that made Dr. Johnson shudder, has turned out to be a distinguishing characteristic of the United States."[18]

EXCEPTIONAL FOREIGN POLICY

For the first century of its existence, the United States was preoccupied internally with its westward expansion and the Civil War, and largely refrained from "foreign entanglements." As it grew and prospered, however, the nation came to believe it had a special mission to help others. At times this notion stimulated hyperbole from the country's leaders, such as Woodrow Wilson's words after World War I that "America had the infinite privilege of fulfilling her destiny and saving the world." In World War I, the United States was, in the popular phrase, "making the world safe for democracy."[19]

Throughout the Cold War, American foreign policy held as a principal objective the promotion of democracy, human rights, and capitalism in response to the ideological force of Communism and the Soviet nuclear threat. At the same time, its leaders practiced the realpolitik of balancing national interests, seeking security by preserving stability, and, when necessary, dealing with governments as they existed. Critics complained of America's inconsistency in not practicing what it preached, but few voices claimed the United States sought to impose its will on the world. For example, as former ambassador Stephen Sestanovich, a senior fellow at the Council on Foreign Relations, has pointed out, there was relatively little public outcry in Europe when Washington, following the collapse of the Berlin Wall, pushed for the immediate reunification of Germany. Objections from Britain and France, whose leaders were worried about the stability of the Warsaw Pact, failed to carry the day.[20]

But the change from a multipolar to a unipolar world without an overarching nuclear threat led to a new willingness to criticize the United States and its now unrivaled power. Discomfort with and even suspicion of the United States has become one of the most significant elements driving public attitudes toward America. During the Cold War, especially in the first two decades after World War II, Europeans embraced America's protection.

Before the September 11 attacks, while the world acknowledged American superpower status and resented it to some extent, few, with the exception of some Islamic extremists, considered the United States a threat. America was not on the offensive, nor at that time was it threatened. The terrorist attacks changed that. America's new offensive stance has made the world's only superpower and its policies the global issue of our time. Now U.S. power is resented even by America's oldest friends. As Robert Cooper, a former special adviser to British prime minister Tony Blair, has written, "[T]he rest of the world reacts to America— alternately because it fears America, lives under American protection, envies, resents, and plots against, and depends on America."[21]

Some may argue that the terrorist assaults were merely a catalyst that hastened the world's changing view of America, an inevitable metamorphosis given the great disparity of wealth and power between the United States and the rest of the world. Others will maintain that it was Bush administration policies, before and after September 11, that precipitated the change. In either case, it is clear that strains between the United States and its old allies, and indeed between America and the rest of the world, predated George W. Bush.

In any event, the post-Communist resentment of American power emerged clearly in the run-up to the Iraq invasion. Before the war, Pew polling found most Western Europeans sharing American concerns that Saddam Hussein's regime was a danger to the world, yet saying the real purpose for American intervention would be to take over Iraq's oil. Following the war, Middle East oil has been even more broadly accepted by the global public as both America's real motive for invading Iraq and its rationale for the war on terrorism. At the same time, the Bush administration's declarations that U.S. actions stand as an effort to instill democracy in the Middle East have spurred anxieties that the United States has adopted a mission to spread American values. Europeans in particular felt threatened when President Bush declared, "This great nation has a chance to help change the culture [of the past]." As *The Economist* reported, the president appealed to a view in which "America is not exceptional because it is powerful;

America is powerful because it is exceptional." What makes America different keeps it rich and powerful, it continued, so the Bush administration, by encouraging the growth of American wealth and power, "tend[s] to encourage intrinsic exceptionalism." Bush policies, the magazine concluded, "embody American exceptionalism."[22]

A year later, Bush set his administration's goals even higher. In his second inaugural address, he stated:

> There is only one force of history that can break the reign of hatred and resentment, and expose the pretensions of tyrants . . . and that is the force of human freedom. We are led by events and common sense to one conclusion. The survival of liberty in our land increasingly depends on the success of liberty in other lands. The best hope for peace in the world is the expansion of freedom in all the world. America's vital interests and our deepest beliefs are now one. . . . It is the policy of the United States to seek and support the growth of democratic movements and institutions in every nation and culture, with the ultimate goal of ending tyranny in our world.[23]

With that address, Bush's foreign policy doctrine "transcended the war on terror," applauded columnist David Brooks in the *New York Times*. With his words, the United States embarked on "transformational diplomacy," moving away from the realpolitik of previous U.S. administrations toward a near-utopian goal of a world built in America's image. In a later address, the president asserted that "decades of excusing and accommodating tyranny in the pursuit of stability have only led to injustice and instability and tragedy."[24] It was unclear whether he considered the prolonged stability during the Cold War, which ended in the collapse of the Soviet Union, to have been "accommodating tyranny," but Bush's grand vision and zeal reminded one former Soviet dissident of the old Communist adage: "Philosophers throughout history have been trying to understand the world; we will change it."

The recent foreign policy manifestations of American exceptionalism have been called various names and characterized in different ways. Walter Russell Mead of the Council on Foreign Relations termed it "American revivalism," which he vaguely defined as "not an explicit ideology but a pattern of beliefs, attitudes, and instincts." Some Europeans describe the new policies as "American maximalism," an arrogant unilateralism. Stephen Sestanovich prefers to consider America's new stance as "reach[ing] for big solutions that cut against the grain of events," citing former Secretary of State Madeleine Albright's comment that the United States is exceptional because "we see further than other countries into the future." Similarly, a commentator in *Der Spiegel,* Claus Christian Malzahn, observed that German politicians ridiculed Ronald Reagan's "tear down this wall" speech in 1987 because they could not imagine an alternative to a divided Germany. He added, "We Europeans always want to have the world from yesterday, whereas the Americans strive for the world of tomorrow."[25]

SOURCES OF ANTI-AMERICANISM

Some see the breach between Americans and Europeans as primarily a difference in attitudes about national security and sovereignty. Political scientist Robert Kagan points to Europe's experiences over the last half-century—two continent-wide wars and their aftermath as well as the creation of the European Union—to explain why Europeans' views on the uses and morality of power have taken a very different shape from Americans'. "If the strategic chasm between the United States and Europe appears greater than ever today, and grows still wider at a worrying pace, it is because these material and ideological differences reinforce one another," Kagan observes. "The divisive trend they together produce may be impossible to reverse."[26]

A telling example of these different ideals and principles is the entity to which a nation looks for protection. Americans, although they seek allied backing and support in confronting international threats, continue to rely primarily on their own forces for their own defense.

Europeans look to international organizations rather than to their own states. A 2005 German Marshall Fund survey found Americans more willing than Europeans to ignore the United Nations if U.S. vital interests were threatened. And Pew surveys have found Europeans less disposed than Americans to support preemptive military actions. America's oldest friends fault it for this Lone Ranger tendency in approaching global problems.

They also are highly critical of American ways of governance and business. Pew surveys in 2002 found British, French, Germans, and Italians divided over whether they liked or disliked the American practice of democracy, but pluralities in all four countries disliked the way Americans do business. Of forty-four nations polled by Pew in 2002, only the people of the Muslim world generally expressed more consistent criticism than Western Europeans of U.S. ideals of democracy and free enterprise.

Globalization is increasing the antagonism in the world toward the spreading influence of America, even though the publics of many countries, including many Muslim countries, continue to say they enjoy American movies, songs, and TV programs. And in nearly every country of the world, U.S. scientific and technological achievements are admired. Yet large majorities in all countries say they deplore the spread of American customs and ideas. From nearby Canada to the far reaches of Africa and Asia, majorities of people believe that there is too much America in their worlds.

THE VALUES GAP

Essentially, Americans are set apart from other peoples of the world by their values. There are profound differences between the way Americans and other people—especially Western Europeans—think about themselves and their governments. Americans are more action-oriented, individualistic in their behavior, and more opposed to the intrusions of government than Europeans and others. They are also among the least compassionate in principle. Among forty-four nations surveyed by Pew in 2002, Americans were among the strongest believers that most people who fail in life have themselves to blame rather than society.

Americans care more about personal freedom than about government guarantees of social justice. While most Americans support a social safety net, they are less strongly committed than other peoples to the concept that their government is responsible for taking care of those who cannot care for themselves. This may appear surprising in a country that is both the most religious and the richest—indeed, the only religious rich country—in the world. But it is consistent with a people who are more personally freewheeling, self-reliant, and adverse to government involvement. In contrast, Europeans are among the least devout people in the world and are dismayed at the use of religious concepts in political discourse, as when President Bush invoked the "axis of evil" to describe adversarial nations.

The values gulf between America and the rest of the world is not merely a matter of academic interest. Even America's close friends are concerned that an imperial America will try to remake the world in its own image. For example, Robert Cooper worried that "since 9/11 the United States has acquired a steely determination that frightens even some of its friends. The gap between Europe and the United States is not just about capability: it is also about will."[27]

EXPLORING THE AMERICAN CHARACTER

America's "steely determination" to change the world may not be as great as feared, but its self-image and worldview are certainly distinctive. In what manner the United States is distinctive is a question that has increasingly engaged political analysts, who have, in a sense, put the American character on the couch in recent years.

Of course, attempts to explain how national character and values shape history are not new. Among the most notable was Max Weber's grand effort in the nineteenth century, which contended that the Protestant ethic was the basis for Northern European economic development. Many less sweeping claims run through popular thinking about the values and traits of various nationalities: British reserve, French cultural sophistication, German orderliness, Asian industriousness. In times of conflict, definitions of national character become part of war chants. American characterizations of Germans as inherently cruel and blindly obedient, and Japanese as fanatical and savage, were prevalent during World War II. Such characterizations, both the positive and the negative, are often little more than stereotypes but they nonetheless provide enduring and pervasive ingredients in a nation's identity as seen from abroad.

A leading foreign policy commentator, Robert Kagan, has encapsulated the cultural differences and policy gaps on the continental level: Europeans are from Venus, Americans are from Mars. To him, European thinking reflects a new idealism based on diplomacy, negotiations, patience, and forging economic ties. Americans, he maintains, generally see the world divided between good and evil, between friends and foes, and generally favor policies of coercion rather than persuasion. But there have been a variety of internationalist strains in the American disposition, depending on the times. In his book *Special Providence,* Walter Russell Mead devised a typology based on the U.S. leader who most exemplified it. Hamiltonians looked at the world as interconnected through commerce; Wilsonians urged promoting American values with missionary zeal; Jeffersonians favored a minimalist internationalism to protect American values; and Jacksonians took a prickly, populist "don't tread on me" attitude toward the world. Mead's four categories raise the question: Is the American character so dependent on the person in charge?[28]

Most characterizations of the American people usually start with, or owe much to, Alexis de Tocqueville's depictions of early-nineteenth-century America. Even back then, American exceptionalism was a complaint as well as a thesis. The thesis was that the American condition was unique in the nineteenth-century world; the complaint was that it could metastasize into something ugly and dangerous, not only for Americans, but also for other political systems. Tocqueville's thesis has changed only somewhat, but the complaints today are of an entirely different order, given the extraordinary role that the United States now plays in the world.

What the multinational surveys prove, disprove, or leave open about American character and American exceptionalism constitutes the primary content of this book. But we will also examine how American distinctiveness plays out in American policy and the consequences of the differences between Americans and other peoples around the world—including, foremost, the rise of anti-Americanism. We will look in detail at the most significant components of American character and their effects on cultural issues, commerce, and democracy, personal freedoms and social justice, religion, multilateralism, and the use of force. We will also ask: Is there a political divide in America so great that it sunders the American character? By looking in the mirror—in the contours and shadings of extensive multinational data—America and Americans can begin to understand why America is disliked, how Americans are distinct, and why these two traits are inextricably linked.

2

THE RISE OF ANTI-AMERICANISM

THE PUNCTUATED RISE in anti-Americanism is not lost on Americans. They harbor no illusions about the popularity of their country around the world. Americans believe the United States is "generally disliked" by people in other countries, and identify the loss of regard for the United States as a major foreign policy problem. To understand exactly what is going on—if there is a growing rift between America and the world, and why—it is useful to start by looking at what polls tell us about how the world views both America and Americans.

Of course, Americans have their own doubts about the characters and behaviors of the citizens of other countries. And that mutual antipathy is not without an element of ambivalence. As British writer Tina Barney wrote in 2004, Europeans and Americans have long viewed each other with a conflicting mixture of "jealousy and admiration, mistrust and understanding, ignorance and familiarity." Antipathy toward the United States has been endemic among European intellectuals, particularly the English, since the founding of the Republic. In 1842 Charles Dickens found Americans rude, addicted to sharp business practices, hypocritical about liberty in light of their treatment of blacks, and careless about where they spit tobacco. Excepting the last complaint, many foreigners still see Americans in the same negative light.[1]

But while anti-Americanism is not a new phenomenon, today's anti-Americanism is an amalgam of discontents. Some of it is a reaction to the impact on foreign societies of American popular culture, with the commercial television programs and music and uniform McDonald's and Starbucks diet that threaten other countries' indigenous cultures. A second source of disgruntlement is resentment that American-style business practices are forcing changes in industrial and societal practices—longer work days and the opening of shops on Sunday—and that such acceleration in the pace of modernization threatens to overwhelm traditional ways of life.

While the popular concept of globalization is relatively new, the negative reaction to the United States for its global reach has been apparent for at least two decades. A 1983 Gallup poll in six countries—France, West Germany, Great Britain, Japan, Brazil, and Mexico—found that majorities or pluralities in four of the six complained of too much American influence on their pop music, movies, and television, and in five of the six nations, majorities or pluralities complained of too much American influence in business. In retrospect, these findings appear as harbingers of the cultural anti-Americanism of today.[2]

A third category of anti-Americanism, the one we will examine, is the world's reaction to U.S. foreign policies. It also is not new. For centuries, Latin Americans have struggled under the overbearing power and influence of the colossus to the north, manifested in such events as the mob that attacked Vice President Richard Nixon's motorcade during his visit to Caracas in 1958 and the anti-American riots that greeted President Bush on his visit to Argentina in the fall of 2005.

Elsewhere, however, the rise in anti-Americanism in reaction to U.S. foreign policy is relatively recent and, like other anti-American backlash, it extends to all parts of the globe. For two decades after World War II, most of the world acknowledged a debt to American power for defeating the Axis powers. In particular, Western Europeans, though at times critical, were largely grateful for the Marshall Plan aid that had revived their societies, and appreciated the U.S. military umbrella that protected them against Soviet ambitions. In the late 1960s, as European disillusionment with the Vietnam War grew, these pro-America attitudes began to unravel. In the 1980s, the Reagan administration's hardline approach to Moscow, which resulted in the NATO decision to station Pershing intermediate-range missiles in Western Europe to counter the Soviets, spurred huge anti-American demonstrations.

The 1983 Gallup European poll documented broad discontent with Reagan's policies at that time. It also found widespread distrust of American power. In five of the six countries, majorities or pluralities said a strong U.S. military presence around the world increased the chance of war. Only in West Germany, the single country in the survey abutting the Soviet bloc, did people (by a 39 to 25 percent plurality) believe that the American military presence on their territory increased the chances for peace. Washington tended to brush off such findings of discontent, citing its own polls by the U.S. Information Agency. Since the mid-1950s, the USIA had found that attitudes toward the United States depended heavily on the news of the day, suggesting that anti-Americanism was a transitory phenomenon.

Moreover, despite European opposition to U.S. government policies, the 1983 Gallup poll found little dislike of the American people and substantial approval of the American way of life in every country except France. Even the French disapproved by a mere 4 percent margin (40 to 36 percent). A *Newsweek* cover story that year summed up the poll results as showing that "Americans are seen as a good and productive people with an erratic or even dangerous government. And while the policies of the Reagan administration—like those of some of its predecessors—heighten skepticism about American power and intentions, the world guilelessly embraces America's products and popular culture."[3]

SOMETHING OLD, SOMETHING NEW

But that was then. Today's anti-Americanism runs broader and deeper. Not only is U.S. foreign policy more strongly opposed, but now the influence of the American lifestyle is also rejected even as American products are still widely accepted. And, for the first time, the American people are also less liked. Judging by trends in international surveys, the negative image of many things American seems unlikely to change anytime soon in much of the world. Whatever global goodwill the United States had in the wake of the September 11 attacks appears to have quickly dissipated as U.S. policymakers broadened the focus of the war against terrorism.

In 2002, a Pew survey of 38,000 people in forty-four countries found that the U.S. global image had slipped when contrasted to the results of comparable prior polls conducted by the U.S. State Department. Favorable attitudes toward America had declined most sharply in majority Muslim countries, but slippage was also observed among longtime NATO allies, in Eastern Europe, and in most regions of the world. By the following spring, after the March 2003 launch of the U.S.-led invasion of Iraq, a follow-up Pew survey of 16,000 people in twenty countries found that favorable opinions had more than slipped. They had plummeted.

The most striking finding was how broadly anti-Americanism had spread geographically by 2003. It was no longer limited to Western Europe or to the Muslim world. In Brazil, for example, where 52 percent of the public expressed a favorable opinion of the United States in 2002, the pro-American portion of the population had dropped to 34 percent. In Russia, there was a 25-percentage-point decline in the U.S. favorability rating, from 61 percent to 36 percent, in the course of less than a year.

In the Muslim world, the image of America had been dismal for some time. In 1999, State Department surveys found only 23 percent of Pakistanis expressing a favorable view of the United States, but after the invasion of Iraq, antipathy toward America spread to majority-Muslim countries far outside of the region. For example, only 15 percent of Indonesian Muslims looked favorably upon the United States in 2003, a mere quarter of the 61 percent who had expressed positive sentiments a year earlier.[4]

Moreover, there was considerable evidence that Muslim loathing of the United States was also rooted in fear. In the wake of the Iraq invasion, majorities in seven of eight predominantly Muslim nations were afraid that the United States might one day militarily threaten their country. Most strikingly, these included 71 percent of people in Turkey, a U.S. NATO ally.

Such distrust of America was shared in Europe. A Eurobarometer survey conducted in fifteen European Union countries in October 2003 found that people saw the United States and Iran to be equal threats to world peace. And in four countries—Greece, Spain, Finland, and Sweden—the United States was viewed as the greatest threat to stability, more menacing than either Iran or North Korea. Even in the United Kingdom, America's most trusted ally, a majority of 55 percent considered the United States to be a danger.[5]

A Pew survey in 2004, one year after the start of the Iraq war, echoed these findings. It found very little improvement in the image of the United States. The French and the Germans were at least as negative in their opinion of America after the success of the initial invasion as before, and the British, whose troops joined American forces on the ground, were decidedly more critical. Negative perceptions of American unilateralism remained widespread in European and Muslim nations.

America's credibility had also suffered. Doubts about the motives behind the U.S. war on terrorism multiplied, while an increased segment of European publics supported developing foreign policy and security arrangements independent of the United States. Across

Europe, there was considerable support for the European Union to become as powerful as the United States.

REPAIRING AMERICA'S IMAGE

In 2005, two years after the invasion of Iraq, anti-Americanism eased slightly—compared with the nadir of the previous year. But the United States remained broadly disliked in most countries surveyed by Pew, and opinion of the American people continued to be less favorable than it once was. Even popular U.S. policies and actions did little to repair America's image. President Bush's calls for greater

TABLE 2.1

FAVORABLE OPINION OF THE UNITED STATES

	1999–2000 %	2002 %	2003 %	2004 %	2005 %
Canada	71	72	63	—	59
Britain	83	75	70	58	55
Netherlands	—	—	—	—	45
France	62	63	43	37	43
Germany	78	61	45	38	41
Spain	50	—	38	—	41
Poland	—	79	—	—	62
Russia	37	61	36	47	52
Indonesia	75	61	15	—	38
Turkey	52	30	15	30	23
Pakistan	23	10	13	21	23
Lebanon	—	35	27	—	42
Jordan	—	25	1	5	21
Morocco	77	—	27	27	49
India	—	54	—	—	71
China	—	—	—	—	42

Source: Office of Research, U.S. Department of State and Environics (Canada), 1999–2000; Pew Global Attitudes Project, 2002–2005.

democracy in the Middle East and U.S. aid for tsunami victims in South Asia were well received in many countries. But only in four of sixteen countries—Indonesia, India, Morocco, and Russia—was there significant improvement in overall opinions of the United States.

Anti-Americanism remained entrenched in most countries. In Europe, more than half the French and Germans, and half the Spanish, maintained an unfavorable view of the United States, although their anti-Americanism had declined somewhat since 2004. And even in Great Britain, where a majority of the population still liked the United States, support had eroded considerably since 2002. Moreover, belief in the U.S. war on terrorism had collapsed in Spain—only one in four Spaniards supported it—and was down by 24 percentage points in France, 20 points in Germany, and 18 points in Great Britain since 2002.

As for the Muslim world, attitudes there toward the United States continued to be quite negative, although hostility toward America softened in some countries. Pew's 2005 poll found many Muslims who believed that Americans do support authentic democracy in their countries and were optimistic about the prospects for democracy in the Middle East as a whole; moreover, they gave at least some credit to U.S. policies for the change. But significant improvement of America's image in these countries remained distant; solid majorities in five predominantly Muslim countries continued to express unfavorable views of the United States. And while the survey found that support for suicide bombing and other terrorist acts in defense of Islam had declined significantly in most majority-Muslim countries, about half of Muslims in Morocco, Jordan, and Lebanon said suicide bombings against Americans and other Westerners in Iraq were justified.

In the face of entrenched anti-Americanism and the United States' perceived global domination, China appeared to gain both friends and influence. Strikingly, China had a better image than the United States in most of the European nations as well as in the Arab countries and most of Asia surveyed by Pew in 2005. But given the decline of America's reputation, other major nations also now outpoll the United

TABLE 2.2

WESTERN PUBLICS RATE MAJOR NATIONS

% Favorability Ratings for . . .

Rating Given by . . .	United States	Germany	France	Japan	China
Canadians	59	77	78	75	58
British	55	75	71	69	65
French	43	89	74	76	58
Germans	41	64	78	64	46
Spanish	41	77	74	66	57
Dutch	45	88	69	68	56
Russians	52	79	83	75	60
Poles	62	64	66	60	36
Americans	83	60	46	63	43

States in popularity. Japan, France, and Germany are now all more highly regarded in Europe than is the United States. Even Americans' cultural cousins—the British and the Canadians—share this relatively dim view of the United States.

For their part, Americans are well aware of their country's declining reputation. Two out of three Americans surveyed by Pew in 2004, and slightly more in 2005, recognized that the United States was less respected in the world. Two decades earlier, about a third of the public thought America's image was in trouble. Of those who recognized the diminished regard for America in 2005, 66 percent believed it was a major problem for the country.[6]

AMERICA VS. AMERICANS

In the past, foreigners' distaste for U.S. policies, be they in regard to Vietnam or the Middle East, did not lead to antipathy toward the American people. The first few Pew Global Attitudes surveys, beginning in 2002, continued to find that the rest of the world held Americans in higher esteem than America. This held true until 2005, although the gap narrowed in several countries. Nowhere was this more apparent than in Indonesia, where favorability ratings for America as a nation more than doubled between 2003 and 2005, from 15 percent to 38 percent, but opinion of the American people fell from 56 percent to 46 percent.

TABLE 2.3

DECLINING VIEW OF THE AMERICAN PEOPLE

	% Favorable			
	2002	2003	2004	2005
Great Britain	83	80	73	70
Poland	77	—	—	68
Canada	78	77	—	66
Netherlands	—	—	—	66
Germany	70	67	68	65
France	71	58	53	64
Russia	67	65	64	61
Spain	—	47	—	55
Lebanon	47	62	—	66
Indonesia	65	56	—	46
Jordan	53	18	21	34
Turkey	31	32	32	23
Pakistan	17	38	25	22
India	58	—	—	71
China	—	—	—	43

The decline in favorable views of Americans all around the world suggests that people are now increasingly equating the U.S. people with the U.S. government. The drop in favorable opinions has been most precipitous in the Muslim world, but heightened dislike for Americans is widespread. Between 2002 and 2005, the favorability ratings of the American people declined in nine of the twelve coun-tries for which trend data exist. These include the ancestral homes of many current U.S. citizens—Great Britain, Poland, Germany, France, and Russia; our cultural and geographic neighbor, Canada; Jordan and Turkey, both Washington allies in the Middle East; and Indone-sia. Only in Pakistan, India, and Lebanon did people's estimation of the American people improve.

U.S. tsunami relief efforts—including the millions of dollars in private donations that flowed to south and southeastern Asia immedi-ately after the disaster—drew a favorable response from the Indone-sian people, among whom nearly eight in ten said the aid had led them to look more favorably on the United States. But that goodwill did little if anything to improve their image of the American people. In fact, favorable attitudes toward Americans declined among In-donesians from 56 percent in 2003 to 46 percent in 2005. A similar pattern—a rising image for the United States coupled with a declin-ing image of Americans—occurred in Pakistan, Turkey, and to a lesser extent in Russia over the same period.

What is it that the people of other nations see in Americans that evokes such positive or negative feelings? In 2005, Pew asked people around the world, including in the United States, to judge Americans on seven character traits, three of them positive (hardworking, inven-tive, honest) and four negative (greedy, violent, rude, immoral). The resulting portrait of Americans is both complex and nuanced.

Despite generally less favorable views of Americans, many people still acknowledged positive American traits. For example, while only 46 percent of Indonesians viewed Americans favorably, 84 percent said Americans were hardworking and inventive. Likewise, many who admired Americans generally nonetheless discerned weak points in their character. Two-thirds of the Dutch public had a favorable over-all view of the American people, for instance, but an equal proportion said Americans were greedy and 60 percent said they were violent.

There is considerable unanimity on the positive side of the ledger with respect to the characteristics most readily associated with

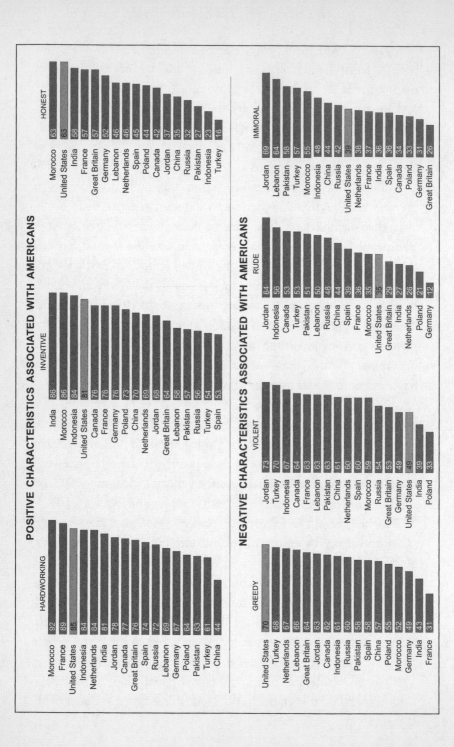

POSITIVE CHARACTERISTICS ASSOCIATED WITH AMERICANS

HONEST

Morocco	63
United States	63
India	58
France	57
Great Britain	57
Germany	52
Lebanon	46
Netherlands	46
Spain	45
Poland	44
Canada	42
Jordan	37
China	35
Russia	32
Pakistan	27
Indonesia	23
Turkey	16

INVENTIVE

India	86
Morocco	86
Indonesia	84
United States	81
Canada	76
France	76
Germany	76
Poland	73
China	70
Netherlands	69
Jordan	68
Great Britain	64
Lebanon	58
Pakistan	57
Russia	56
Turkey	54
Spain	53

HARDWORKING

Morocco	92
France	89
United States	85
Indonesia	84
Netherlands	84
India	81
Jordan	78
Canada	77
Poland	76
Great Britain	74
Spain	72
Russia	69
Lebanon	67
Germany	64
Poland	63
Pakistan	61
Turkey	44
China	

NEGATIVE CHARACTERISTICS ASSOCIATED WITH AMERICANS

IMMORAL

Jordan	69
Lebanon	64
Pakistan	58
Turkey	57
Morocco	55
Indonesia	48
China	44
Russia	42
United States	39
Netherlands	38
France	37
India	36
Spain	36
Canada	34
Poland	33
Germany	31
Great Britain	26

RUDE

Jordan	64
Indonesia	56
Canada	53
Turkey	53
Pakistan	51
Lebanon	50
Russia	48
China	44
Spain	39
France	36
Morocco	35
United States	35
Great Britain	29
India	27
Netherlands	26
Poland	21
Germany	12

VIOLENT

Jordan	73
Turkey	70
Indonesia	67
Canada	64
France	63
Lebanon	63
Pakistan	63
China	61
Netherlands	60
Spain	60
Morocco	59
Russia	54
Great Britain	53
Germany	49
United States	49
India	39
Poland	33

GREEDY

United States	70
Turkey	68
Netherlands	67
Lebanon	66
Great Britain	64
Jordan	63
Canada	62
Indonesia	61
Russia	60
Pakistan	58
Spain	58
China	57
Poland	55
Morocco	52
Germany	49
India	43
France	31

Americans. Hardworking tops the list. The French were the most likely to see the American people in this light, with nearly nine in ten crediting Americans for their industriousness, and majorities in every country agreed—except in China. Fewer than half the Chinese, long known as hard workers, claimed to see that same trait in Americans. Majorities in every country said Americans are inventive, ranging from 86 percent of Indians to 53 percent of Spaniards. However, in only four countries, excluding the United States, did majorities believe Americans were honest. Even among Canadians, only slightly more than four in ten felt their neighbors to the south were generally trustworthy in their dealings.

On the negative side, foreigners were inclined to view Americans as greedy and violent, although they were disinclined to call them rude and immoral. Two-thirds of the Dutch, roughly three-fifths of the British, Canadians, and Spanish, and half the Germans, criticized Americans for their avarice. (Americans agreed; in fact, they were more critical of their own greediness than were non-Americans.) The French and Canadians were especially disapproving of what they saw as Americans' proclivity for violence. Not unexpectedly, the American people generally fared worse on these measures in Muslim countries than they did among traditional allies.

ALIENATING VALUES

With its military might, its economic power, and its culturally pervasive movies, music, and television America is "the inescapable country" for most of the world. And much of the world resents the impact of American pop culture on their traditional values. More telling perhaps, Europeans and others are also dubious about the two pillars of the American system, U.S.-style democracy and U.S.-style business practices.

American society has been discredited in the eyes of the world, according to University of Toronto professor in human rights Michael

Ignatieff. "Once a model to emulate," he wrote in the summer of 2005, it "has become an exception to avoid." Ignatieff cited the world's judgment of America's lack of health care for the poor; its retention of capital punishment; the curious "constitutional right" of every citizen to have guns; the religiosity of American conservatives; the arguably unjust outcome of the presidential election of 2000; and "the phenomenal influence of money on American elections."[7]

More than a million legal and illegal immigrants enter the United States every year, but when presented with a choice people around the world say they no longer see America as the prime land of opportunity. Asked where a young person should go to lead a good life, no more than 10 percent of respondents to a 2005 Pew survey in thirteen of sixteen countries recommended the United States. Australia, Canada, Great Britain, and even Germany were all preferred destinations. Only in India was America still the most popular place if one's children were thinking of emigrating.

The rise in anti-Americanism and the disillusionment with American values have been particularly strong among young Europeans. In 2002, prior to the war in Iraq, 38 percent of the French ages eighteen to twenty-nine had an unfavorable opinion of the United States; by 2005, 64 percent did. There was a similar rise in animosity among the young in Germany. Even in Great Britain, long a U.S. ally, anti-Americanism doubled—from one in six to one in three young men and women. Significantly, by 2005 the younger generation in France, Germany, Spain, and the Netherlands held the strongest anti-American sentiments of any age group in those countries.

Such generational criticism of the United States is clearly a product of the times. Over the course of even the last few years, attitudes among age groups in various countries have shifted back and forth. In 2002, for example, the strongest anti-American sentiments among Germans were held by those over age sixty-five; by 2005, it was Germans under age thirty who disliked the United States in overwhelming numbers. Similarly, in France those under age fifty had about the same view of Washington in 2002: a little over a third dis-

WHERE IS THE LAND OF OPPORTUNITY?*

People from
this country ...   pick this destination

People from this country ...	pick this destination	
United States	Canada	16%
Canada	Australia	18%
Great Britain	Australia	31 %
France	Canada	14%
Germany	Australia/Can.	11%
Spain	Great Britain	14%
Netherlands	Australia/Canada	16%
Russia	Germany	22%
Poland	Great Britain	21%
Turkey	Germany	18%
Pakistan	China	18%
Lebanon	France	19%
Jordan	United Arab Emirates	17%
Indonesia	Japan	24%
India	United States	38%
China	Canada	12%

(Most frequently named country)

* Note: Question wording was "Suppose a young person who wanted to leave this country
asked you to recommend where to go to lead a good life—what country would you recommend?"

liked America. By 2005, younger French people were the most un-
happy with the United States, with two-thirds considering themselves
anti-American.

President George W. Bush fueled the anti-Americanism among
many young Europeans. In Great Britain, France, and Germany, those
under thirty were the most likely to have the least confidence in the
U.S. president. Two-thirds of young Britons, four-fifths of young Germans, and nine-tenths of young French men and women held anti-
Bush sentiments.

Opposition to the U.S. war on terrorism may also have been a driving force behind the anti-Americanism of youthful Europeans. The young were the most opposed to the crackdown on terrorism in Great Britain, France, Germany, and Spain. This opposition has grown rapidly. In early 2005, opposition in France stood at 68 percent, up from 60 percent the year before; in Germany it was 66 percent, up from 51 percent. Youthful criticism of the U.S. antiterrorism campaign has also risen in Britain, but the 2005 polling in that country was conducted before the July subway and bus bombings in London, an incident that may have tempered opposition to such efforts.

Finally, even more than many of their elders, the young wanted a more independent Europe. Across the continent, those under thirty were the most likely to support another country becoming as powerful as the United States and they wanted Western Europe to take a more independent approach to security and diplomatic affairs.

The recent rise in unfavorable feelings toward Americans, as distinct from animosity toward the United States, was also most marked among younger groups in some key societies. In Britain, about one in five people under the age of thirty had an unfavorable view of Americans in 2005, double the one in ten who said so in 2002. Disdain for Americans among the young was also on the rise in France, Russia, and Poland (although not in Germany). Even if much anti-Americanism can rightfully be dismissed as headline-driven and transitory, a product of one U.S. leader and recent events, the emergence of widespread anti-American sentiment among Europe's future leaders could pose long-term challenges for U.S. diplomacy and activities in the world.

POLICIES AND POWER

The data from Europe, in particular, raise the question: Is widespread antipathy toward the United States the symptom of a generalized anger at America and Americans or is it merely a more specific hostility toward President Bush and his policies? To find out more about why people around the world have lost faith in the United States, Pew asked those who expressed a negative view of America to be more specific.

Majorities in most countries blamed the president, not his country. Mr. Bush was personally unpopular internationally from the first days of his first administration, owing to his opposition to the Kyoto Protocol to curb global warming and his perceived tendency to adopt a unilateral approach to many international issues. With the U.S.-led invasion of Iraq, his ratings went from bad to worse. In 2005, of Europeans who had an unfavorable view of the United States, three out of four Spaniards, two out of three Germans, French, and Dutch, and more than half of Britons said their problem was mostly with President Bush. Such antipathy toward the president carried over to Europeans' attitudes toward the United States more generally. Strong majorities throughout Western Europe said the reelection of President Bush in 2004 led them to have a less favorable opinion of the United States.

Yet such sentiments do not tell the whole story. Undoubtedly, President Bush has been the lightning rod for anti-American feelings. But while the Bush administration brought these anxieties to the surface and intensified distrust of America, the roots of anti-Americanism run deeper. American power itself, as well as U.S. policies, fuel resentment toward the United States throughout the world. Global publics believe the United States does too little to solve world problems and supports, if not advances, policies that increase the gap between rich countries and poor countries.

Similarly, opposition to strong American support for Israel long predates the Bush administration. For Muslims, it has become an article of faith that the United States unfairly supports Israel in its conflict with the Palestinians. Almost all people in the region—99 percent of Jordanians, 96 percent of Palestinians, and 94 percent of Moroccans—think Washington sides with Israel. As do most Western Europeans. The only dissent comes from Americans, where a 47 percent plurality sees U.S. policy as fair. Even in Israel, as many as 38 percent of those surveyed viewed U.S. policy as unfair to Palestinians.

These broad-ranging indictments transcend the current administration and will likely remain. Short-lived jumps in favorability produced by transitory events such as tsunami relief aid cannot sustain a long-term shift in the world's view of America. Resentment of American power, as much as its policies or leadership, drives anti-American sentiments. People around the world—particularly in Western Europe and the Middle East—are anxious about the consequences of America's exercise of its unrivaled military might, not only in Iraq but in the amorphously defined war on terrorism. By 2004, growing numbers of Europeans believed that the United States overreacted after September 11. Only in Great Britain and Russia did large majorities continue to feel that the United States was right to be so concerned about the threat of terrorism. In France and Germany, many had come to accept the view, widespread in Muslim countries, that the Americans had gone overboard.

Moreover, Europeans expressed considerable skepticism about U.S. motives in its global struggle with Al Qaeda and other Islamic extremists. When asked why they thought U.S. action was insincere, large percentages in France and Germany expressed belief that the United States was conducting the war on terrorism in order to control Middle Eastern oil and to dominate the world. People in predominantly Muslim nations who doubted the sincerity of American antiterrorist efforts saw a wider range of ulterior motives, including helping Israel and targeting unfriendly Muslim governments and groups.

For their part, Americans acknowledge that their views are somewhat out of step with the rest of the world, particularly with Europeans. But the role their values now play suits the American temperament at this time and place in the country's history. As we will discuss in more detail in the next two chapters, Americans believe they can get what they want in the world. Indeed, they are accustomed to getting what they want, as most rich people are. They believe that they, not others, are responsible for getting what they want—or for failing to do so. Americans are also optimistic—by nature, by experience, by belief that God is on their side. That optimism has many positive effects, but it can also lead to decisions about such issues as global governance and environmental resources that other countries may view as short-sighted and selfish.

Americans are somewhat defensive about how their policy positions and attitudes interweave with anti-Americanism. On global environmental issues, they argue that the Kyoto Protocol put an unfair burden on the United States to reduce emissions and would have never passed in Congress anyway. They broadly support the concept of preemptive military action if an enemy has the means and intent to strike the United States. They have limited enthusiasm for global institutions, particularly the United Nations, where they see small, insignificant nations engaged in political bargaining to produce coalitions that vote against American interests. They have little appetite for global welfare in the form of foreign aid because they believe in the value of hard work rather than handouts, whether at home or abroad. And they recognize that the world is becoming more anti-American, but to this point they seem disinclined to change their own behavior.

Still, anti-Americanism is a pervasive problem, one of the principal challenges facing the United States in the years ahead. Dealing with it will require that Americans distinguish among the differing sources of this antagonism and address them appropriately. Much of what currently irritates or even infuriates other countries about the United States are the ways in which U.S. policies and American attitudes rub up against happenings on the world scene. The differences that arise in how Americans view these problems and how the people of other countries do may be bridged in the course of events by modifications in policy or by tactful efforts to persuade others of the rightness of U.S. views and actions. The positive reaction to U.S. tsunami-relief efforts demonstrates the potential positive impact of American cooperation and generosity.

But more difficult cases emerge when relatively permanent and intractable differences in opinions and behaviors provoke discord in global decisions. Perhaps most prevalent, however, and most amenable to amelioration are those antagonisms that arise out of misunderstood beliefs about America and the American character that have no solid basis in reality.

Chief among such misapprehensions are the prevailing fears about the use of American military might for imperialistic or self-serving ends. Foreigners hear the rhetoric of particular U.S. leaders and assume such sentiments reflect broad public attitudes. But do they? Do Americans seek to save, reform, or convert the world into their own image, as many people around the world fear? Do they wish to export or impose their culture and their values? Do Americans wish to save the world for democracy, adopting President Woodrow Wilson's ideals and President George W. Bush's rhetoric? Do they hope to convert others to their particular faith? Are there crusades that motivate the agenda of the American people? To address these fears, Americans—and the world—must understand the essence of the American character. As we will see, judging from the data, the answer to all these questions is most often no, but this message has not reached the larger world—or Americans' own depictions of their interests.

3

THE AMERICAN WAY

BY OBJECTIVE STANDARDS, America's position vis-à-vis the world has not changed much since 2000. Now, as then, the United States is the richest and most powerful country, the sole superpower. But in subjective ways, in the eyes of the world, America's global posture has indeed undergone a transformation. From the reluctant superpower with quasi-isolationist leanings in the 1990s, the United States has morphed into an assertive hyperpower in the opening years of the new century.

The worldview of the American people has also changed in profound ways. A decade ago Americans questioned the need for global engagement. They enjoyed, for the first time in a half-century, the luxury of no longer standing on the barricades against an ideological, nuclear-armed adversary. Then, in 2001, the world came crashing in on the United States. Americans found themselves facing a new enemy, one that had thrust itself onto their home soil to claim the lives of nearly three thousand people and to threaten even greater mayhem. Fear of international terrorism, not confined to the lingering threat of Al Qaeda and its offshoots, now informs and animates

American views of the world. This and the high costs of the Iraq war will shape U.S. politics and leadership choices for years to come.

That this is occurring at a time when the United States seems all-powerful has raised disturbing concerns around the world about the U.S. global approach and intentions. Much of the "American way" is increasingly not the ideal to which people in many parts of the world aspire but rather is seen as an unpredictable and threatening force bent on empire. Ordinary Americans are almost stunned by the accusation. They cannot understand the reason and the extent to which the United States and its "ideology" have come to be resented. Average Americans have no imperial aspirations. Indeed, they have only limited interest in international affairs and little appetite for bearing the burdens of the world. They see their country as an exemplar of democracy whose citizens enjoy unparalleled personal freedom and opportunity. The gap between the self-image of America on a white horse and the dim view of America from abroad has never been greater. Moreover, this gap in perceptions comes at a time when global public opinion has emerged as an important force in international politics, the by-product of economic globalization, transnational opinion polling, and the connectivity of peoples through mass communications.

The combination of policy and circumstance has spawned a widespread resentment of America and a considerable public recognition of anti-Americanism around the world. In virtually every country the Pew Research Center has surveyed from 2002 through 2005, whether friendly to the United States or not, people decry the spreading influence of America. Yet they do so only up to a point. They dislike the exercise of American power, they envy its wealth—and they admire its products. They resist American ideas and culture—even as they embrace them. Anti-Americanism is not a simple problem. All of this brings new urgency to understanding the attitudes and values of the increasingly dominant American character. Who are Americans as a people? How different are they from the rest of the world? And are they different in the ways America's detractors suggest?

In approaching these questions, a more nuanced definition of exceptionalism will emerge. There will be aspects of the American character, such as religious belief and nationalism, whose impact on U.S. policies and actions is widely misinterpreted in the larger world; these aspects are *misunderstood*. There will be aspects of the American character, such as America's equivocal internationalism, that are subject to the course of events and the influence of American leadership; they are *conditional*. Finally, there will be aspects of the American character, such as America's strong individualism, that are both a source of vitality and the wellspring of many of the differences between U.S. citizens and other people; in their essence, they are *problematic*, in that the possibility for change is slight. We will consider these aspects of exceptionalism over the course of this book, particularly in analyzing those differences that pose special problems for U.S. policy in today's world.

THE ESSENCE OF AMERICAN EXCEPTIONALISM

As Alexis de Tocqueville described it in his classic *Democracy in America*, the essence of American exceptionalism is a unique mixture of liberty, egalitarianism, individualism, populism, and laissez-faire values. These concepts emanated from the egalitarian nature of the early American society that had no experience with—indeed a profound distaste for—monarchies and hereditary privilege. Tocqueville saw much to praise in these features, but he also found in Americans a feeling of superiority and even arrogance. "Do not lead an American to speak of Europe," he wrote. "He will ordinarily show great presumption and a rather silly pride" by lecturing Europeans about liberty and freedom. Tocqueville suggested that a gnawing insecurity underlay such posturing.[1]

Does this presumption and pride grow out of Americans' belief that they are more pragmatic and less ideological than the peoples of the Old World? Is it part of the American creed—not a religious doctrine but perhaps derived from religion—that disposes Americans to impose their values on the rest of the world? How is American nationalism linked to the defining values of the American people and their way of life? Is there a distinctive American way of thinking that determines how Americans view the rest of the world? Finally, are Americans unaware that their way of thinking about themselves and the world causes resentment abroad?

Stereotypes aside, Americans are indeed distinctive among the world's peoples. But they are most distinctive in ways that go beyond Tocqueville's nineteenth-century characterizations and the mythology of American exceptionalism. As we will discuss in greater detail in later chapters, Americans are more strongly individualistic than Europeans, more patriotic, more religious, and culturally more conservative. Some of these differences do not necessarily result in permanent divides, while others are more problematic.

Americans are chauvinistic, but not with the usual connotations. The charge that Americans are more nationalistic is true, but comes with an important caveat. Americans have greater feelings of national superiority and are more patriotic than the citizens of many other advanced countries. Fully 60 percent of Americans agreed with the broad statement "Our people are not perfect, but our culture is superior to others"—a proportion almost twice that found in France (33 percent), somewhat more than in Britain and Germany, and approached only by neighboring Canada (49 percent). But despite the sharp contrast with Western Europe, American nationalism is close to the norm of the forty-four nations surveyed by Pew in 2002. Peoples of developing nations, particularly in Asia, hold nationalistic views much closer to those of Americans. And American nationalism pales in comparison with the nationalism expressed in many other parts of the world. More than two-thirds of Japanese feel culturally superior to others, for example, and the number rises to 80 percent and higher for such nations as Mali, the Philippines, Turkey, and India. South Korea and Indonesia top the scale with an astonishing 90 percent of the public believing their culture is superior to other cultures.[2]

Much as Tocqueville found, national pride is another trait on which Americans stand out compared to Europeans. Many more U.S. citizens say they are very proud of their nationality (71 percent) than the Spanish (51 percent), who are in turn prouder than the British, French, and Italians, and far prouder than the Germans (21 percent). But again, Americans are matched or surpassed in their pride by the peoples of Asia, Africa, and Latin America. Among those proudest of their nationality are Pakistanis (81 percent); still prouder are Salvadorans, Filipinos, and Moroccans; most chauvinistic are Venezuelans (92 percent).[3]

In most nations, a significant segment of the population believes that its way of life needs protection from foreign influences. This feeling is more pervasive than the sense of cultural superiority or of national pride. Again, the sentiment is strongest among people in developing countries.

TABLE 3.1

VERY PROUD TO BE . . .	%
American	71
Canadian	66
Spanish	51
British	45
French	38
Italian	38
German	21
Venezuelan	92
Moroccan	89
Filipino	87
Salvadoran	86
Pakistani	81
Nigerian	72
Indian	67
South African	66
Japanese	21

Source: World Values Survey, 2000.

In general, Europeans and Canadians feel less anxious about protecting their culture than Americans do. Barely more than one in two Britons, French, and Germans feel in need of cultural protection, compared to almost two-thirds of Americans; in Europe, Russians feel most beleaguered in this respect, with more than three in four wanting to protect their culture. But beyond Europe the threat of foreign influence looms. Almost nine out of ten Turks fear being overwhelmed by foreign culture, followed closely by Indonesians, Ugandans, Kenyans, Senegalese, and Egyptians. This pattern recurs time and again: Americans are different from Europeans, especially Western Europeans, but they are closer to people in developing nations on many key attitudes and values, including cultural insecurity.

Moreover, there is no evidence in the polls, contrary to some foreign commentary, that Americans have become more nationalistic in recent times. Strong expressions of patriotism have long been characteristic of Americans. But for the last decade and a half, a period including the September 11 attacks, the level of patriotism in the United States has remained remarkably stable. In a 1988 survey, 89 percent of Americans agreed with the statement "I am very patriotic." In 1991, and again in 2003, 91 percent agreed. Following the 2001 terrorist attacks, the number of Americans who "completely agreed" (as distinct from "mostly agreed") with the statement rose from 51 percent in 1994 to 56 percent in 2003, a negligible increase considering the recent terrorism on American soil.[4]

Still, 70 percent of Americans believe it is a good thing that U.S. ideas and customs are spreading around the world, which is of two minds on this issue. Pew's surveys found that America is nearly universally admired for its technological achievements, for being the engine that drives modernity; and people in most countries say they enjoy U.S. movies, music, and television. Majorities in almost every country studied said they disliked the general global influence of the United States. This sentiment is prevalent in friendly nations such as Canada and Britain, and even more so in less friendly countries such as Argentina and Pakistan.

But does it follow that Americans, out of their national pride, are deliberately intent on spreading their values and ways of doing things around the world? Or do Americans merely feel that these concepts "work for us; they're certain to be good for others"? Available evidence suggests the latter. The findings of Pew's Global Attitude Project suggest that the American brand of chauvinism leads to indifference toward the world rather than a messianic desire to change it by spreading American ideas and culture. The default disposition of the average American is to ignore the rest of the world. For its part, the rest of the world seems to have reversed itself over the past decade, from complaining in the 1990s that the United States was isolationist and ignoring it to now charging that the United States is too active around the globe and intent on building an empire.

Moreover, among the foreign policy priorities of Americans, little support can be found for promoting U.S. values—including democracy. When asked in 2004 which of nineteen potential foreign policy problems should get top priority, Americans ranked promoting democracy abroad eighteenth. Fewer than one in four said it should have top priority, down marginally from early in September of 2001, a few days before the terrorist attacks, when the issue reached its high point of the decade (29 percent). And despite the Bush administration's rhetoric about building democracies and ending tyranny around the world, support among Americans for promoting democracy abroad has actually fallen further, to 24 percent in several surveys conducted in 2004 and 2005. Exporting American-style democracy has in fact scored consistently low since at least 1993, when 22 percent gave it top priority.[5]

It is noteworthy that little significant partisan difference can be found on the issue: 27 percent of Republicans and 22 percent of Democrats gave promoting democracy a top priority. Only the goal of improving the living standards in poor nations was rated lower by Americans. At the other end of the scale, protecting the homeland from terrorist attacks and protecting the jobs of U.S. workers was the top priority for more than eight in ten Americans.

Beyond being equivocal about promoting democracy abroad,

TABLE 3.2

AMERICANS' FOREIGN POLICY PRIORITIES IN 2004

Rank		% Naming as Top Priority
1	Protect against terrorist attacks	88
2	Protect jobs of American workers	84
3	Reduce spread of AIDS/diseases	72
4	Stop spread of WMD	71
5	Ensure adequate energy supplies	70
6	Reduce dependence on foreign oil	63
7	Combat international drug trafficking	63
8	Distribute costs of maintaining world order	58
9	Improve relationships with allies	54
10	Deal with problem of world hunger	50
11	Strengthen the United Nations	48
12	Protect groups threatened with genocide	47
13	Deal with global warming	36
14	Reduce U.S. military commitments	35
15	Promote U.S. business interests abroad	35
16	Promote human rights abroad	33
17	Solve Israeli/Palestinian conflict	28
18	**Promote democracy abroad**	**24**
19	Improve living standards in poor nations	23

Americans are ambivalent about what kind of role their country should play on the global stage. Over the last four decades, most Americans have rejected the isolationist view that the United States should mind its own business internationally. In 1964, when the Gallup Organization began asking the question, seven in ten respondents rejected the notion. The internationalist proportion dropped to 47 percent in 1976, in the aftermath of the Vietnam War, but it gradually revived, reaching two-thirds in 2002 and declining only slightly in 2004. With frustration with the casualties in Iraq mounting, isolation-

TABLE 3.3

AMERICA TWO-MINDED ABOUT INTERNATIONAL ENGAGEMENT

The U.S. should mind its own business and let other countries get along on their own.	October 2005
Agree	42%
Disagree	51%
Don't know/Refused	7%

We should not think so much in international terms but concentrate more on our own national problems.	
Agree	71%
Disagree	23%
Don't know/Refused	6%

Source: Pew Research Center for the People & the Press, 2005.

ist sentiment reemerged in 2005, when Pew found 42 percent of Americans again thinking the United States should tend to its own affairs.

But even as most Americans have on balance rejected isolationism, they also believe their government should focus more on domestic rather than on foreign concerns, a view that has prevailed over the last forty years. In 1964, in the same Gallup poll, 55 percent of Americans agreed with this statement: "We should not think so much in international terms but concentrate more on our own national problems and building up our strength and prosperity here at home." In 1972, this view was considerably more prevalent, rising to 76 percent, a level that persisted through the rest of the century. In 2002, it dropped—but modestly—to 65 percent.[6]

These data indicate that while Americans reject a purely isolationist foreign outlook, they are more concerned with addressing problems at home than with exporting their values and ideals abroad. Other results, in surveys asking about America's role in the world, point in the same direction. Since the passing of the Cold War, no more than 13 percent of Americans have said the United States should be the single most important leader in the world. More than three-quarters of Americans feel the United States should play a shared leadership role; and, of these, most prefer that America be no more or less active than other nations. Certainly there is no desire, let alone a mandate, for American empire-building.

TOCQUEVILLE UPDATED

But what about those components of the American creed that Tocqueville identified in the early nineteenth century? Are they still characteristic of Americans? Or, over the past two centuries, have American beliefs become broadly shared in all parts of the world? The short answer to both of those questions is yes. Americans are still defined by our belief in liberty, egalitarianism, individualism, populism, and laissez-faire economics, but these values are by no means uniquely American today.

Americans prize liberty and freedom. But Pew polling and the World Values Survey have found that Western Europeans feel not so differently from Americans about these ideals. Germans and Americans, for example, attach about the same importance to the freedom to openly criticize the government, as well as to having multi-party elections and a fair judiciary system. More Germans put great importance on these democratic features, incidentally, than do most people of the former Soviet bloc countries of Central and Eastern Europe, which are newcomers to democracy and less familiar with the importance of these values in a civil society.

Americans and Europeans are similar in yet another respect: their cynicism toward government. Majorities in the United States and throughout most of the European continent agreed in a 2002 Pew survey that when something is run by the government, it is usually inefficient and wasteful. An earlier Times Mirror survey, conducted in 1991, found that Americans and Western Europeans responded similarly, in the negative, when asked whether they have any say in what government does. Eastern Europeans were even more cynical and alienated in this respect, but presumably these attitudes have improved over the past decade and a half, since the fall of the Soviet Union.

On the limits of liberty, majorities of Americans and most Western Europeans surveyed in 1991 supported free speech even for fascists. The only exception was Germany. Americans and Britons narrowly rejected the idea of banning books with dangerous ideas, while majorities in France, Spain, Italy, and especially Germany would have banned such literature. And majorities in the United States and France favored allowing all parties to compete in elections, including antidemocratic parties; Italians and, again, the Germans favored outlawing some parties.

Americans are indeed egalitarian—but not so much more so than Western Europeans, who are as likely as Americans to say they don't judge people by their level of education, which can be a proxy question for class prejudice. And there was little difference in how much Americans and Europeans say they have in common with their own countrymen who have less education. Along the same line, the World Values Survey found few transatlantic differences on whether individual incomes should be made equal. Of course, there is today less disparity in Europe between the rich and poor than in the United States. The surveys also indicate that Americans and Europeans have the same egalitarian attitudes toward community affairs and the workplace.

On questions of ethnicity and ethnic minorities, however, Americans are more open-minded. This may be less a reflection of an egalitarianism than of a greater acceptance of ethnic diversity, the American embrace of the "melting pot." Whatever the reason, in 1991 Americans were more likely than Western Europeans to reject the notion that they had little in common with people of other ethnic groups and races; despite European unification efforts, foreigners remain highly unpopular on that continent. A Pew 2002 survey found again that Americans, compared to British, French, and Germans, less often said that they had little in common with people of other races and ethnicity.

Americans and Western Europeans also differ on the value that immigrants bring to their new countries. In general, immigrants and minority groups are seen in most parts of the world as having a bad influence on the way things are going in a particular nation. Aside from Canada, where a strong majority holds a positive view toward immigrants, the greatest support for immigrants in advanced nations is found in the United States. And while four in ten Americans feel immigrants are bad for the country, Europeans by comparison are more hostile. Half or more of the people in France, Britain, Germany, and Italy consider immigrants bad for the society, even as these nations are hosts to large and growing minorities for the first time in modern history.

But such value differences are mutable and not inherent. A 2005 survey by the German Marshall Fund underscores that fact. By a margin of 33 to 27 percent, Americans were found more likely than Europeans to believe that large numbers of immigrants and refugees would be an extremely pressing threat to their country over the next ten years. These views could be a precursor of shifts in broader attitudes.

Americans for their part take an overwhelmingly positive view of the country's two largest minorities: African-Americans and Hispanics. Nearly eight in ten say blacks have a good influence on the country and two-thirds say that about Hispanics.

Tocqueville observed that Americans were open to a populist leadership that emanated from the common man rather than from an aristocratic elite. There is little in the way of comparative survey data to trace a line to modern American politics that might prove or disprove his assertion. Among recent U.S. presidents two—Reagan and Clinton—come from poor backgrounds; the two Bushes, father and son, come from privilege. Our leaders may or may not be populist icons, but on the other hand, populism in recent times has more often been defined as a political philosophy focused on the needs of common people and advocating a more equitable distribution of wealth and power. In this sense it clashes with the laissez-faire values that are, if anything, a more significant element in the concept of American exceptionalism.

Two elements of the American creed clearly continue to set Americans apart from other people. Americans continue to be more skeptical of the role of government and more resistant to government regulation than people in other countries. Americans are less supportive of a government social safety net, for example, than are the peoples of the social democracies of Western Europe. Americans want government help in the form of unemployment insurance, Social Security, and some medical care for the poor. But they value personal freedom more. In this regard, Americans are unique among the populations of wealthy nations.

Majorities in every European country, West and East, as well as Canada believe it is more important for government to ensure that no one is in need than it is for individuals to be free to pursue goals without government interference. For Americans, the opposite is true: a majority (58 percent) values individual freedom more than government welfare. Among forty-one countries around the world for which data exist, two-thirds favor protecting the needy. Still, one in three countries favors individualism, often by even larger majorities than in the United States.

Americans show relatively weak support for the social safety net even when there is no potential cost to personal liberty from the government. When asked simply if government has a responsibility to care for the poor, 73 percent of Americans said yes, but this proportion was smaller than in any other country except Jordan and Japan. When the intensity with which respondents held this view was probed, these differences were even sharper: merely three in ten Americans "completely agree" that the government should help the poor, half the level of support that exists in Eastern Europe and Great Britain. Since the 1991 Times Mirror survey, several Western European countries have shown a decline in the proportions that "completely agree" about government responsibility for the poor. Nonetheless, Europeans overall are much more committed to a safety net for the poor than are Americans.[7]

But it is the individualism of Americans that really sets them apart. Unlike most of the rest of the world, Americans believe that individuals,

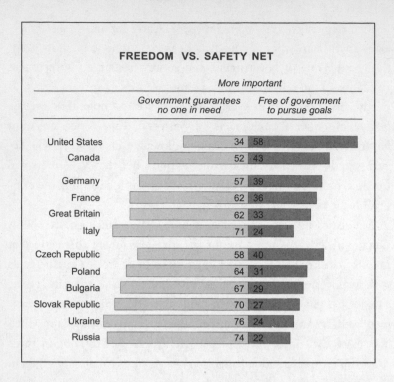

FREEDOM VS. SAFETY NET

More important

	Government guarantees no one in need	Free of government to pursue goals
United States	34	58
Canada	52	43
Germany	57	39
France	62	36
Great Britain	62	33
Italy	71	24
Czech Republic	58	40
Poland	64	31
Bulgaria	67	29
Slovak Republic	70	27
Ukraine	76	24
Russia	74	22

themselves, not the larger forces of society, determine whether a person will be successful in life. In a view consonant with their laissez-faire attitudes, two-thirds of Americans rejected the notion that outside forces determine success in life. Most Canadians felt the same way, as did the Japanese, although to a lesser extent. The rest of the world disagreed. Moreover, this view is becoming even more widely held among Americans: the percentage of the U.S. public that blames outside factors for failure has fallen over the past decade and a half from 41 percent in 1988 to 32 percent in 2002.

Americans also overwhelmingly believed in 2002 that individuals are to blame for their personal failures; merely 12 percent blamed society. Only Indonesians and the Czechs hold this view as strongly as Americans. Yet most Western Europeans agree, if less strongly, that individuals are responsible for their own failures. Interestingly, Europeans' attitudes appear to be shaped partly by the individual's economic

TABLE 3.4

SUCCESS IN LIFE DETERMINED BY FORCES
OUTSIDE OUR CONTROL

	Agree %	Disagree %
United States	32	65
Canada	35	63
Germany	68	31
Italy	66	31
France	54	44
Great Britain	48	48
Poland	63	29
Ukraine	62	35
Russia	52	36
Bulgaria	52	28
Slovak Republic	49	48
Czech Republic	47	48

status, though this is not the case among Americans. In France, Germany, and Italy, and even in Britain to a lesser extent, lower-income citizens were more likely to blame society. More than eight in ten Americans, regardless of income, blame individuals. In fact, the least affluent Americans were less likely to blame society for individual failures than were the most affluent Europeans. On a similar question, one in five low-income Americans completely disagree with the notion that success in life is determined by outside forces. In France, Italy, and Germany, fewer high-income respondents reject the idea completely.

Thus, Tocqueville's American exceptionalism still describes the constellation of core American values, but these values are no longer unique to Americans. Today many such attitudes are shared worldwide. Aspirations of liberty and equality, and a discredited view of the welfare state are evident in much of the world. Admiration of the way America practices democracy and commerce is significant around the world, although this is less true in advanced nations. Pew's 2002 survey

TABLE 3.5

LACK OF SUCCESS IN LIFE DUE TO . . .

	Society %	Individual %
United States	12	82
Canada	18	76
Great Britain	19	75
Germany	22	74
France	28	68
Italy	31	57
Indonesia	11	87
Czech Republic	14	82
Slovak Republic	20	76
Russia	38	52
Ukraine	48	50
Bulgaria	47	38
Poland	55	32

of forty-four nations found much more approval for American-style democracy and economic practices in Africa and Asia than in Western Europe and Canada. But comparisons with Europeans and the people of other developed countries provide the most incisive information; the gap in living standards is much less likely to color their expressed values and outlook.

There are, however, some remarkable differences between Americans and the peoples of wealthy nations that are not captured under Tocqueville's exceptionalism rubric. Among these are Americans' abiding optimism and profound religiosity.

A NATION OF TWO FAITHS

Americans are more optimistic and happier than most people and consistently express more satisfaction with the way that their lives are going. In the 1950s, pioneering social psychologist Hadley Cantril and his collaborator Lloyd Free developed a questioning sequence for public opinion surveys that explicitly investigated national levels of personal contentment and compared these levels country to country, taking into account the differing hopes and concerns of different people around the world. In this so-called self-anchoring model, respondents are asked to describe their best possible life and their worries about how things could go wrong. Then they rate their current position on a "ladder" of life, from 0 to 10. Finally, they recall their position on the ladder five years earlier and forecast where they will be five years ahead. The question series has been used for nearly fifty years by Pew, Gallup, and others. Response patterns are stable and provide a wealth of comparative information about the way diverse people see their lives.[8]

In nearly every survey of this kind taken, Americans have rated their lives higher than people anywhere else in the world. Not too surprisingly, Western European publics generally rank second and people in the developing nations for the most part rank much lower in their self-assessment. One of the world's truisms, that "money buys happiness," has been found in fact to be largely, but not completely, true. Rich people in America are more satisfied with their lives than middle-income and poor Americans. This is generally true in other countries as well. For the forty-four nations Pew surveyed in 2002, there was a strong correlation between per capita income and how people rated their lives: the people of wealthy nations were generally more content than those of poor nations. Notable exceptions include Canadians, who are more satisfied with life than their wealth would predict; the Japanese, who are less satisfied; and Central Americans, who have a remarkably rosy view of their lives despite their income levels.

In this rating scheme, Americans are quite exceptional in their assessment of how far they have progressed from the past and in their optimism about the future. On these measures, they stand higher than their very high incomes would predict, topping even the more self-satisfied Canadians. A 1974 Gallup global poll had remarkably similar results to those in Pew's recent surveys.[9]

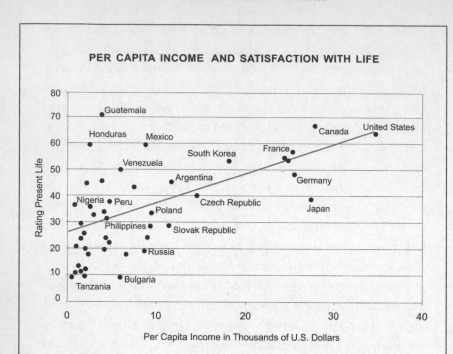

PER CAPITA INCOME AND SATISFACTION WITH LIFE

This confidence and positive attitude are defining characteristics of Americans. Every successful U.S. politician recognized this, and those who speak otherwise do so at their peril. One of President Jimmy Carter's greatest mistakes was to tell Americans during the 1979 energy crisis that they were suffering a "crisis of confidence." He failed to understand how fundamentally upbeat Americans are about their futures, whatever their immediate situation.

A further manifestation of this optimism is reflected in the unwavering consensus that Americans can always find a way to solve their problems. Two out of three respondents have subscribed to this view in Pew surveys since the mid-1980s. To be sure, some segments of U.S. society are less self-confident than Americans overall. But majorities of every major demographic and political group in the nation—whites and blacks, rich and poor, Republicans, Democrats,

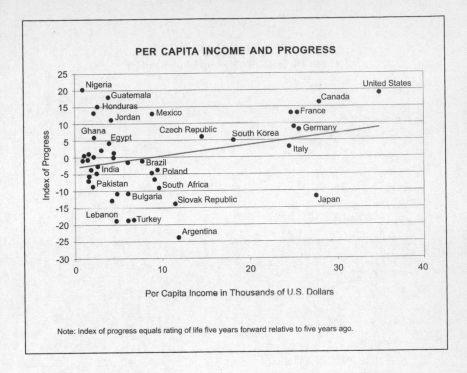

PER CAPITA INCOME AND PROGRESS

Note: Index of progress equals rating of life five years forward relative to five years ago.

and Independents, conservatives and liberals—believe in the country's problem-solving ability.

Americans' faith in technology plays no small part in this outlook. It is as strong and as deep as any other belief in explaining why Americans are optimistic. In 1999, Pew conducted a poll to commemorate the millennium and found that Americans lauded technology as the greatest achievement of the United States in the twentieth century.

Americans see the last century as a time of great economic, social, and technological progress. Among individuals, among families, among members of various social and demographic groups, nearly two-thirds say they have improved their own circumstances since the 1950s; even larger proportions believe that many segments of U.S. society have achieved economic and social gains over the period. Science and technology are widely seen as the vehicles of the nation's economic prosperity in the twentieth century. Americans particularly

TABLE 3.6

GREATEST ACHIEVEMENT OF THE
TWENTIETH CENTURY FOR U.S. GOVERNMENT

	Views of Americans
Science/Technology	19%
Space program, technology, computers	
World peace	12%
Peace	
Winning World War II	
End of the Cold War	
Freedom/Civil Rights	9%
Civil rights/ending segregation	
Equal rights	
Freedom/liberty	
Social Safety Net	6%
Social Security	
Public assistance, welfare, work first	
Economy/Jobs	5%
Maintaining a stable economy	
More/better jobs, lower unemployment	

Source: Pew Millennium Survey, July 1999.

celebrate the inventions and conveniences that have made their lives better today, from the automobile to birth control pills to the Internet. When Americans think about government's achievements, science and technology lead the way, outstripping the advent of Social Security, the victories of World War II and the Cold War, the advance of civil rights, and the maintenance of a stable economy.

The boom years that ushered in the new millennium refreshed Americans' faith in the future. After the deep recession in the early 1980s, the 1987 stock market crash, financial scandals, and years of recovery without many new jobs, "the 1990s reinforced the belief that technological advances will naturally lead to prosperity," wrote Jeff Madrick, the director of policy research at the New School for Social Research. "To many, the U.S. economy was apparently back on its rapid historic track and, in light of relative foreign stagnation, the case for American exceptionalism had found new justification."[10]

From this perspective, most Americans view the rest of the world as a place their forefathers thankfully left, choosing instead America, the land of opportunity and of broader freedoms. As for the future, a vast majority of Americans in the Pew Millennium Survey said they believed that if life is to improve, science and technology must play a major role. Evangelicals were marginally more dubious about this proposition. Americans were also more likely than most Europeans to agree that scientific advances will help rather than hurt mankind. More than half of Americans believed this, compared with one in two Germans, only four in ten British, and three in ten Italians.[11]

On the face of it, Americans' faith in science would seem to contradict a faith in religion. Certainly evangelicals, and perhaps others, are dubious about some aspects of science, including some significant areas of biology, and particularly cosmology and anthropology. About the same number of Americans say they believe in creationism as in evolution, for example. But on issues that directly affect their lives, such as health and protecting the quality of life, science wins. An example is the increasing support for stem cell research. In 2004, by a 52 percent to 34 percent margin, Americans said it was more important to conduct such research, which might result in new cures for human diseases, than to avoid destroying the potential life of embryos. Two years earlier, only a plurality of Americans supported stem cell research (43 percent in favor to 38 percent against).[12] As Tocqueville observed:

> [The Americans] have all a lively faith in the perfectability of man, they judge that the diffusion of knowledge must necessarily be advantageous, and the consequences of ignorance fatal; they all consider society as a body in a state of improvement, humanity as a changing scene, in which nothing is, or ought to be, permanent; and they admit that what appears to them today to be good, may be superseded by something better tomorrow.[13]

A positive technology-driven outlook and substantial national wealth reinforce Americans' view that the world offers boundless opportunities. It is a world in which the individual rules, limited only by his or her ability to achieve the American dream; a world in which the individual, not society, is responsible for personal failure; in which faith in God and in a nation that exists "under God" legitimizes, even sanctifies, their optimism.

And nowhere is the unique global positioning of America more apparent or important than with respect to religion. The long-running World Values Survey has characterized Americans as unique in holding the "self-expressive" values—those relating to personal responsibility, competition, technological advance, and the roles of government and private business—of an advanced nation while subscribing to the traditional social values—those relating to family, patriotism, and religious belief—more associated with less advanced nations. The survey developed a map to graphically represent these differences.

As *The Economist*'s article accompanying this map pointed out, "America's position is odd. On the quality-of-life axis [survival values to self-expression values], it is like Europe: a little more 'self-expressive' than Catholic countries, such as France and Italy, a little less so than Protestant ones such as Holland or Sweden. This is more than a matter of individual preference. The 'quality of life' axis is the one most closely associated with political and economic freedoms." Yet, the magazine's editors went on to say, America is also "more traditional than any place at all in Central or Eastern Europe. America is near the bottom-right corner of the chart, a strange mix of tradition and self-expression."[14]

Polls show huge transatlantic gaps in religious behaviors and attitudes. Compared to Europeans, Americans express more faith in God, attend church more often, pray more often. They are closer to Muslims than to Europeans with respect to observance and commitment, as well as on attitudes of personal morality such as homosexuality. One striking difference: Americans think belief in God is a prerequisite of morality. Most Europeans disagree.

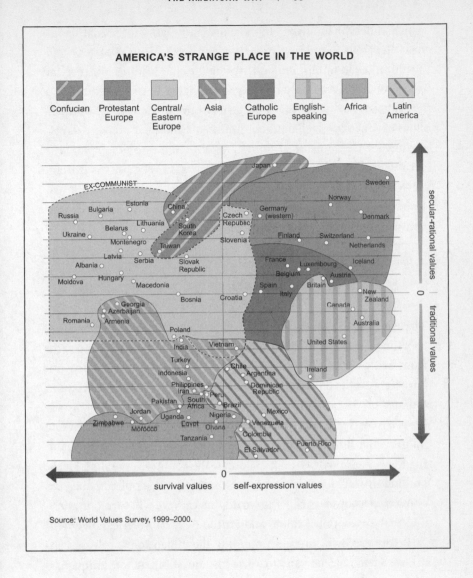

AMERICA'S STRANGE PLACE IN THE WORLD

Confucian | Protestant Europe | Central/Eastern Europe | Asia | Catholic Europe | English-speaking | Africa | Latin America

secular-rational values

traditional values

EX-COMMUNIST

Japan • Sweden • Norway • Denmark

Russia • Bulgaria • Estonia • China • Germany (western) • Switzerland • Netherlands

Belarus • Lithuania • Czech Republic • Finland

Ukraine • Montenegro • South Korea • Slovenia

Latvia • Serbia • Taiwan • France • Luxembourg • Iceland • Austria

Albania • Slovak Republic • Belgium • Britain

Moldova • Hungary • Macedonia • Spain • Italy

Georgia • Bosnia • Croatia • New Zealand • Canada • Australia

Azerbaijan

Romania • Armenia • Poland • United States

India • Vietnam

Turkey • Chile • Ireland

Indonesia • Argentina

Philippines • Dominican Republic

Iran • Peru • Brazil

Pakistan • South Africa • Mexico

Jordan • Uganda • Nigeria • Venezuela

Zimbabwe • Egypt • Ghana • Colombia

Morocco • Tanzania • El Salvador • Puerto Rico

0

survival values | self-expression values

Source: World Values Survey, 1999–2000.

Tocqueville, writing in the nineteenth century, also pointed to this standout characteristic. Indeed, he characterized American religiosity in extreme terms: "Here and there in the midst of American society you meet with men full of a fanatical and almost wild spiritualism, which hardly exists in Europe. From time to time strange sects arise which endeavor to strike out extraordinary paths to eternal happiness. Religious insanity is very common in the United States." Still, Tocqueville did not list religion among the core features of American exceptionalism. And only recently has religion been recognized as a key element distinguishing Americans from Europeans. (The dimensions of Americans' religious commitments and their possible ramifications for U.S. policies at home and abroad are topics explored in greater depth in chapter 5.) Whether American religiosity is extreme or closer to the global norm, Europeans see it as conflated with American exceptionalism and as the driving force behind American conservatism and its evangelic worldview.[15]

BUT HOW EXCEPTIONAL IS AMERICAN EXCEPTIONALISM?

There is no question that the United States is exceptional in terms of its national history: Americans are descended from people who came from everywhere, and since 1814 they have not been invaded nor have they ever been conquered. The United States is the first country founded on the basis of an idea: the primacy of the individual. America is a historically unique hegemon, with a fearsome and unrivaled military. But it has largely conquered not with tanks but blue jeans, Big Macs, and movies—and, of course, the country's founding ideals. Our inquiry will focus less on America, writ large, a military and economic superpower astride the world. Instead, we will turn our attention to the exceptional values and attitudes of the American people.

Before exploring and documenting the dimensions of this exceptionalism, it is important to raise the question of the uniqueness of American uniqueness. As we will illustrate throughout this book, Americans do have basic values and attitudes that are distinctively American. But are they alone in that regard? And, more important, are Americans so different from other publics that they cannot understand and accept the points of view of people in other parts of the world? A careful reading of the data suggests that the value gaps between Americans and non-Americans are not, in fact, so great—except in a few cases. And where such differences exist, they are not greater than those found in peoples of other major countries. In short, many publics are exceptional, and, as it turns out, Americans are clearly *not* the most exceptional on the planet.

The Pew Research Center's largest global survey, of forty-four nations in 2002, specifically investigated this question. People in all walks of life—men and women, rich and poor—were asked about their opinions on social issues, government's role, religion, individualism, and political beliefs. These gross comparisons reveal a number of "outlier nations," including the United States, that hold consistently different views from other countries with similar cultures and levels of economic development.

To be sure, when compared with the citizens of other postindustrial societies, that is, with Western Europeans and Canadians, the American public stands out. But in its relative uniqueness, the United States is not alone. Among South Americans, Argentines are distinct. Among Eastern Europeans, the Czechs and the Russians are those who hold distinctive views. And the Japanese stand apart from other Asian publics.

In fact, if the Japanese are compared with people from other rich nations rather than with other Asians, they are the most exceptional in the world, not only in Pew research but in other multinational surveys. Poll after poll finds the Japanese to be the most pessimistic of people, expressing far less satisfaction with their lot in life than might be expected given their relatively high per capita incomes. Yet, compared to other Asians, the Japanese are, like Americans, highly self-reliant and distrustful of government and, like Europeans, secular. It is the Japanese public, not the American public, that is most exceptional in the world. (The Chinese might one day take this prize, but there is not yet enough data because of state controls on independent polling.)

Thus American exceptionalism itself is not unique. Moreover, American differences with other Western publics are not so great that

TABLE 3.7

WHO'S EXCEPTIONAL

Western Democracies	Exceptionalism Index	Eastern Europe	Exceptionalism Index
United States	**220**	**Czech Republic**	**192**
France	102	**Russia**	**191**
Italy	101	Slovak Republic	141
Germany	98	Ukraine	129
Canada	84	Bulgaria	128
Britain	77	Poland	125
Latin America		*Muslim Nations*	
Argentina	**240**	**Jordan**	**236**
Brazil	142	Uzbekistan	211
Honduras	132	Turkey	207
Guatemala	114	Pakistan	150
Bolivia	111	Lebanon	102
Venezuela	109	Egypt	92
Peru	91		
Mexico	89	*Africa*	
		Angola	**235**
Asia		Uganda	148
Japan	**338**	South Africa	143
India	218	Mali	135
Korea	203	Tanzania	122
Bangladesh	191	Kenya	105
Indonesia	178	Nigeria	105
Philippines	174	Ivory Coast	94
		Ghana	87
		Senegal	86

Note: Index computed by the Pew Research Center for the People & the Press as the sum of the percentage difference between each nation's score and the average of all countries *in the region* on each of sixteen values.

the United States could not find common ground with traditional allies on many global issues. These differences are bridgeable because the values of liberal democracies—and most especially many Anglo-American values—triumphed in the twentieth century. Had public opinion surveys been conducted in the nineteenth century, American beliefs about democracy might well have stood out more. And had the polling been conducted thirty years ago, Americans' apparent anti-government attitudes and soft support for a social safety net would likely have stood out more than they do today.

In short, Americans are different from other peoples on many counts. But most of these differences do not portend a widening rift with the rest of the world. Despite the current negative image of America, its people and policies, there is broad global acceptance of the fundamental economic and political values that the United States has long promoted. Its free-market model and democratic ideals are accepted in all corners of the world.

4

THE PROBLEM OF AMERICAN
EXCEPTIONALISM

AMERICA'S EXCEPTIONALISM IS relative, not absolute. Nevertheless, differences in American values and attitudes, modest as many may be, do matter in the daily relations among nations because of the status of the United States as an unprecedented superpower and the driving influence of American business and culture. Even minor differences between American views and those held by people in other parts of the world can become points of friction.

Argentine and Japanese exceptionalism do not face such resistance because Argentina and Japan do not impose themselves in the way the United States dominates the globe. Americans' exceptionalism is America's problem, not so much because Americans are that different from others, but because any dissimilarities in attitudes or values are magnified by the United States' place in the world, and others often resent those differences.

In pursuing these questions it is helpful to differentiate between three types of American exceptionalism, mentioned in chapter 3, that shape the ways U.S. citizens look at the world and the way the world looks at them:

- *Misunderstood exceptionalism*—American values and attitudes that many in the United States as well as those abroad regard as part of the problem, though there is little evidence to support this contention.
- *Conditional exceptionalism*—Aspects of the American character that are distinctive, though not so much that they are destined to consistently divide the American people from the rest of the world. These aspects include values and attitudes that are products of the times or subject to the course of events and subject to the influence of American leadership with respect to foreign policy.
- *Problematic exceptionalism*—How Americans view themselves, their country, and the world in ways that reflect potentially unbridgeable, persistent gaps in opinions on important issues.

Not all of the characteristics that distinguish Americans fall neatly into one or another of these categories, of course, but one point bears repeating. As noted in the previous chapters, we use the term *exceptionalism* without the normative judgments often associated with it. Our references to the distinctiveness of the American public carry no implication of superiority. Whether the special qualities of American attitudes and values have encouraged a sense of American superiority is an issue we will revisit throughout this book.

MISUNDERSTOOD

Two aspects of the American character—American nationalism and religiosity—are assumed to drive Americans' views of the world and significantly influence the way the United States conducts itself in the world. As Minxin Pei of the Carnegie Endowment for International Peace has put it, "Today's strident anti-Americanism represents much more than a wimpy reaction to U.S. resolve or generic fears of a hegemon running amok. Rather, the growing unease with the United States should be seen as a powerful global backlash against the spirit of American nationalism that shapes and animates U.S. foreign policy."[1]

Similar concerns are expressed about how Americans' faith influences U.S. foreign policy. Reflecting the world's worries at the time of the run-up to the war in Iraq, the editors of *The Economist* opined, "Only one thing unsettles George Bush's critics more than the possibility that his foreign policy is secretly driven by greed. That is the possibility that it is secretly driven by God." The magazine's editors saw the potential for the disastrous "clash of civilizations" envisioned by Samuel P. Huntington, a confrontation in which Christians and Jews aligned against Muslims. "War for oil would merely be bad," they concluded. "War for God would be catastrophic."[2]

Such punditry makes convincing reading because it reinforces long-standing prejudices about the American people. And certainly, long-term U.S. support for Israel and, more recently, strong support among Christian evangelicals for the repossession by the Jewish people of the land promised in the Bible, have heightened concern in predominantly Muslim countries—as well as in Europe—that America is on a religious crusade. But little hard data support the idea that either religiosity or nationalism plays a significant role in Americans' actual opinions about how the United States should relate to the world in general or how Americans form their views about specific international issues.

The City on a Hill Syndrome

Nothing is more vexing to foreigners than Americans' exalted view of their country, their belief that the world would be a better place if people everywhere thought and acted like citizens of the United States. The criticism goes something like this: America sees itself as a shining city on a hill—a place apart where a better way of life exists, one to which all other peoples should aspire. American intellectual and political leaders from Governor John Winthrop of colonial Massachusetts to President Ronald Reagan have used this image to suggest that America is somehow different and special.

Compared with Western Europeans, average Americans are more likely to see their culture as superior to that of others and to express more patriotism. U.S. citizens are particularly inclined to think highly of their democratic ideals and their form of democracy. To the latter point, in 1999, when Americans were asked to account for their country's success in the twentieth century, they credited the "American system." And although many Americans were distrustful of government, wary of the news media, and disinterested in politics, they resoundingly endorsed the economic and democratic systems on which their nation is grounded. When looking back on the accomplishments of the twentieth century, overwhelming majorities agreed that the Constitution, free elections, and the free enterprise system were major reasons for the success the United States enjoyed during the twentieth century. The public may have been frustrated by how the system operated, but they liked the design.

There is little question that Americans take great pride in "their system." The immigrant experience—leaving the "old country" for a better life in America—has helped convince them that the U.S. way is better. At the same time, Americans also hold a number of other attitudes that mitigate their nationalism, rendering it a less potent factor in the way they look at the world.

Most important, contrary to widespread misconceptions, Americans' pride in their country is not evangelistic. The American people, as opposed to some of their leaders, seek no converts to their ideology. To be sure, seven in ten Americans think it is a good idea to promote "American-style" democracy in the world, but the American public evidences no missionary zeal for this task. This point was dramatically driven home by the results of a Gallup poll taken in February 2005, just days after President George W. Bush's State of the Union address in which he made far-reaching and eloquent calls for increased democracy in the Middle East. The survey found that only 31 percent of the American public thought that building democracy should be a *very* important goal of U.S. foreign policy. Their real priorities were preventing terrorism, controlling the spread of weapons of mass destruction, and maintaining U.S. military power, not planting the flag of American-style democracy in faraway places. A subsequent poll for the Chicago Council on Foreign Relations, conducted in September 2005, found that only 27 percent of the public said they were strongly committed to spreading democracy.[3]

Similarly, while U.S. citizens are alone in thinking it is a "good thing" that American customs are spreading all around the world, they see people from other countries benefiting more from such Americanization than themselves. These are hardly the sentiments of cultural imperialists, as Americans are so often portrayed. Americans just do not see a personal or national benefit to increasingly exposing the world to the best (and worst) of U.S. culture and technological innovation. In fact, Americans have as many of the same qualms about globalization as the people of other nations do.

Americans are nationalistic, but Americans' nationalism is largely passive. They are accused of believing, "Aren't we great? Do as we do!" In reality, Americans are far more likely to say, "We think the American way is great; we assume you want to be like us, but if you don't, that's really not our concern." This distinction—between love of country and the desire to impose it upon others—undercuts the criticism that Americans' nationalism and patriotism are the driving forces behind particular U.S. foreign policies that foreigners (and many Americans) find objectionable.

The ordinary American's modest appetite for spreading U.S. ideals around the world goes hand in hand with the public's lack of imperial aspirations. Consider the American reaction to the collapse of the Soviet Union and the end of the Cold War. At the time, pundits and politicians made much of the vindication of democracy and capitalism. But ordinary Americans barely paid attention. In fact, just barely half the public very closely followed the news about the fall of the Berlin Wall in November 1989, according to the Times Mirror Center for the People & the Press surveys at the time. And that level of interest represented the high point of public engagement with the events that ultimately dismantled the Soviet Union. The immediate reaction in the United States to the fall of the Iron Curtain was neither one of triumph nor of hunger for world domination. On the contrary, the American public became even more indifferent to international affairs than it had been. And the size of the isolationist minority in the United States surged.

Having become the world's sole superpower at the end of the Cold War, the American people rejected the imperialist role that often comes with such hegemony. Polls in 1993 and again in 1997 found that one in eight Americans thought that the United States should be the "single" leader of the world. Only one in five thought that the United States should play a first-among-equals role with other leading nations. This lack of imperial appetite is as great today as it was in a safer, less contentious time. Polls in 2005, for example, showed that the number of Americans who aspire for their country to play a world leadership role has not grown. Even the opinions of American elites—academics, journalists, business leaders, and so forth—show few aspirations for empire and little appetite for proselytizing American-style democracy. While two out of three American opinion leaders believe that the United States should play a strong leadership role in the world (twice the proportion of the public at large), fewer than 10 percent think the United States should be the single world leader. This has been a consistent finding in surveys throughout the 1990s and into 2005. Further, American elites have *not* given the spread of democracy around the world significant greater priority than the average citizen.[4]

It is true that the idea the United States should play the evangelist because its values are the "right" ones has in recent years echoed in speeches by America's leaders, from the president and vice president of the United States to the secretary of defense. The idea has likewise appeared in commentary pieces and essays by political scholars, particularly those from the "neoconservative" school, and been heard in countless press briefings and congressional testimony. Writing in the *Weekly Standard*, Robert Kagan and William Kristol asserted in 2002 that "September 11 really did change everything. . . . George W. Bush

TABLE 4.1

DESIRED U.S. LEADERSHIP ROLE

	World's Single Leader %	Shared Leadership			Don't Know/ Refused %
		Most Active %	No More Active %	None %	
Influentials	10	45	36	—	2
General Public	12	25	47	10	4

UNITED STATES PROMOTING DEMOCRACY ABROAD

	Top Priority %	Some Priority %	No Priority %	Don't Know/ Refused %
Influentials	21	68	9	2
General Public	24	54	19	3

Source: Pew Research Center for the People & the Press, 2005.

is now a man with a mission. As it happens, it is America's historic mission."[5]

But while Bush administration officials and many neoconservatives have given the impression that American nationalism is proactive and evangelistic, their views do not reflect general public opinion. Americans may have a very high regard for the "American way," but its relevance to their views on foreign policy is limited. For example, in the second Clinton administration, American foreign policy opinion makers—and especially academics and the leaders of labor unions—strongly supported an extension of the U.S. military mission in Bosnia. But the American public was split down the middle on putting more boots on the ground in the Balkans. To them, it was overreach. Foreigners should be wary of confusing the ambitions of America's elites with the attitudes of the American public.

The case that Americans are dangerously nationalistic is further undermined by their striking lack of hubris. Whatever their faults or pretensions, Americans have a refreshing penchant for self-criticism. Although the public has a pretty positive opinion of the U.S. economic and political systems, it has even greater reservations about some aspects of the American character than people in many other parts of the world.

Pew's 2005 global survey asked people in sixteen countries and the United States what words or phrases they associated with the American people. The results were striking. Fully 70 percent of Americans described their fellow countrymen as greedy, a harsher criticism than that leveled by any non-Americans in the survey. About half of Americans, 49 percent, saw themselves as violent, a self-criticism with which majorities agreed in thirteen of the sixteen other countries surveyed. And 39 percent of Americans characterized their own people as immoral, a self-critique stronger than that leveled at Americans by any Western Europeans.

Americans embrace their historical legacy, their culture, and their system of government and business. The "American way" works for them. And they are so sure it will work for others that they believe foreigners will benefit more from the spread of American ideas and customs than they will in the United States. Still, despite commonly held beliefs, Americans harbor no hegemonic ambitions. And their significant reservations about their own character suggest a healthy self-doubt that tempers imperial hubris.

America, the Blessed Nation

The religiosity of Americans is also a growing concern to many foreigners who misunderstand how religion plays out in American lives. It is especially worrying to America's traditional European allies, who are among the most secular people in the world. However, American religious fervor also influences the views of people in some Muslim societies.

Any assessment of American religious exceptionalism is relative and must distinguish between personal belief and influence on public policy. In their faith and religious observation, Americans are not particularly distinctive compared to the citizens of the entire globe. Americans believe and act on their beliefs much like many people in the Middle East, Africa, Latin America, and parts of Asia. Where America stands out in its religiosity is among economically developed countries. In particular, there is a transatlantic religious divide that has added fuel to the fire of anti-Americanism in Europe and contributed to misperceptions around the world of the impact of religiosity on U.S. foreign policy.

The United States has a long tradition of separating church from state—but an equally powerful inclination to mix religion with politics. Throughout the nation's history, great political and social movements—from abolition to women's suffrage to civil rights to today's struggles over abortion and gay marriage—have drawn upon religious institutions for moral authority, inspirational leadership, and organizational muscle. But for the past generation, religion has come to be woven more deeply into the fabric of partisan politics than ever before.

Within the United States, there is little question that the religious views of the American public have a decided impact on many social issues. The U.S. debates about abortion, end-of-life decisions, stem cell research, and homosexuality are all driven by the public's religious beliefs, or lack thereof.

Little wonder, then, that a great many European respondents in Pew's 2005 poll described the American people as "too religious." It is also not surprising that critics of President Bush would see his religious and moralistic rhetoric—especially in his use of the phrase "axis of evil"—as just the kind of American religious fervor they fear in U.S. foreign policy. Upon hearing that Christian fundamentalists in the United States link their support for Israel to their own apocalyptic vision of history, it is understandable that Muslims

TABLE 4.2

INFLUENCES ON POLICY ISSUES

	Personal Experience %	Friends/ Family %	Media %	Religious Belief %	Education %	Something Else %	Don't Know/ Refused %
Foreign Policy							
Views about . . .							
Send troops to Bosnia							
(June 1996)	15	7	35	6	18	16	3
Favor	14	6	40	6	21	12	1
Oppose	16	7	32	7	17	19	2
Opinion on Iraq war							
(March 2003)	16	7	41	10	11	11	4
Favor	18	8	41	9	11	11	2
Oppose	16	5	44	10	13	10	2
Sympathize with . . .							
(Early July 2003)	8	4	33	20	21	10	4
Israel	7	6	34	26	18	7	2
Palestinians	10	2	37	11	30	9	1
Preventing genocide							
(March 2001)	12	4	34	13	18	12	7
Agree	12	4	37	12	21	12	2
Disagree	14	7	35	16	14	12	2
Life Issues (March 2001)							
Views about . . .							
Gay marriages	12	8	9	40	12	15	4
Favor	20	15	13	4	24	23	1
Oppose	7	3	6	65	6	11	2
Human cloning	6	2	21	35	19	13	4
Favor	10	3	27	6	36	16	2
Oppose	5	2	20	42	17	13	1
Physician-assisted suicide	24	8	13	27	11	13	4
Favor	35	12	15	4	16	17	1
Oppose	11	4	10	59	6	9	1
Helping people in need	35	12	11	18	10	12	2
Agree	35	12	11	20	10	11	1
Disagree	35	13	14	4	10	20	4

might fear that religious conservatives are driving U.S. policy in the Middle East.

Yet there is little evidence that Americans make their judgments about world affairs based on their religious beliefs. For nearly a decade, Pew has surveyed national samples of the American public about a range of concerns, from social issues to foreign policy decisions, to discover what factors were most influential in shaping their opinions. On personal issues, such as gay marriage, euthanasia, and cloning, those who take conservative stances largely credit their religious beliefs. But this link between religion and policy did not exist when it came to the use of force in the Balkans and Iraq, or even in preventing genocide. Only when people were asked about their basic sympathies in the Israeli-Palestinian dispute did religion emerge as a significant factor in their opinions on a foreign policy issue. But even then Pew's surveys found Americans cited media coverage as a stronger influence on their support for Israel. Further, opinions on foreign policy issues were generally not correlated with a person's religiosity when his or her partisanship was taken into account.

Although there is little evidence that Americans' deep religiosity shapes their views of the world, the public's religious conception of the United States as "one nation under God" cannot be ignored as an important ingredient in the almost boundless stock of American optimism. Separation of church and state is written into the Constitution. Most important, there is little indication that strong religious beliefs have much direct bearing on how Americans see the United States' role in the world.

Thus, while Americans are clearly nationalistic and quite religious, there is little evidence that either their patriotism or their faith drives public support for the more activist and unilateralist American foreign policy that has fueled anti-Americanism in recent years. If misunderstandings about what makes Americans different are not always the root cause, then conditional or problematic American exceptionalism might offer some answers.

IT ALL DEPENDS

The world's biggest complaint about the United States is that Washington too often acts unilaterally, without concern for the interests of others. Certainly the American public bears at least some responsibility because of their ambivalence about multilateralism. True to a conditional exceptionalism, Americans run hot and cold on whether the United States should cooperate with allies or adopt a go-it-alone approach to international problems. This tension in American public opinion is evident on almost every major foreign policy concern.

Americans of course want good relationships with others and, at least in principle, want to be cooperative. But for the U.S. public, national defense comes first, especially in times of trouble. If asked to choose, Americans prefer proactive, assertive unilateral action to multilateral efforts beset by delay and compromise.

This conflict in public thinking was clearly illustrated in opinion polls taken during the 2004 U.S. presidential election campaign. An August 2004 Pew and Council on Foreign Relations poll found that Americans believed that deteriorating relationships with allies in the wake of the Iraq invasion was a major U.S. foreign policy problem. Americans were both highly aware of and concerned about the loss of international respect for the United States, with two-thirds of the public saying that the United States was less respected globally than in the past and by roughly two to one viewed this loss of respect as a major problem for the nation.[6]

But in the same poll Americans ranked improving relations with allies a low ninth out of nineteen international objectives. The survey also showed that, despite internal discontent with the war in Iraq and broad international disapproval, a majority of the American public continued to believe that preemptive military action to protect the United States from a perceived threat could be justified—at least sometimes. Further Pew polls that year found that Americans, unlike Europeans, felt their country did not need to seek U.N. approval in order to take preventive military action to protect itself. And the U.S. public, which in the 1990s disapproved of military spending hikes, believed that the United States should assert a policy that will assure that the country remains the sole global military superpower.

Three months after the August 2004 survey, despite believing that tensions with allies and rising anti-Americanism abroad were significant problems, voters reelected George W. Bush, the arch villain of America's foreign critics. And not only did voters reelect him, they did so mostly because they liked the president's leadership style and his stewardship of the war on terrorism. While Bush's hard-line approach to foreign policy galvanized opposition among Democrats and liberals, it appealed to many Independent voters and even to some conservative Democrats.

The 2004 election results seemed to indicate that the majority of American voters placed themselves squarely in the quasi-unilateralist camp. On balance, American voters were saying: "We want good relations with our allies. We need their help. But we need to put first things first. We are ultimately responsible for protecting ourselves from another terrorist attack and we take comfort in George Bush's get-tough stance around the world." This tension in public sentiment was nicely captured in Bush's approval ratings at the time of the election. Most surveys then found pluralities of the public disapproving of the way Bush handled foreign policy, but approving of the way he dealt with terrorism.

History suggests that Americans' conflicting views about going it alone or working with others are driven by leadership and response to external threat. The American public's two-mindedness about unilateralism and multilateralism—and, further, Americans' propensity to embrace the use of military force—vary significantly over time, driven by events and changes in American leadership. In his illuminating *Surprise, Security, and the American Experience,* Yale University historian John Gaddis points out that an aggressive U.S. response to an international threat is not unique to our times. Reactions to the September 11 attacks, he asserts, were consistent with the way America responded to the only other attack on its home soil by a foreign power, the British invasion of the United States in the War of 1812. According to Gaddis, preemption, unilateralism, and hegemony were a three-pronged U.S. response to both attacks. "Despite some obvious differences in personality," he writes, "John Quincy Adams and George W. Bush would not have had much difficulty, on matters of national security, in understanding one another."[7]

While we have no public opinion data dating to the War of 1812, it is fair to say that unilateralism and hegemony (at least with regard to the Western Hemisphere) have been accepted by the American people for most of their history—as they certainly were by many Europeans in the nineteenth century. In Gaddis's view, it was not until the mid-1930s, during the administration of Franklin Delano Roosevelt, that the United States began to pursue a more multilateralist course in foreign affairs. And even then, to sell this U-turn to a skeptical American public Roosevelt had to convince voters that working closely with others was the best way to preserve American resources and to get the Allies "to do most of the fighting."[8]

President Woodrow Wilson had begun the transformation, moving away from John Quincy Adams's unilateralism toward the notion that U.S. security would best be served through efforts to spread democratic and capitalistic values. Wilson overreached but, Gaddis writes, "Roosevelt now revived the Wilsonian project, taking care, though, to couple it to a cold-blooded, at times even brutal, calculation of who had power and how they might use it."[9]

This shift in Americans' views about their relations with the rest of the world carried the nation through World War II and the Cold War, defining American foreign policy for the remainder of the twentieth century. Thinking multilaterally, and supporting international institutions, albeit tepidly, were valued by the American public throughout the period. And they remain so. But the September 11 attacks and the Bush administration's response—invading Afghanistan and then Iraq and conducting an American-led war on terrorism—have rekindled Americans' acceptance of unilateralism. Gaddis might argue that this is not at all unexpected given U.S. history, yet, in today's world, that stance has clearly divided the U.S. public from its traditional allies.

Pew's seventeen-nation poll in 2005 found that 69 percent of Americans believed that the United States was "generally disliked" by people in other parts of the world. This was the most downbeat assessment of a country's global popularity given by any nationality in the survey. In only two other nations—Turkey and Russia—did a majority of the public believe that their country was generally disliked by people in other lands. However, the same polling found that while most people around the world believed that the United States ignored their interests in making foreign policy, 67 percent of Americans believed, quite to the contrary, that their country paid attention to foreigners' interests. This is a disconnect of a major order. The American public's appreciation for their country's stature in the world and, more broadly, their understanding of international affairs remains modest at best.[10]

Americans' reawakened affinity for unilateralism also resonates with their opposition to ceding sovereignty over international endeavors. Polls have consistently found public opposition to U.S. troops serving under U.N. command in "blue helmet" operations. Americans, unlike a majority of Europeans, are not prepared to allow their soldiers to be tried in international criminal courts when charged with war crimes. And U.S. citizens are considerably less willing than other Westerners to give an international organization final say on global environmental policies.

But such go-it-alone American exceptionalism is both equivocal and conditional. While Americans are protective of their sovereignty and jealous of their right to protect themselves, the urge to be good world citizens and cooperate with allies is never far from the surface. The 2004 Pew poll that found continued support for preemptive military action also showed that, by a 49 to 35 percent plurality, Americans continued to believe that U.S. foreign policy should take into account the interests of allies rather than be based mostly on U.S. interests. It also found rising criticism of President Bush for paying too little attention to the interests of close allies.

Furthermore, it is now the American public that seeks a closer working relationship with traditional allies, while Europeans want more space. In Pew's 2005 survey, sizable majorities in Great Britain, France, Germany, Spain, and Holland said that their governments should take a more independent approach to security and diplomatic affairs than they have in the past. However, two in three Americans felt that the United States and Western Europe should remain as close as ever. Such equivocation about foreign relations is not new. Since the mid-1960s, Gallup and Pew surveys have documented the public's long record of saying that, on the one hand, the United States should take into account the views of its major allies, while, on the other, the United States should not be so internationally minded and should concentrate more on domestic problems.

American public opinion on international engagement is also conditional, a product of its times, and highly responsive to leadership. In the relatively peaceful 1990s, President Bill Clinton tapped into Americans' internationalist sentiment to build bare public majorities in support of U.S. participation in multilateral peacekeeping and peacemaking in the Balkans. The September 11 attacks changed the international context, enabling President Bush to win, at least initially, broad public support for a largely unilateral invasion of Iraq. Each president appealed to a different face of the American public, demonstrating that when it comes to U.S. international engagement, the American public is subject to persuasion and to changes of heart.

A PROBLEM, YOU SAY?

While nationalism and religiosity are misunderstood manifestations of American exceptionalism, and U.S. internationalism is conditional on the tenor of the times and who is in the White House, a problematic deep-seated individualism, coupled with an inherent optimism, truly distinguishes Americans. The American ethic of self-reliance and independence, coupled with the unparalleled economic and military success of the United States since its founding, have given Americans boundless optimism.

But these traits pose a number of problematic consequences for the United States' relationship with the world. The American public has four interrelated tendencies: first, to downplay the importance of America's relationship to other nations; second, to be indifferent to global issues; third, to lack enthusiasm for multinational efforts and institutions; and fourth, to have oversized, if not unrealistic, expectations about what the world offers the United States.

Americans' self-reliance leads them to believe that they really don't need the rest of the world. This often manifests as an inattentive self-centeredness unmindful of their country's deepening linkages with other countries. For example, Pew's surveys have found majorities of Americans saying that what happens in Europe and Asia has little, if any, impact on their lives. There was similar disinterest in events even in our neighbor countries Mexico and, especially, Canada. Although these polls date to the 1990s and the early days of September 2001, little suggests that these attitudes have changed. Americans have

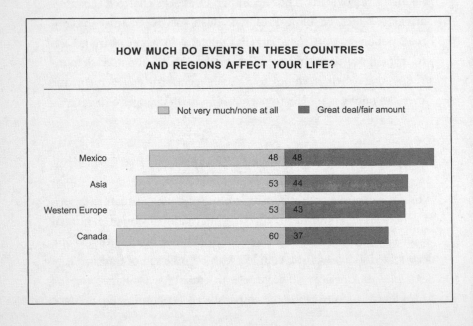

HOW MUCH DO EVENTS IN THESE COUNTRIES
AND REGIONS AFFECT YOUR LIFE?

Not very much/none at all   Great deal/fair amount

Country	Not very much/none at all	Great deal/fair amount
Mexico	48	48
Asia	53	44
Western Europe	53	43
Canada	60	37

remained disinterested in foreign news except when it deals directly with the United States or the war on terrorism.

Polls conducted by the University of Maryland's Program on International Policy Attitudes (PIPA) also found that despite being citizens of the world's leading trading economy, Americans believed that other countries benefit more from global trade than the United States does. Not recognizing the mutual benefits of an interdependent global economy has no doubt fueled a lack of public support for eliminating trade barriers as well as scant appreciation of foreign fears about the Americanization of their cultures.

Indeed, Americans' self-confidence breeds indifference and inertia toward dealing with problems generally and international problems in particular. Americans tend to minimize challenges even as they acknowledge them. In mid-1999, Pew conducted an in-depth national survey asking Americans to look back on the twentieth century and ahead to the twenty-first. The public's optimism in the face of anticipated problems captured America's "what, me worry?" disposition. Respondents to the survey anticipated many perils in the twenty-first century, but none of the travails, no matter how grave, could dim the public's positive view of the future. Despite gloomy consensus forecasts of natural disasters, environmental calamities, and international terrorism, Americans were highly confident that life would get better for themselves, their families, and the country as a whole.[11]

A resounding 81 percent of adults were optimistic about what the twenty-first century held for them and their families, and 70 percent believed the country as a whole would do well. Eight in ten Americans described themselves as hopeful, anticipating that the new millennium would usher in the triumph of science and technology. Majorities predicted that it was most likely cancer would be cured, AIDS would be eradicated, and ordinary people would travel in space.

At the same time, nearly two-thirds of the public anticipated a serious terrorist attack on the United States within the next fifty years (little did they know it would only take two years). And more than

TABLE 4.3

DON'T WORRY, BE HAPPY

About . . .	Optimistic %	Pessimistic %	Don't Know %
Self and family	81	15	4
Nation	70	27	3

| Expectations for Next Fifty Years Hope for the Future . . . | Probably/Definitely | | |
	Will Happen %	Won't Happen %	Don't Know %
Cure for cancer	81	18	1
Cure for AIDS	79	20	1
Improve environment	78	20	2
Men on Mars	76	22	2
Citizens in space	57	41	2
Jesus Christ on Earth	44	44	12
But Gloomy Predictions . . .			
Earthquake in California	91	6	3
Global warming	76	19	5
Terrorist attack on United States	64	32	4
Major energy crisis	63	34	3
Epidemic worse than AIDS	56	41	3
Nuclear war	41	57	2
United States in nuclear war	37	58	5
Asteroid will hit Earth	31	62	7

Source: Pew Millennium Survey, July 1999.

half said an epidemic worse than AIDS was at least likely. Vast numbers of Americans believed that by the middle of the twenty-first century it was probable there would be a major earthquake in California, global warming, and a severe energy crisis. But for all their worries, the public's faith was just as strong that science and technology would expand their horizons. Americans overwhelmingly said science and technology, medical advances, and education would play major roles in creating a better future.

Such confidence in the face of looming problems is a key element in Americans' "can do" reputation. But optimism can also reinforce a "muddle-through" mentality, which, in turn, can foster passivity rather than activism in the face of challenges and make it more difficult to bring public pressure to bear on elected leaders to deal forcefully with problems that Americans see on the horizon.

This inertia, especially when dealing with faraway international problems, is clearly evident in the PIPA polls. These surveys have shown that a strong majority of the American public believe that global warming is a real and serious problem. Yet large majorities also expressed little urgency to deal with the issue. As many as 21 percent of respondents stated that unless global warming is a certainty, no steps should be taken to deal with it, and another 42 percent responded that since warming is a gradual problem, only gradual, low-cost steps should be taken to deal with it. Just 34 percent of the public said it was necessary to deal with global warming right now.

High confidence and scant concern about long-run problems are certainly part of Americans' indifference to and lack of interest in international issues. Such attitudes also often lead to mistaken impressions about U.S. policies among Americans. The PIPA global warming survey found 68 percent of a nationwide sample of respondents thinking that the United States was either doing more than other Western countries to limit greenhouse gases or about as much as other advanced nations.

Americans' lack of attentiveness, if not indifference, to U.S. policies is often not shared by the publics of other Western nations. For example, in August 2001, when many Americans were indifferent to the Kyoto Protocol and President Bush was withdrawing U.S. support from the deal, Europeans knew all about it, and 80 percent or more of Britons, French, Germans, and Italians disapproved of Bush's decision. Americans were generally indifferent to an internationally controversial policy decision that was simply not on their radar screen.[12]

This combination of indifference and inattention applies more broadly to the American public's views of the U.S. role in dealing with international problems in general. For decades, U.S. polls have found that Americans overstate their contribution to international efforts, whether it is foreign aid in general or the number of troops in peace-keeping missions overseas. At the same time, foreign publics believe the United States is not doing enough.

American individualism likewise disposes the public to be suspicious of, and lend only soft support to, international bodies such as the United Nations and its multilateral efforts. Given Americans' general unease with government, it is not too surprising that U.S. citizens are less comfortable with and supportive of multinational organizations and multilateral efforts. Americans have certainly wanted allies to support them in Afghanistan and Iraq. But they are far more resistant than Europeans to international constraints on America's use of force. Americans' opinions of the United Nations are currently less positive than in the 1990s, largely because of the Security Council's failure to bless the war in Iraq. Even so, their opinions have fluctuated over the years, and most often have been less positive than the views of Europeans toward the world body.

Finally, Americans' strong sense of individual freedom combined with their almost boundless optimism leads many to think they can have it both ways. Nowhere is this more clearly evident than in their attitudes toward the use of energy. Americans have long acknowledged the risk of dependence on foreign energy sources. Yet, support for energy conservation and more fuel-efficient cars increased only slightly when fuel prices began their rise in 2004; it was not until the sharp spurt in prices in late August and early September 2005 that support for policies such as tighter automobile fuel-efficiency standards and incentives for alternative energy-source development were apparent in Pew surveys. For most Americans, the high cost of gasoline represents a challenge to their assumed right to low-priced fuel, an integral part of the SUV culture of modern America.[13]

Even the September 11 attacks, carried out largely by nationals of Saudi Arabia, America's largest oil provider, had minimal impact on attitudes toward the car culture. A *Newsweek* poll taken shortly after the terrorist attacks found that only 42 percent of Americans thought it *very* important that SUV owners be encouraged to switch to more fuel-efficient vehicles in order to reduce dependence on imported oil.[14]

A similar two-mindedness is apparent with respect to trade policy. On the one hand, Americans deplore the loss of U.S. jobs because of imports and they support protectionist measures to curb foreign goods from entering the U.S. market. But in recent years they have happily purchased record amounts of imported goods, citing their high quality and relatively low prices. In effect, Americans are saying, "Protect our jobs but keep those affordable frocks and electronic gadgets coming."

In the following chapters we will probe more deeply into specific areas of American attitudes and opinions, how misunderstood, conditional, and problematic exceptionalism has become entangled in them, and the myriad ways in which the larger world has reacted. Our analyses deal with the intensity of Americans' religious values and practices; their zeal for democracy and capitalism; the global spread of U.S. culture; U.S. ambivalence toward multilateral approaches to global problems; U.S. approaches to conflict and the use of force and the tensions created with traditional allies. Finally, we will address (and reject) the notion that, given the political differences that have so divided Americans in recent years, it is no longer meaningful to speak of a single American character or set of values.

Many aspects of these subjects, while of considerable interest in their own right, do not fall neatly into one or another category of American exceptionalism. It is, for instance, not so simple as saying

American values on issues of globalization are misunderstood rather than problematic, and then moving on, and we will not attempt to shoehorn each American value into a single mold. But, as appropriate, we will note where particular American attitudes or opinions fall into each of the categories of exceptionalism and how they might affect U.S. policies and America's place in the world.

5

A BLESSED PEOPLE

IN OCTOBER 2003, when *NBC Nightly News* and the *Los Angeles Times* revealed that a senior U.S. general had been giving speeches to church groups across the nation in which he characterized America's war on terrorism in starkly religious terms, there was a chorus of dismay. Among the inflammatory comments captured on video and audio tapes, Lieutenant General William James Boykin told audiences that America's true enemy was neither Osama bin Laden nor Saddam Hussein but "a guy called Satan"; that terrorists wanted to destroy the United States "because we are a Christian nation"; and that President George W. Bush was "in the White House because God put him there for such a time as this."[1]

President Bush later said he disagreed with the general's comments, and a U.S. Defense Department investigation concluded the next year that Boykin had violated Pentagon rules by not making it clear he was speaking in a personal, not official capacity. But Boykin remained in his job as deputy under secretary of defense for intelligence and the matter continued to be cited in the media outside the United States as a prime example of America's messianic impulses, which many in Europe, the Middle East, and elsewhere believed to be guiding current U.S. foreign policy.

"America's founding fathers insisted on a separation of church and state because they wished to be free of the coercive power that the church, of various denominations, used to exercise in the Old World. The ironic result of that separation is that the church is now more influential in the New World than it is in the Old," wrote Janadas Devan of *The Straits Times*/Asia News Network, adding that, "If [Boykin] had been French, he might have hardly made it to the rank of Sergeant-Major." "Ugly comments," the *Japan Times* called Boykin's remarks. An "unwanted mixing of religion and the war on terror," headlined a commentary in the *Turkish Daily News*. In the *National Jewish Post & Opinion,* Rabbi Dennis Sasso warned that Boykin's statements were "a dangerous proclamation of divine imprimatur that confuses a legitimate war against terrorism with a religious crusade against infidels." More recently, in the *South China Morning Post,* an article asked, "Is America increasingly being perceived as no longer championing a political system that constitutionally institutionalizes the rightful separation of church and state? The very fact that anyone could plausibly ask this question tells us that America now has some kind of serious image problem in the world."[2]

Religion's role in American life is both complex and contradictory, whether viewed from within the United States or abroad. A majority of Americans believe their country is not religious enough, for example. But a plurality of Americans also think organized religion has too much political influence in the country. They think churches should express their views on political questions, but even larger numbers of Americans think it is wrong for the clergy to discuss political candidates from the pulpit.[3]

One in three Americans believes the Bible is the actual word of God and should be taken literally. And three in five believe in creationism or evolution guided by a supreme being. But, contrary to the views of many religious conservatives, most Americans support a woman's right to abortion, approve of stem cell research, and take a decidedly commercial approach to religious holidays. When religion competes with materialism, pragmatism, and other American values, it often loses.[4]

The view from abroad of religion in America is similarly complex and contradictory. In France, three in five people, and nearly as many in the Netherlands, think Americans are too religious, while large majorities in many Muslim societies believe Americans are not religious enough. Clearly the French, Dutch, Indonesians, and Pakistanis look at Americans through the filter of their own values and beliefs.

To Europeans, Americans' religiosity skews what should be secular policy decisions, such as on teaching creationism in the schools, and the death penalty, abortion, and gay marriage. To Muslims, the wrong kind of religious beliefs drive U.S. attitudes and actions in the world. Two in three Jordanians and half of all Moroccans, for example, think Jews have the most influence on U.S. foreign policy, more than the military or the business community or the press. Little wonder, then, that in the turmoil after the September 11 attacks, the rest of the world is curious, anxious, and critical of America's religiosity and how it affects U.S. actions in the world, seeing fearful parallels between the jihads encouraged by Islamic fundamentalists and the crusading zeal of Christian fundamentalists. As Josef Braml, a researcher at the German think tank SWP, writes, "The religious/moral engagement of the Christian Right is polarizing the United States and has caused and will continue to cause some ruptures in the transatlantic relationship: not only when deliberating about whether to use military force or diplomatic means, but also when taking concrete steps to deal with conflicts, especially in the Middle East."[5]

The widespread view that President Bush owed his reelection in 2004 to the votes of religious Americans' "moral values" has reinforced the broader belief that the United States is an increasingly religious society dominated by evangelical Christians.[6] A flawed exit poll that asked voters to choose among a half-dozen concrete reasons for their vote, such as "Iraq" and "terrorism," plus one amorphous reason, "moral values," was responsible for the confusion. But there is enough truth, both historical and contemporary, in the larger perception about the influence of religion on American politics to give it the patina of credibility.[7]

Certainly President Bush's faith informs his rhetoric and probably many of his decisions—witness his justifying the war on terrorism as a battle between "good and evil." Certainly religion and morality play a larger role in American life—especially around the issue of abortion—than in most other Western nations. And it is true that the United States has historically supported the state of Israel, a policy that many Europeans and many Muslims believe reflects religious influence over U.S. foreign policy. So it is little wonder that many non-Americans see religion influencing much of what the United States does in the world. But the vision held by many Europeans and other non-Americans of a United States run by religious fanatics is a caricature that distorts the American religious experience and invites serious misunderstanding of its role and importance in civic and foreign affairs. The manifestations of American religiosity that so trouble people of other countries are a classic case of misunderstood exceptionalism. Whatever their own religious views, most Americans have no interest in imposing their faith on others and, with the exception of policy toward Israel, religion has little bearing on how they think about international affairs.

But in some respects, Americans' faith in God and their religious practices spill over into conditional and problematic exceptionalism as well. The outspoken faith of many of America's current leaders and the religious values that shape many U.S. foreign and domestic policies are to some extent a product of the times. Further, the intensity of Americans' personal religious beliefs caricatures the image of the United States and its separation of church and state, particularly when religious extremists are a main target of U.S. policy abroad.

Nonetheless it is important to bear in mind that Americans' faith in God and their religious practices are actually not exceptional at all when compared with most other people of the world. When it comes to religion, Americans look an awful lot like Muslims in the Middle

East. In matters religious, it is Europeans who are exceptional for their secularism. It is only in this historical and global context that American religious exceptionalism can be understood.

EARLY AWAKENINGS

From its very beginning, America has impressed the world as a deeply religious society. In *Democracy in America,* Alexis de Tocqueville observed that "the religious atmosphere of the country was the first thing that struck me on arrival in the United States." As he traveled throughout the young American democracy, Tocqueville marveled at the centrality of religion in both private and public American life: "In the United States the sovereign authority is religious . . . there is no country in the world where the Christian religion retains a greater influence over the souls of men than in America. . . . Religion in America . . . must be regarded as the foremost of the political institutions of that country." Modern students of the colonial era agree. According to the best estimates, 80 percent of northerners were "churched" at the time of the American Revolution, as were 56 percent of southerners.[8]

American history has been periodically marked by dramatic expansions in religion's impact on politics, sometimes associated with "great awakenings" in which the variety, size, fervor, or public presence of religious groups increased dramatically. Some scholars, including the economic historian Robert Fogel, believe that the first great awakening, during the colonial period, set the stage for the American Revolution by preaching that individual conscience was sovereign even over kings and that common people also had certain rights. The second great awakening contributed to the Civil War by preaching that slavery was evil. The religious revivals of the late nineteenth and early twentieth centuries, considered by some to be a third awakening, were felt through the prohibition and women's suffrage movements, and later within the anti-Communist crusade, the civil rights movement, and the protests against the Vietnam War. It is argued that the current religious ferment in the United States represents a fourth awakening.[9]

Individual Americans' affinity for religion, the unique place they accord faith in daily life, and the "special" relationship they see between God and America's destiny is quite evident today. Nearly half of all Americans think that the United States has had special protection from God for most of its history. "I've always believed that this blessed land was set apart in a special way," said President Ronald Reagan, "that some divine plan placed this great continent here." Among those Americans who perceive that the United States has a unique tie to God, white evangelical Protestants stand out in this belief. "We do believe that God has providentially blessed America," Richard Land, president of the Southern Baptist Convention's Ethics and Religious Liberties Commission, told a Council on Foreign Relations meeting in September 2005. This, said Land, "is not a doctrine of pride but of special responsibility to be the defender of freedom anywhere in the world."[10]

Evangelicals were nearly twice as likely to hold this view compared with less fervently religious white mainline Protestants, such as Episcopalians and Presbyterians, as well as white non-Hispanic Catholics. The belief that the United States has a "special place" in God's eyes was most widely found among those most deeply religious members of all Christian denominations, whether evangelical, mainline Protestant, or Catholic. Beyond the religious, such sentiment is also well established in American folklore, as reflected in the expression, "God takes care of drunks, fools, and the United States of America."[11]

Nonetheless, the sentiment is not universal. A significant minority of Americans reject the idea that the United States enjoys divine protection. "There is no greater human presumption than to read the mind of the Almighty, and no more dangerous individual than the one who has convinced himself that he is executing the Almighty's will," warned Arthur Schlesinger, Jr., in 2005. As for self-righteous claims of national innocence, Schlesinger reminded readers that "whites coming to these shores were reared in the Calvinist doctrine of sinful humanity, and they killed red men, enslaved black men, and later on imported yellow men for peon labor—not much of a background for national innocence."[12]

Still, for many Americans, those whom God protects, God also rewards. Most people in the United States see their religious beliefs as the basis for America's success in the world. Not surprisingly, a person's own religious faith, and the strength of his or her beliefs, shape these views. An overwhelming majority of white evangelicals said religious faith is at the core of America's strength; a much weaker majority of white mainline Protestants and white Catholics agreed. Within each of these groups, people with high religious commitment were much more likely to attribute American success to God than were those with low religious commitment.

Aspects of this belief in a providential relationship with the divine extend into American governance. "In God We Trust" is inscribed on the back of the U.S. dollar. The Pledge of Allegiance, including, since 1954, the phrase "under God," is recited by American schoolchildren at the beginning of each day; this religious oath was affirmed as constitutional by the U.S. Supreme Court in 2004. (Coincidentally, in the same year, the European Union decided not to reference God or Europe's Christian roots in its draft constitution.)

In a somewhat ambivalent view, however, most Americans do not consider their nation's relationship with God to be exclusive. Even though nearly half of Americans said the United States enjoys this special protection, only a small number believed that other nations do not enjoy the same divine guardianship. This view was consistent across all religious, political, and demographic lines, which suggests that while Americans believe they are blessed, they believe God watches over others as well.

Unlike Tocqueville, modern-day Europeans find Americans' religiosity unappealing at best; many consider it disturbing, even threatening. "To Europeans," write the editors of *The Economist*, "religion is the strangest and most disturbing feature of American exceptionalism. . . . They find it extraordinary that three times as many Americans

TABLE 5.1

FEW AMERICANS SEE SPECIAL PROTECTION FROM GOD

	%
United States has had special protection from God	48
Other nations also have special protection	37
Other nations do not have special protection	7
Don't know if others have protection	4
United States does *not* have special protection from God	40
Don't know/refused	12

believe in the virgin birth as in evolution. . . . The persistence of religion as a public force is all the more puzzling because it seems to run counter to historical trends. Like the philosophers of the Enlightenment, many Europeans argue that modernization is the enemy of religion. As countries get richer, organized religion will decline. Secular Europe seems to fit that pattern. America does not."[13]

American evangelicals are scathing in response to such European criticisms. "There is a new 'dark continent'—the land that used to be known as Christian Europe," wrote Dale Hurd, a senior reporter for evangelist Pat Robertson's Christian Broadcast Network. A more moderate rejoinder is that Europeans seem to ignore the fact that after many centuries of conflict, most European nations settled for having one "established" religion imposed on all its (primarily homogeneous) peoples, usually the faith of the king and the aristocracy. The United States, rather than having a single religion, has a multiplicity of competing faiths—which some Americans believe contributes to their country's strength and unity. As political scientist James Q. Wilson puts it, "Religion may be important in the United States because governmental indifference allows so many religions to prosper. Voltaire foresaw as much when he observed that a nation with one religion has oppression, a nation with two has civil war, and a nation with a hundred has peace."[14]

Setting aside transatlantic squabbles about the historical momentum behind religiosity, Americans are much more pious, at least outwardly, than most Europeans. By any standard—behavior, commitment, belief, or views on personal morality—religious views and religious practice play a greater role in Americans' lives than in those of Europeans. But this does not make Americans exceptional. The people of Latin America, Africa, and the Muslim world are often even more devout than those in the United States. Moreover, there is little evidence that developing countries shed their religiosity as they modernize. Europe is the exception in this case, not America.

But it is not only that the private religious beliefs and practices of Americans trouble Europeans and others in the world. It is Americans' blurring of lines separating faith and public policy, especially U.S. foreign policy, that others find so alarming. Non-Americans (as well as some Americans, of course) eschew President Bush's use of religious language and imagery to justify the U.S. war on terrorism. "We've come to know truths that we will never question: Evil is real, and it must be opposed," the president said in his State of the Union address four months after the September 11 attacks; he went on in the speech to label North Korea, Iran, and Iraq as the "axis of evil." Later in the spring of 2002 he intoned, "We are in a conflict between good and evil, and America will call evil by its name."[15]

The European response highlights how such misunderstandings hurt America's image abroad. "He's convinced he's right, and he's almost got this feeling he has a quasi-divine mission to fill as president of the United States," observed the Reverend Michel Kubler, the executive religion editor of *La Croix*, a Roman Catholic newspaper in France. Along the same line, Daniel Keohane, a senior analyst at the Center for European Reform, a London think tank, said, "It's not that most Europeans have a problem with religion per se. It's more whether they suspect religion affects a politician's choice on policy."[16]

Peter Singer, the Australian philosopher, extended the argument to the conditions of global politics after September 11. "Bush represents a distinctively American moral outlook," he writes in *The President of Good and Evil*, "not, of course, one shared by all Americans, but nevertheless one that plays a more central role in American public life than it plays anywhere else." In times of crisis especially, Americans cast national challenges in religious terms. By nearly two to one, Americans said the lesson of the terrorist attacks was that there is too little, not too much, religion in the world; even after September 11, an overwhelming majority said religion's influence in the world around them is for the good. But while the linkage between the American public's faith and U.S. public policy has been highlighted and amplified by the war on terrorism, it has long been a cornerstone of American life since the founding of the Republic.[17]

AN AMERICAN PRINCIPLE

In the seventeenth century, the quest for the freedom to practice their faith as they saw fit brought Puritans to Massachusetts, Quakers to Pennsylvania, Catholics to Maryland. It led Roger Williams to flee Massachusetts and found Rhode Island. Virginia's "Act for Establishing Religious Freedom," written by Thomas Jefferson in 1786, enshrined the principle of religious freedom even before the United States became a unified nation. His authorship of this seminal legislation is remembered on his tombstone, reflecting the significance with which Jefferson viewed it.

George Washington saw faith and public life in the young United States to be inexorably intertwined. "Do not let anyone claim to be a true American," he said, "if they ever attempt to remove religion from politics." A generation later, Daniel Webster, one of the first and foremost advocates of American nationalism, went even further. "Whatever makes men good Christians," he proclaimed, "makes them good [American] citizens."[18]

Despite these exhortations, American leaders in the century following the Civil War were inclined to treat their religious beliefs as a private matter, one between themselves and God, and there were relatively few loud public expressions of faith. Americans preferred that church and state be clearly separate, and that when it did become a public issue, it would sit comfortably with the Protestant majority in America. In the 1928 presidential election, Al Smith's Catholicism—with its overtones of split loyalties between the Vatican and Washington—helped deny him the White House, and fears that John F. Kennedy might obey the pope and not the Constitution almost kept him from winning the presidency in 1960. Overt religious observance declined enough for *Time* magazine in 1966 to ask on its cover, "Is God Dead?"

Yet reports of Americans' abandoning their faith were premature. In 1965, a Gallup poll found that fully 70 percent of Americans considered religion "very important" in their lives. Eleven years later, the country elected Jimmy Carter, the first modern president to speak often in public of his evangelical convictions. His immediate successors did not parade their religious views in the same way—President George H. W. Bush was notable in considering his religion to be a personal concern—but Bill Clinton was often his most compelling when preaching from a Baptist pulpit. George W. Bush, much more than Carter, spoke often of his personal faith during his election campaigns. "I don't see how you can be president . . . without a relationship with the Lord," Bush said. These different attitudes toward religious expression reflect a deeper divide in the nation as a whole about the proper relationship between religion and government. According to New York University Professor Noah Feldman, evangelical Christians, in particular, believe the correct answers for government "must come from the wisdom of religious tradition," while more secular Americans view religion as a matter of personal belief and choice. Indeed, many Americans feel that values derived from religion are likely to divide Americans.[19]

Since the 1960s, the number of Americans who say religion is "very important" in their lives has fluctuated, and by July 2005 the number stood at 60 percent. Conversely, the proportion saying religion was "not very important" doubled from 7 percent in 1965 to 14 percent in 2005. Despite the role attributed to religion in the 2004 presidential elections, it is striking that Americans as a whole regard religion as less important than they did four decades before.

Still, almost all Americans believe in God—a far higher proportion than among the people of Great Britain, France, or Germany; even higher than in Catholic Spain and Italy. In their belief in a deity, Americans are most like the people of Poland and the developing world, where almost all Indians, South Africans, and Mexicans believe in God.[20]

TABLE 5.2

BELIEVE IN GOD

	%
United States	94
Poland	96
Italy	88
Spain	80
Great Britain	61
Russia	60
France	56
Germany	50

Source: World Values Survey, 1999–2000.

In contrast, the citizens of almost all other major industrial nations see their faith as less significant in their lives than Americans do in theirs. Only one in ten people in France, two in ten in Germany, and one in three of those in both Great Britain and strongly Catholic Poland said religion is "very important" to them. The Reverend David Cornick, general secretary of the United Reformed Church in Great Britain, encapsulated the trend when he voiced his worries that "in Western Europe, we are hanging on by our fingernails. The fact is that Europe is no longer Christian." The role of religion in an individual's life distinguishes the United States from Canada and Japan, too. Only three in ten Canadians, and even fewer Japanese, rate religion as very important in their lives. A gender gap over religion exists in many countries, including the United States, with more women than men valuing religion highly. Nevertheless, European women were far, far less likely than American women to be intensely religious.[21]

As for public expressions of faith, an overwhelming percentage—90 percent—of American white evangelicals surveyed in 2004 believed it is important to spread their faith by converting others, responding perhaps to the Bible's missionary injunction in Mark 16:15 to "go ye into all the world and preach the Gospel."[22]

The anomaly is striking. By almost every measure, the United States is the most religious rich nation in the world. Indeed, it is the *only* religious rich nation in the world. Why this should be so is a matter of conjecture, with a recent sociological theory drawing on supply-side economics in its explanation: Americans are more religious than other wealthy, educated peoples because they live in a more open religious market, with more churches and a greater variety of religious perspectives competing for their devotion. With more options, Americans have blossomed into greater consumers of religion. Secular Europeans, in contrast, live in an uncompetitive market. "Wherever you've got a state church," argues Baylor University sociologist Rodney Stark, "you have empty churches." The comparable resurgence of religiosity and religious fundamentalism in developing countries is attributed to the risks and vagaries of life in weak and vulnerable societies. According to political scientists Pippa Norris and Ronald Inglehart, life in rich and secure countries lessens the importance of religious values, except—again—in the United States. They argue that the high level of religiosity in America is due to an "existential insecurity" derived from social and economic inequality together with the massive immigration of people with traditional worldviews, mainly from Hispanic countries.[23]

DIFFERENT IN PRACTICE

Religion manifests itself in American life through the importance of everyday religious practices. In 2004, four in ten Americans said they attended religious services once a week or more, a proportion that has not changed significantly in a decade. Intensity of religious belief determines practice, with evangelical Americans much more likely than Americans in general to attend church more than once a week. Moreover, two-thirds of white evangelicals talk about religion informally with their friends on a weekly basis. Fewer than half of other Americans have such conversations.[24]

By comparison, only one in five British and fewer than one in twenty Russians said they attend a religious service regularly. Americans are also more likely than Europeans to be active members of a church or some other religious organization. At the turn of the century, more than half of Americans had some affiliation with a church or mosque or synagogue, compared with fewer than one in ten in Great Britain and France. Again, American religious observance is most like that in Africa, Asia, and Latin America, where more than half of Mexicans, two-thirds of Indonesians, and nearly all Nigerians told pollsters they regularly attended a church or mosque.[25]

But religious practice is not the sole measure of commitment, and a closer view suggests a less sharp divide between Americans and Europeans. If religious behavior is defined as active soul searching rather than institutional attendance, American piety is not that much greater than that claimed by many in Europe. An overwhelming proportion of the American public says they think often or sometimes about the meaning and purpose of life. However, the French are almost as introspective and the Italians are as likely to ask themselves such questions. Almost all Americans believe in God but many other European nationalities—Polish, Italian, and Spanish—believe to a similar degree. Most Britons are believers, even if far fewer than their American cousins. And even in secular France, only a minority rejects belief in God.

Americans, however, are distinguished in their broader set of religious concepts. An overwhelming majority believes in life after death, a fundamental, distinguishing religious question. Most Western Germans, and the French, share that belief. Similarly, almost all Americans believe people have souls. Far fewer Spanish, British, and French agree.[26]

Americans and Europeans are even more at odds over issues of good and evil and their consequences, which may explain why President Bush's rhetoric after September 11 resonated so well with his fellow citizens and so poorly with Europeans. Satan and hell are religious conceptions that divide Americans from Europeans. Americans are more than twice as likely as the British and nearly four times more likely than the French or the Western Germans to believe in the devil, the embodiment of evil. An overwhelming majority of Americans say hell is real, twice the percentage of Britons and nearly four times the percentage of French and Germans who hold this belief.

The transatlantic gap is slightly narrower with regard to heaven. Nearly all Americans said heaven exists and they share that faith with a strong majority of the British, although fewer than half of Germans agreed. There was an even closer accord on the existence of sin. More than half of Germans, and a strong majority of British and Italians, said they believe in sin, and almost all Americans agreed.

MORAL VALUES

Such differences would probably be limited to theological and philosophical debates if they did not inform the moral values that can influence public policies in the real world. It is not so much the belief in God but the perceived relationship between this belief and moral behavior that separates Americans from Europeans.

In his farewell address, George Washington said that "reason and experience both forbid us to expect that national morality can prevail in exclusion of religious principles." Today, most Americans agree, saying it is necessary to believe in God in order to be a moral person and have good values. Europeans overwhelmingly reject that notion. Moreover, strong majorities of Europeans, from both Eastern and

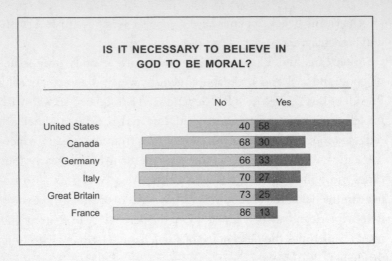

IS IT NECESSARY TO BELIEVE IN
GOD TO BE MORAL?

	No	Yes
United States	40	58
Canada	68	30
Germany	66	33
Italy	70	27
Great Britain	73	25
France	86	13

Western Europe, contend that the opposite is true, that it is not necessary to believe in God to be a moral person.[27]

These transatlantic differences are found among both the young
and the old. In the United States, majorities in every age category said
belief in God is a prerequisite for morality, though younger Americans
were somewhat less likely to express this opinion than those ages sixty-
five and older. In Canada and Western Europe, majorities in every age
group said that belief in God is not a prerequisite for morality; in these
countries, younger respondents were again more likely to hold such
views. As might be expected, white evangelical Americans believed
most fervently that God and morality are linked; however, a strong minority of white mainline Protestants and white Catholics agreed.

For Americans, more so than others, piety, morality, and faith are
inextricably connected to family life. More than half of all Americans
said it is especially important for children to learn religious faith at
home. Only a small portion of the British and the French agree. Further, Americans have a strong sense that religion is central to the
moral development of children. A majority stated that children are
more likely to grow up to be moral adults when they are raised in a religious faith. Again, evangelicals held such sentiments most strongly,

but the view was shared to a lesser extent with white mainline Protestants, white Catholics, and black Protestants.

These strongly held religion-based beliefs lead naturally to sharp reactions to any perceived challenges to the family, such as abortion and homosexuality, and, by extension, to a cluster of public morality issues that include suicide, euthanasia, and prostitution. To Europeans, American attitudes on these matters are rooted too deeply in religious faith, with scant concern for the societal concerns involved. Yet there is more complexity here than Europeans may recognize. On some of these high-profile issues, for example, religious Americans are more traditional in their views than their secular European counterparts. On other issues, American attitudes are actually more liberal than those held in at least some European societies. More significantly, on many issues, American views have converged with those in many European countries.

Absolute American opposition to prostitution, abortion, suicide, and euthanasia actually weakened somewhat in the 1990s, although roughly half of Americans still think killing oneself or selling one's body is always wrong. Among those who said such activities are never justifiable, American views tend to look more like those of traditionally Catholic Italians and Poles than they do of the French. But it is the convergence of transatlantic views that is most striking, especially on abortion and suicide.

On the issue of homosexuality, the 2002 Pew Global Attitudes survey found Americans differing from the rest of the industrial world to a greater degree. Most German, French, British, and Italian respondents felt that homosexuality should be accepted by society. Canadians, who have subsequently legalized gay marriage, closely mirrored Western Europeans. Americans were split, with a bare majority believing gay people should be accepted. In this regard, Americans were more in tune with attitudes in Latin America, where publics in 2002 were also split.

When homosexuality became a contested public issue, as it did around the issue of legalizing gay marriages in the United States in

TABLE 5.3

SOME CONVERGENCE ON SOCIAL ISSUES

	1990 %	1999–2000 %	Change %
Prostitution Never **Justifiable**			
United States	58	48	−10
Poland	73	—	—
Italy	56	56	0
Spain	47	29	−18
France	45	—	—
Great Britain	41	40	−1
Germany	31	35	+4
Abortion Never **Justifiable**			
United States	33	30	−3
Poland	40	42	+2
Spain	29	27	−2
Italy	22	31	+9
Great Britain	19	25	+6
France	18	14	−4
Germany	17	22	+5
Suicide Never **Justifiable**			
United States	59	57	−2
Poland	71	61	−10
Italy	65	60	−5
Spain	64	48	−16
Great Britain	38	38	0
Germany	36	50	+14
France	31	25	−6
Euthanasia Never **Justifiable**			
United States	30	24	−6
Poland	62	47	−15
Italy	39	38	−1
Spain	34	22	−12
Germany	27	27	0
Great Britain	21	20	−1
France	21	12	−9

Source: World Values Survey, 1999–2000.

SHOULD HOMOSEXUALITY BE
ACCEPTED BY SOCIETY?

	No	Yes
Germany	15	83
Italy	20	72
France	21	77
Great Britain	22	74
Canada	26	69
United States	42	51

2004, the intensity of religious belief fueled anti-gay sentiment. A slender majority of the American public supported civil unions for homosexuals, and support for gay marriage had increased, though it remained a minority position. But white evangelical Americans were overwhelmingly opposed to such marriages, and a strong majority were against civil unions. Indeed, the spectacle of mass marriages of gay couples in San Francisco, coupled with the Massachusetts Supreme Judicial Court ruling overturning the state's ban on gay marriage, was credited with energizing President Bush's religious base during the 2004 presidential campaign. However, it is not certain that religiosity alone determines attitudes on homosexuality. American women were more willing to accept homosexuals than were American men, although religion played a more important role in women's lives. A similar pattern of beliefs was found among European women. Larger cultural attitudes, rather than narrow religious persuasion, may be a more central factor.[28]

At first glance, attitudes toward prostitution appear to be loosely driven by religion. In 1999, roughly half of Americans said sex for money is never justifiable, reinforcing the stereotypical view of

Americans as Puritans. They shared this view with people in traditionally Catholic Italy. Far fewer of the more secular British and Germans agreed. But pitting Puritanism against libertinism fails to explain why, in 1990, nearly half of the supposedly cosmopolitan French said prostitution was never justified. Again, religion is an indicator of moral values but not necessarily an ironclad determinant, for either Americans or Europeans.

Attitudes on abortion seem more clearly linked to religion and the depth of religious belief. A Pew survey in July 2005 found that more than two-thirds of American evangelicals felt that abortion should be illegal in most or all cases, compared with about 40 percent of the general U.S. population who held such views. In this, Americans were twice as likely as the French to say abortion is never justifiable. Such American views resembled those of Catholic Spain and Poland. But Americans as a whole were deeply divided, with somewhat contradictory polls suggesting that Americans supported abortion in principle but had doubts about it in practice. In January 2005, somewhat fewer than half of Americans surveyed told the Gallup Organization that they were satisfied with the nation's policies on abortion; however, just over half of Americans said they believed the decision about an abortion should be left up to the woman and her doctor. But at the same time, nearly two-thirds of respondents in another poll said that abortion should not be permitted or should be permitted only with stricter limits.[29]

But there is no ambivalence about American attitudes with respect to capital punishment. Although support for the death penalty has fallen substantially since 1996, in 2005 two out of three Americans supported executing those convicted of murder. Still, religion's role in the bitter transatlantic debate over the death penalty is, at best, exaggerated by America's critics. Substantial support for imposition of the death penalty exists in much of Europe, a fact that might undermine the European criticism that stark moral judgments about good and evil drive the American justice system as well as U.S. foreign policy.

Over the past few years, outrage over capital punishment in the United States has triggered street protests and angry public demonstrations in many European capitals. The U.S. embassy in Paris once received an anti-death penalty petition signed by 500,000 French citizens. For several decades, European Union governments have refused to extradite criminal defendants to stand trial in the United States—even when they were suspected terrorists—without commitments by American prosecutors to forgo the death penalty.

The chorus from abroad was well summed up by the wife of British prime minister Tony Blair: "The observation 'Americans are from Mars and Europeans are from Venus' is illustrated by the two nations' differing reactions to use of the death penalty," complained Cherie Blair in February 2004. "The reality is that too many people—innocent people—are executed for the system to be able to claim a just precision." Reflecting on the international costs to the nation of enforcing the death penalty, former high-ranking U.S. State Department official Harold Hongju Koh wrote that "the practice has caused allies and adversaries alike to challenge our claim of moral leadership in international human rights, and probably helped contribute to the embarrassing, temporary loss [in 2001] of America's seat on the U.N. Human Rights Commission."[30]

Still, while fewer people in other industrial societies support putting criminals to death, there is not all that much difference between foreign and American attitudes. In 2003, for example, just over half of people in Mrs. Blair's United Kingdom supported the death penalty, according to Gallup, as did nearly half of Canadians. Similarly, a 1996 Dutch poll showed half of the public there favored capital punishment. And strong minorities of Italians and French agreed, according to *Time* magazine. So though it is true that there is less support in Europe for the death penalty, there is no great transatlantic divide on this issue among the publics.

Religious fervor does not fully explain sentiments about capital punishment. Many of those Americans who "strongly favor" the death penalty may fervently believe in the Old Testament's call for an eye for an eye, but supporters of capital punishment are not solely the deeply religious. White evangelicals with high levels of religious commitment are no more likely to back the death penalty than other Protestants who are not as religiously committed. In fact, Catholics and mainline Protestants with a high degree of religious commitment actually show less support for the death penalty for those convicted of murder than do fellow churchgoers with less commitment. Moreover, Americans who oppose the death penalty cite their religious beliefs nearly three times more often than do death penalty supporters who say their views are rooted in religious teachings.

Finally, neither American nor European attitudes toward divorce appear to be driven by religious conviction and its associated commitment to the family. Expedience seems to trump traditional attitudes toward the indissoluble nature of wedlock. Fewer than one in ten Americans said divorce is never justified, a reflection of the practical reality that one in two American marriages end in divorce. Americans were no more opposed to divorce than the worldly French and slightly less opposed than the British and Germans.

Nonetheless, American attitudes on public morality for the most part follow strong religious beliefs. Except for divorce, Americans are more moralistic than Europeans. But, again, Americans are not exceptional in these attitudes. Their views closely track those in many parts of Latin America and Africa, and are often less rigid than those in parts of the Muslim world. For example, in 2002 people in Africa and the Middle East objected more strongly to societal acceptance of homosexuality than did Americans; in some African countries—notably Kenya and Senegal—opposition was virtually unanimous. Still, in some Latin American countries such as Mexico, Argentina, Bolivia, and Brazil, tolerance for homosexuality was greater than in the United States.

MORAL POLICY

It should not be surprising that the religiosity that frames many of the debates about public morality in the United States might affect government decisions on domestic and foreign policy. As mentioned earlier, there has been a sea change in American attitudes toward the church's role in such public deliberations over the past two genera-tions, with a majority of Americans now in favor of churches speak-ing out on contemporary political and social issues. Even as fewer Americans see their religion as "very important" to them, they have become more willing to see a positive role for religion in affairs of state. In 1968, a Gallup poll found that by a margin of 53 to 40 percent Americans believed churches should refrain from involvement in pol-itics, and a 1965 Gallup survey found that only 22 percent felt it was acceptable for clergy to discuss political issues or candidates from the pulpit. By 2005, a Pew poll detected significant changes: by a margin of 51 to 44 percent, Americans said churches should express views on political and social issues of the day, and 31 percent supported out-right politicking from the pulpit.[31]

Other surveys have revealed similar sentiments. In 2003, a Pew survey found that three in five Americans not only believed that Pres-ident Bush relied on his own religious convictions a great deal or a fair amount in making policy decisions, but a similar proportion thought

TABLE 5.4

AMERICANS VIEW THE ROLES OF THE CHURCH IN POLITICS

	1965 %	1968 %	1996 %	2001 %	2005 %
Churches should keep out of politics	—	53	43	43	44
Churches should express views	—	40	54	51	51
No opinion	—	7	3	6	5
Is it ever right for clergy to discuss political candidates or issues from the pulpit?					
Yes	22	—	29	28	31
No	68	—	66	65	63
Don't know/Refused	10	—	5	7	6

Source: Gallup, 1965 and 1968; Pew Research Center for the People & the Press.

that was "about the right amount." The next year, more than half of likely American voters told *Time* magazine that "religious values should serve as a guide to what our political leaders do in office," and just short of half of voters reported they thought the president should allow his personal religious faith to guide him in making decisions as president. This signals a dramatic shift away from the separation of church and state that candidate John F. Kennedy signified in 1960 with his promise to American Baptists that he would not allow his Catholicism to affect his presidential decisions.[32]

To be fair, religion has long been used to justify or rationalize U.S. action at home and abroad. From the Plymouth Colony in the seventeenth century to Manifest Destiny in the nineteenth century, Americans have seen themselves as divinely inspired to conquer the wilderness and extend American influence, chosen by God for the task because of their innate goodness and morality. In 1898, President William McKinley conquered the Philippines to "uplift and civilize and Christianize" its people, and in the process extend American power in Asia and the Caribbean.

Religious views continue to frame some opinions about foreign policy and religious pressure groups have significant influence these days in Washington. The concept of a "just war," for example, first propounded by Saint Augustine, finds far more adherents in the United States than in Europe. More than three-fourths of all Americans believe that under some conditions war is justified to obtain justice; only about one in four Europeans agree. In the 1990s, America prodded and led a reluctant Europe to intervene in Bosnia and Kosovo to prevent genocide, even though no direct U.S. interest was at stake.

More concretely, Americans' attitudes toward Israel are heavily influenced by religion. One in three Americans who sympathize with Israel said their sympathy for the Jewish state comes from their religious beliefs. Beyond sympathy, two in five Americans believed Israel was given to the Jewish people by God, and one in three said creation of the state of Israel is a step toward the Second Coming of Christ. "The return of Jesus to the Holy Land was the beginning of the fulfillment of the scriptures," explained the Southern Baptist Convention's Richard Land. But, Land added, "that does not mean blind acceptance" of every action by Israel's government.

In the case of Israel, at least, intensity of belief is correlated with much of this sentiment. White evangelicals are much more pro-Israel than Americans in general. More than half of evangelicals say they sympathize more with Israel in its dispute with the Palestinians, compared with four in ten Americans overall who hold this view. This support appears to be reinforced by political orientation: white evangelicals who identified themselves as political conservatives were more than three times as likely to back Israel as were moderate evangelicals. On Palestine, evangelicals differed little from the general American population, which voiced weak support for the Palestinian cause.[33]

The most recent and controversial bleeding of faith into American foreign policy was apparent in the U.S. reaction to the September 11 attacks. In the wake of the tragedy, President Bush insisted that the

TABLE 5.7

AMERICAN VIEWS OF ISRAEL LINKED TO RELIGIOUS BELIEFS

	%		
Israel fulfills Biblical prophecy			
Yes	36		
No	46		
Don't know	18		

| | | Believe Israel Fulfills Prophecy . . . | |
| | | Yes | No |
	%	%	%
Sympathize more with			
Israel	41	57	34
Palestinians	13	9	18
Both	8	6	8
Neither	18	10	23
Don't know	20	18	17

U.S. war on terrorism was not a holy war or a clash of religions. But his public rhetoric returned again and again to religious themes to bolster and justify the American public's support for the U.S. effort. In the days immediately following September 11, the president characterized the terrorists as motiveless "evildoers," a word harkening back to the description in Psalms of malefactors or offenders of God's law. "They have no justification for their actions," he said. "There's no religious justification, there's no political justification. The only motivation is evil." A few days later he declared war on this evil, asserting that "the great goodness of America must come forth and shine forth." His speeches later called forth America's founding principle of religious freedom. "The terrorists hate the fact that . . . we can worship Almighty God the way we see fit," he told a convention of religious broadcasters in Nashville. The terrorists not only attacked the United States; they attacked its religion.[34]

In the run-up to the U.S.-led invasion of Iraq, President Bush used much the same religious imagery and justification. "He decided that Saddam was evil," wrote Howard Fineman in *Newsweek,* "and everything flowed from that." Fineman quotes then Palestinian prime minister Mahmoud Abbas as saying that Bush told him, "God told me to strike Al Qaeda and I struck them, and then he instructed me to strike at Saddam, which I did." Concluded Fineman, "Bush is dwelling on faith-based foreign policy of the most explosive kind."

In *The President of Good and Evil,* Peter Singer tallied it up: "Bush has spoken about evil in 319 separate speeches, or about 30 percent of all the speeches he gave between the time he took office and June 16, 2003." Further:

> In these speeches he uses the word "evil" as a noun far more often than he uses it as an adjective—914 noun uses as against 182 adjectival uses. Only twenty-four times, in all these occasions on which Bush talks of evil, does he use it as an adjective to describe what people do—that is, to judge acts or deeds. This suggests that Bush is not thinking about evil deeds, or even evil people, nearly as often as he is thinking about evil as a thing, or a force, something that has a

real existence apart from the cruel, callous, brutal and selfish acts of which human beings are capable. His readiness to talk about evil in this manner raises the question of what meaning evil can have in a secular modern world.[35]

For all of Bush's religious imagery, its impact on Americans' views on foreign policy issues has been unclear. Religion clearly shapes people's positions on social issues such as abortion. White evangelicals who reported intense belief showed relatively strong support for the Iraq war, with about seven in ten calling the decision to invade Iraq the right decision. However, an even higher proportion of Republicans (more than eight in ten) also endorsed the decision. Since about half of white evangelicals identified themselves as Republicans, it is not possible to say with confidence whether their support for the conflict reflected their party affiliation or their identity as proselytizing Christians.[36]

Bush's religiosity—a condition of his leadership—leaves many Americans and non-Americans anxious, particularly when it is applied to international affairs. The most outspoken of the president's critics fear that his pursuit of a faith-based foreign policy will lead to an even worse conflict. Bush's justifications of the Iraq war that used "religious rhetoric and . . . his Christian faith . . . played into the hands of Muslim fundamentalists who see the looming battle as a 'crusade' against Islam," complained the *Los Angeles Times* before the Iraq war began. Pope John Paul II urged Bush to quit invoking God's name to justify war.[37]

A RELIGIOUS MOMENT

In the American experience, nothing is exceptional about religiosity in public life. But there is something exceptional about the level of religiosity in American public life today. "In the United States of America, religious attitudes have more of an influence on political choices than in any other western democracy," argues Josef Braml of the SWP think tank.[38]

Voting patterns in U.S. presidential elections over the last four decades show that religion has played an increasing role in explaining how people vote; in particular, it is a better predictor of attitudes toward social, sexual, and cultural issues than age, gender, or education. It is clear that the United States is undergoing another period of religious enthusiasm, whether on the scale of a "great awakening" or not, marked not only by high-profile manifestations of religiosity but also, and equally important, by the greater involvement of religious persons in the nitty-gritty of politics.

And such religious adherents have become an increasingly cohesive force within the Republican Party. In 1987, white evangelical Protestants were divided in their partisan attachments. In 2004, Republicans outnumbered Democrats among evangelicals by more than two to one. Reflecting their conservative outlook, evangelicals are more supportive of the military and the war in Iraq than their fellow countrymen, and they are more concerned about politically controversial social issues.

In the last four decades, social issues that impinge on religious belief—gay marriage, abortion, homosexuality, school prayer—have gained much more visibility in the American political realm, and religious citizens are much more likely than ever before to take their concerns about such issues into the public arena, linking faith and political engagement. Christian evangelicals, in particular, because they believe in missionary work, assert their values more aggressively than do some other denominations. They are better organized and more active in campaigns, and when their candidates win they have greater influence on policy development, including at the highest levels of government.

In some sense, then, both views of the current state of religiosity in America are true. Contrary to widespread impressions, religion plays no radically new role in American life. And, with the exception of the tremendously important issue of U.S. support for Israel, the American public's religiosity has little influence on most U.S. foreign policies that affect the rest of the world. But it is the case that a minority of the more deeply religious Americans, energized by moral issues, are arguably having a substantially greater influence on current politics and the public discourse. That influence has focused unprecedented attention from abroad on American religiosity and generated fear of a faith-driven U.S. foreign policy that risks endangering American alliances, particularly with countries in Europe. The risk, in turn, to the United States is that such perceptions could feed the level of anti-Americanism that is already high as the result of cultural differences with both secular Europe and the more religious Muslim world.

6

DOING BUSINESS,
PRACTICING DEMOCRACY

THE TELEVISION IMAGES were worth a thousand words. Jubilant Iraqis waved their index fingers in the air—ink-stained to avoid duplicate voting—after having just cast ballots in the first free Iraqi election in decades. The January 2005 selection of an Iraqi national assembly, flawed as it was by violence and a low turnout among Sunni voters, was a vitally important first step toward a self-governing society. In the weeks before the election, 86 percent of Iraqis said they wanted democracy. And they were on the road to getting it. "The world is hearing the voice of freedom from the center of the Middle East," President George W. Bush said, just hours after the Iraqi polls closed. "In great numbers and under great risk, Iraqis have shown their commitment to democracy. By participating in free elections, the Iraqi people have firmly rejected the anti-democratic ideology of terrorists."[1]

The Iraqi parliamentary elections were only one of a series in democratic balloting in the Middle East in 2005. Even before the Iraqis went to the polls, the Palestinian people elected a new president of the Palestinian Authority. In June the people of Lebanon began electing a new parliament. And in September Egypt held its first-ever multicandidate presidential balloting. Democratic values were emerging in a region long known for its autocratic regimes.

Halfway around the world, in Managua, Nicaragua, stooped-shouldered, auburn-skinned women, their faces creased with toil more than age, stretched yard after yard of rough-hewn white organic cotton cloth along a cutting table in a small cement-slab factory. The women were the owners and employees of the Cooperativa Maquiladora Mujeres. They built the factory with their own hands; their products include T-shirts destined for the Presbyterian Church (USA), Bucknell University, and Maggie's Clean Clothes of Ypsilanti, Michigan. In a country where socialism thrived in the 1980s, these women have converted to capitalism, so much so that they successfully lobbied to have themselves declared an Export Processing Zone so they would not have to pay import and export taxes, gaining the same tax benefit accorded to the big American, Taiwanese, and Korean multinational corporations located in Nicaragua. "We decided," said Mike Woodward, who works for Jubilee House, an American organization that advises the cooperative, "to beat the system at its own game." That system is capitalism, a set of economic values that may be widely criticized but are also now widely shared by people all over the world.[2]

Free-market economic principles and individual democratic freedoms—so popular in the slums of Managua and in the streets of Baghdad—are no less enthusiastically embraced by Americans. Indeed, Americans' zeal for democracy and capitalism rivals the fervency of their religiosity. For many Americans, these values are what the United States is all about. As the twin pillars of the American way of life, they define America's nature; they are its cultural legacy. To Americans, capitalism and democracy are universal norms that others would be well served to emulate.

But as recent experience in the Middle East, Latin America, and elsewhere demonstrates, Americans are not unique in their commitment to the fundamental values of a democratic system—the freedom to criticize the government, a fair judicial system, and multiparty elections—and to an economy free of state control. After years of experimenting with socialism and experiencing totalitarianism, most people around the world share these views. To the extent that U.S. support for democracy and free markets has become part of the anti-American critique, such condemnation reflects an American exceptionalism that is misunderstood. These values are not exceptional to Americans. They are widely shared.

At the same time, Americans differ from others in their allegiance to "U.S.-style" democracy and "U.S.-style" business practices—however they define them.[3] While often indifferent to elections, Americans are more likely than Europeans to be politically engaged in other ways. Americans are also more committed to competition and other underlying principles of a free-market system. And they work harder. These value differences reflect aspects of the American character that are distinctive, but they do not necessarily signify an unbridgeable gulf between Americans and other peoples of the world. In this sense, these exceptional American traits are also misunderstood.[4]

For example, Europeans, for their part, see democracy and open markets as guidelines to follow rather than American models to pursue. This disconnect between how Americans view their style of democracy and business and how many in the world see those same practices manifests itself in international policy disputes that range from how to foster democracy in the Middle East to how to approach globalization. The divide reflects fundamental differences of opinion about the functioning of the modern free-market system and a marked divergence of attitudes toward the work ethic. It is, moreover, a dichotomy that often closely parallels foreign attitudes toward the United States in general.

In polls, Americans are fiercely proud of their national experience and overwhelmingly convinced that their Constitution, free elections, and the free enterprise system are major reasons for the nation's political and economic success in the last century. They say that the spread of such American ideas and customs would be a good thing. "It is the policy of the United States to seek and support the growth of democratic governments and institutions in every nation and every culture," President Bush said in his second-term inaugural address. A strong majority of Americans agree, although, as discussed previously, spreading democracy abroad is seen as a low priority by the American people.

Those who are not keen to see the further spread of American governance and business models include people who arguably know America the best: the Canadians and the Europeans. Only half of Canadians like the way the United States practices democracy and only one-third like American ways of doing business. Western Europeans are even harsher judges. Less than half the British, French, Italians, and Germans admire American-style democracy and even fewer support American-style business. Even among most Eastern Europeans— what U.S. secretary of defense Donald Rumsfeld christened the "New Europe"—a bare majority, except in the Czech Republic, expresses affection for American democratic norms.

It is not that Europeans oppose democracy or capitalism per se. They share with Americans strong support for basic democratic principles and a free-market economic system. But many Europeans question the kind of democracy and the kind of capitalism practiced in the United States.

Europeans' preference for social democracy helps to explain their mixed reaction to American-style governance. In Germany, and in many Eastern European countries, people who said it is up to the government to ensure that no citizens are in need tend also to reject American-style democracy. By contrast, people who favor a more minimalist government role in providing a social safety net favor the American form of democracy by higher margins.

American-style business practices are even less popular in Europe since the late 1990s, when the high-tech stock market bubble burst and provided a contradictory lesson to the American claims that the United States had put an end to the business cycle; the Enron

TABLE 6.1

OPINIONS OF AMERICAN-STYLE DEMOCRACY

	Like %	Dislike %	Don't Know/Refused %
North America			
Canada	50	40	10
Western Europe			
Germany	47	45	7
Italy	45	37	18
Great Britain	43	42	15
France	42	53	5
Eastern Europe			
Czech Republic	64	30	6
Slovak Republic	54	38	8
Ukraine	53	35	12
Poland	51	30	19
Bulgaria	50	23	27
Russia	28	46	26
Conflict Area			
Uzbekistan	65	22	13
Lebanon	49	45	7
Turkey	33	50	17
Jordan	29	69	2
Pakistan	9	60	31
Egypt	n/a	n/a	n/a

OPINIONS OF AMERICAN BUSINESS PRACTICES

	Like %	Dislike %	Don't Know/Refused %
North America			
Canada	34	56	11
Western Europe			
Italy	39	43	18
Great Britain	37	44	18
Germany	32	58	10
France	23	73	4
Eastern Europe			
Ukraine	58	23	18
Slovak Republic	52	40	8
Bulgaria	50	12	37
Poland	46	25	29
Czech Republic	44	47	9
Russia	41	30	29
Conflict Area			
Uzbekistan	76	11	12
Lebanon	65	28	7
Jordan	44	52	4
Egypt	34	46	20
Turkey	27	59	14
Pakistan	14	53	33

accounting scandal a few years later suggested to Europeans that American competitiveness was, in part, a product of cooking the books. More broadly, while Europeans envy American innovation, productivity, and economic growth, they tend to reject what they see as the cutthroat deal making that often fuels American business success. In 2002, for example, Jean-Marie Messier of France was forced from his job as chairman of Vivendi Universal for being too American in his business practices. Four years earlier he had taken over the venerable Compagnie Générale des Eaux and, through aggressive U.S.-style acquisitions and mountains of U.S.-style debt, he transformed it from a national utility to a global media and entertainment company (changing its name in the process). The straw that broke the camel's back may have been Messier's move to New York. His investors pulled the plug, apparently calling foul on Messier's push to establish an American identity for the French business. Such antipathy is certainly shared by the French public, nearly three out of four of whom dislike American-style business practices.[5]

Central Europeans, on the other hand, who suffered under two generations of Communism, are generally more favorable toward American-style capitalism. Ukrainians in particular, possibly because they were so short changed under Soviet rule, seem hungry for the fruits of the free market: 64 percent think people are better off in a free-market economy and 58 percent favor American business practices. Czechs, on the other hand, who have the region's most globalized economy, stand as a notable exception; roughly half of them hold a negative view of U.S. business.

Such international differences mask deeper disparities in attitudes toward the social and economic attributes of a market economy and toward work itself. Americans, true to their capitalist image, work more than Europeans, are more likely to consider competition beneficial, are more comfortable with merit-based pay, and are more skeptical of the idea of employee rights. Yet they are not that much more likely to believe that people are better off in a free-market economy.

Attitudes toward the United States in general, and toward its version of democracy and free enterprise, go hand in hand in many parts of the world. People in the Middle East, while embracing democratic principles, harbor great antipathy toward American-style democratic and commercial ideas. Consistent with their largely unfavorable views of the United States, half or more of the publics in Turkey and Jordan also say they dislike these core values of the American political and economic systems. In Lebanon, opinion is split, with about half the public favoring U.S.-style democracy and a strong majority holding a favorable opinion of U.S.-style capitalism. The Uzbeks, who are even more enthusiastic about America's versions of democracy and capitalism, are the only other public of the broader Middle East to join the Lebanese.

But skepticism abroad about the American models of democracy and economic activity is not limited to nations that hold generally unfavorable views of the United States. They extend to many nations, including Great Britain, which supplied the original immigrants to the United States and whose culture helped produce the American character.

DEMOCRATIC VALUES

Americans' belief in democracy is deep-seated. Pew Research Center and other polls show a profound commitment among Americans to democratic values to an extent that at times sets them apart. Although no more or less devoted to free elections and free speech than others, Americans tend to value their democratic freedoms as much if not more than other peoples. Americans complain that their democracy in practice often falls short of its promise, but they are generally satisfied with its functioning. To be sure, democratic participation, as measured by voter turnout, is lower in the United States than in most other major democracies. But Americans tend to be more engaged than Europeans in other aspects of democratic life, such as belonging to political parties or being willing to sign petitions.

After decades of struggle, democracy is now universally embraced in most parts of the world. According to numerous polls, Americans overwhelmingly believe they have the best form of government, despite democracy's many acknowledged problems. They share this faith with people in Asia, Africa, Latin America, and Europe. But Americans are distinct from others in their belief that their own democracy actually lives up to these ideals. Elsewhere, less than a third of Brazilians say they have freedom of speech, less than one in six Russians think their country has fair elections, and only one in four Turks believes Turkey has a fair judicial system. Moreover, Americans are much more likely to accept as normal the squabbling and everyday to-and-fro that mark public dialogue in a healthy democracy. While four in ten Americans think their form of government is indecisive and hamstrung by too much bickering, fully half the Canadians, and three-quarters of the French and the Russians, are critical of their democracies for such perceived shortcomings.

While Americans celebrate their democracy, cherish their democratic freedoms, and bemoan their democratic failings, they are much less likely than most other people to actually exercise the most fundamental of democratic rights: participating in elections. While three in five eligible U.S. citizens voted in 2004, such high voter participation is the exception, not the rule, in the United States.[6]

Nevertheless, Americans appear to be more politically engaged than other peoples in alternative ways. According to the World Values Survey, they were twice as likely as the French or the Germans, for example, and three times as likely as the British, to say politics is very important to them. One in five Americans claimed to be active members of political parties, while acknowledged political party membership in Europe stood in the single digits—and was declining. Moreover, 81 percent of Americans said they signed a petition regarding some political or government matter in recent years. Fewer Europeans engaged in this elemental exercise of their democratic rights.

Americans and Europeans both champion democracy and democratic freedoms as central values, yet their demonstrated ambivalence

TABLE 6.2

PARTICIPATION IN POLITICAL ACTION

% Saying They Have Done Each of These Activities

	Signing Petition	Joining Boycott	Demonstrating	Joining Strike	Occupying Building/ Facility
United States	81	24	20	6	4
Canada	73	18	19	7	3
Great Britain	79	16	13	8	2
France	67	12	38	12	9
Germany	52	8	32	2	1
Italy	52	10	33	5	8
Spain	24	5	24	7	2

Source: World Values Survey, 1999–2000.

about democratic practice—for Americans, by voting; for Europeans, by engaging in other forms of democratic expression—suggests democracy means different things to different people. One explanation for this seeming contradiction may lie in differing views of the state.

People all over the world, including Americans, hold complex and somewhat contradictory feelings about their own governments. There is a widespread sense that government is inefficient, and majorities in Western Europe and the United States feel that the state is too controlling. At the same time, people generally view their governments as being on their side. In effect, publics have a compartmentalized perspective on those who spend their taxes, collect their garbage, and defend their borders. Americans are typical in this regard: a majority said the government is inefficient and overly controlling, but most also believed that the government was run for the benefit of all citizens, not just some. The British held this same view, as did people in Canada, Honduras, Lebanon, Turkey, and many other countries, including several in Africa.

Time and circumstance have a great deal to do with shaping people's attitudes toward the state. In 1991, fewer than half of Americans thought government was run for the benefit of all people; a decade later, in 2002, nearly two-thirds had a positive view of the state. One possible explanation is that the Republican administrations in the 1980s bashed government while the Democratic administration in the 1990s espoused a more government-friendly message.

TABLE 6.3

GOVERNMENT BENEFITS ALL PEOPLE

	% Saying They Agree	
	1991	2002
United States	48	65
Great Britain	52	66
France	48	40
Germany	41	86
Italy	12	88
Poland	31	88
Russia	26	50
Ukraine	22	32
Czech Republic	61	56
Slovak Republic	71	54

The same phenomenon has been seen in Europe, particularly in the former Eastern bloc. In Poland and also in Germany, the percentage of the population with a favorable view of their governments more than doubled between 1991 and 2002, the period spanning the fall of Communism. In Russia, by 2002 half the people saw the government as benefiting everyone, double the level in 1991.

On the question of whether government is overly controlling, Europeans have mixed views. In the 1990s, there was a significant increase in the proportion of Germans who saw their government as too controlling. In contrast, in Russia significantly fewer people said public authorities were overly controlling in 2002 than did so in 1991, apparently reflecting the legacy of the Soviet leadership.

Americans and Europeans are not exceptional in their commitment to democracy. As the 2005 elections in Iraq, Lebanon, Egypt, and the Palestinian Authority attest, large and growing majorities in many Muslim societies believe that Western-style democracy can work in their countries. This is the case in predominantly Muslim states such as Kuwait and Bangladesh, but also in religiously diverse Nigeria. As a corollary, most Muslim publics clearly favor democratic government over a strong autocratic leader. In fact, in two Muslim countries—Lebanon and Turkey—the proportions of the population preferring democracy over a strong leader are about the same as in the United States. And in five of six Muslim countries polled by Pew in 2005, the percentage believing that democracy could work in their country had increased since 2002.

TABLE 6.4

BELIEFS ABOUT GOVERNANCE

Western-Style Democracy Can Work Here . . .	2002 %	2005 %
Turkey	43	48
Pakistan	44	43
Lebanon	75	83
Jordan	63	80
Morocco	64	83
Indonesia	64	77

Moreover, despite soaring anti-Americanism and substantial support for Islamic fundamentalism, there is a considerable appetite in the Muslim world for certain democratic freedoms. People in these countries place a high value on freedom of expression, freedom of the press, multiparty systems, and equal treatment under the law. This includes people living in kingdoms such as Jordan, as well as those in authoritarian states like Uzbekistan and Pakistan. Many Muslim publics express a stronger desire for democratic freedoms than some nations of Eastern Europe. And such confidence in democracy's potential exists among most Muslims in these countries regardless of age or gender.

This is not to say that Muslims necessarily envision democracy in quite the same way as Americans. In Pew polls, fewer than half of Muslims in Pakistan, Indonesia, Uzbekistan, and Jordan, for example, rated honest two-party elections and freedom of the press as very important. Moreover, many supported a prominent and in some cases expanding role for Islam and for religious leaders in the political life of their countries. Nonetheless, Muslims generally are no less supportive of keeping religion separate from government policy than are people in other countries. Indeed, in predominantly Muslim countries with secular traditions, such as Turkey, Senegal, and Mali, a larger portion of the population than in the United States thought that religion should be kept separate from government policy. Moreover, belief in close links between religion and governance did not diminish Muslim support for a system of governance that ensures the same civil liberties and political rights enjoyed by Western peoples.

As in much of the West, in Muslim societies there is a pervasive sense that these democratic aspirations are not being fulfilled. Skepticism is widespread about honest elections and freedom of expression. Perceptions of repression in some Muslim countries, notably Turkey and Lebanon, were as prevalent in 2002 as anywhere else in the world. Solid majorities in both nations said they lack the fundamental rights to freedom of speech, freedom of the press, fair elections, and an impartial judiciary.

Support for democracy in the Muslim world does not, however, improve people's attitudes toward the United States, calling into question the American assumption that Washington's advocacy of the democratization of the Middle East will rebound to the United States' benefit. In Pakistan, for example, those who strongly supported democratic values were just as hostile to America as those who placed little or no importance on such values. This pattern was evident in Turkey as well. Only in Jordan did advocates of democracy also see America in a favorable light.

MARKETPLACE VALUES

Nearly two centuries ago, Alexis de Tocqueville wrote, "The love of wealth is . . . at the bottom of all that the Americans do. . . . It perturbs their minds, but it disciplines their lives." President Calvin Coolidge put it more succinctly during the 1920s: "The chief business of the American people is business."[7]

Both observations still seem accurate in America's third century. According to Pew polls, seven in ten Americans believed that people are better off living in a free-market economy, slightly more than those who expressed such views in Germany, Britain, France, or Canada. But Americans were far from being alone in their enthusiasm for capitalism. With the end of the Cold War, the international struggle between free markets and socialism has ended and capitalism has won.

In the new global economy, almost everyone wants to be a capitalist, particularly the poor, like the women in Managua. In 2002, support for free markets was higher in several developing African countries, particularly Nigeria and Ivory Coast, than it is in the United States. Enthusiasm for capitalism among Czechs and Ukrainians is on a par with support among Canadians and the French. Even in China, seven in ten Chinese thought their nation's turn toward a more market-oriented economy has meant a better life, even though some people get rich and some stay poor.

In fact, while support for free enterprise is greatest overall in wealthier countries, it is also quite high among those with the least wealth. Why this is true is unclear, but it may be attributable to the experience of the rich and the hope of the poor. Support for free markets is notably weaker in middle-income countries, many of which are struggling to make capitalism work. Among them, only a plurality of people in India and a narrow majority of people in Egypt and Indonesia agreed in 2002 that people are better off in free-market societies. Conversely, hard times, even among the rich, engender discontent with free markets. In Japan, where the economy stagnated throughout most of the 1990s, a majority of the public believed people are not better off in a competitive system.

As might be expected, among people who are less well off, some blame capitalism. In Argentina, where the economy collapsed in the late 1990s, only about a quarter of the public felt that people are better off trying to live in a free market. Similarly, many Russians, Poles, and Bulgarians doubt the benefits of capitalism.

Americans and most Europeans support the free-market system in theory, but they hold distinctly different attitudes toward many of the underlying values of capitalism. Almost no one on either side of the Atlantic wants to nationalize industry today, in part because a strong majority in the United States and even stronger majorities in Western

TABLE 6.5

VIEWS OF ECONOMIC COMPETITION

	% Say It's Good
United States	58
Canada	53
Germany	49
Great Britain	42
Italy	42
Spain	37
France	36

Note: Percentages represent the number of respondents answering 1–3 on a 1–10 scale, where 1 means complete agreement with the statement "Competition is good. It stimulates people to work hard and develop new ideas."
Source: World Values Survey, 1999–2000.

Europe think that when something is run by the state it is usually inefficient and wasteful. Three in ten Americans polled believed there should be more private ownership of industry. Since there is relatively little public ownership of enterprises in the United States at this time, such sentiments seem to reflect Americans' philosophical commitment to free enterprise rather than a practical desire for more privatization. In contrast, a plurality of Europeans thought the public-private balance in the economy is just about right.

Many more Americans than Europeans also firmly believed that competition—in many ways the essence of any market economy—stimulates people to work hard and develop new ideas, according to the World Values Survey. As people who more often doubt the value of competition, Europeans may be the odd ones out in the rapidly globalizing world. In the late 1990s, they had more doubts about economic competition than did Brazilians, Nigerians, or Indians.

Reflecting the sharp contrast between America's capitalist tradition and Europe's social democratic history, Americans and Europeans also hold distinctly different views about how to organize the workplace. More than half of Americans believed owners should run businesses or appoint company managers; only a quarter of the French and three in ten Germans agreed. Six in ten French and Germans said owners and employees should participate jointly in selecting corporate managers. Less than four in ten Americans concurred.

THE BUSINESS OF WORK

Americans not only differ with Europeans about how the free-enterprise system should operate; they also view work itself in a different light. "To every reproach," wrote Ralph Waldo Emerson in a nineteenth-century paean to labor, "I know now but one answer, namely, to go again to my work."

Americans surveyed in 1997 were twice as likely as most Europeans to believe that hard work brings a better life. They were more likely to work at a task until satisfied with the result. And Americans were much more likely than Europeans—most notably, the Germans—to think that hard work is a value children should be taught in the home.[8]

TABLE 6.6

CHILDREN SHOULD BE TAUGHT VALUE OF HARD WORK

	Important %
United States	60
Canada	51
France	50
Spain	45
Great Britain	38
Italy	36
Germany	22

Source: World Values Survey, 1999–2000.

Overall, Americans and Europeans value their work in almost equal measure. And even though Americans now labor longer hours than Europeans—Europeans have the shortest workweeks and longest holidays in the world—both think the balance they have struck between work and leisure is about right for them. However, belying their reputation as workaholics, Americans said they value leisure time more than Europeans—presumably because they have less of it. European governments, reflecting the desires of their electorates, choose policies that provide more leisure for their people, such as mandating shorter workweeks.[9]

Why these dissimilar attitudes toward work and leisure exist is open to speculation. The Puritan and, more broadly, the Protestant ethos that links good works to salvation and idle hands to Satan's mischief—and celebrates work as its own reward—is obviously deep and long-lasting among Americans. Moreover, as a nation descended from immigrants, many of whom succeeded in the New World after arriving with virtually nothing, the virtues of hard work are deeply embedded in many family mythologies, passed from generation to generation.

At the same time, the rationale for Americans' exultation of work may simply be pecuniary. Income disparities are much greater in the United States than in Europe, and the opportunity to get rich is a more compelling dream in America. Living in a more egalitarian so-ciety, Europeans may rationally decide that the payoff from laboring harder is simply not worth the effort, and thus they value work less. Since Europeans are as happy with their work/leisure balance as Americans are with theirs, European attitudes toward work may also simply reflect less desire for the consumer benefits derived from earn-ing more money. If owning an Apple iPod or BMW is intrinsically less attractive to a European than to an American, he or she may be less willing to work hard to afford one.

Whatever the reasons for the differences, it is strikingly obvious that more than a century of social democracy in Europe has influ-enced people's views of capitalism and work, just as the U.S. history of cowboy capitalism has shaped American attitudes. There are no public opinion data available from the mid-nineteenth century to demon-strate American and European views on the day-to-day functioning of the free market and the value of work. But there is clearly no shared vi-sion today. Generations of differing experiences have led Europeans to work less, to value competition less, to feel less comfortable with link-ing income to performance, to support more egalitarian incomes and a more egalitarian workplace. It is little wonder that most Europeans look askance at American-style business practices.

Democracy and capitalism have been the foundation of the Amer-ican experience, and it is little wonder that most Americans value them highly. Given the United States' political and economic success, it is also not surprising that many people in the emerging economies of Asia and the impoverished societies of Africa and Latin America also embrace such values, including the particularly American brands of democracy and business. Yet Americans' positive view of their own democratic and economic experience is not universally shared, and their often fervent commitment to certain democratic and capitalist principles has practical ramifications.

Europeans, while no less committed to democracy, have different traditions and historical experiences and, having dealt more with the United States, take a more jaundiced view of the American model of governance. This critical perspective is at the heart of European skepticism about the Bush administration's effort to spread democracy in the Middle East. Europeans' long struggle to embed democracy in their societies leads them to measure potential change in decades, not years. Europeans acknowledge Muslims' desires for fundamental democratic values. But they are more wary than Americans of Muslims' willingness to have religion and religious leaders play a greater role in governance.

Similarly, the caveats with which Europe instituted the free market lead it to quite different positions than the United States on key issues, such as trade rules and business practices. In negotiations at the World Trade Organization, for example, both Brussels and Washington advocate freer trade. But reflecting European sensibilities, the European Union has been unwilling to embrace U.S. calls for the elimination of all tariffs and creation of a completely free market in the trade of goods, or to agree to wipe out all farm subsidies.

These rifts emerge as Americans and the rest of the world juggle with differing visions of democracy and business, a misunderstanding of terms, and a problem of distinct attitudes and practices.

7

GLOBALIZATION AND
AMERICANIZATION

WITH HIS THICK moustache and Gallic brow, French sheep farmer José Bové looks a lot like Asterix, the shrewd and indomitable children's cartoon character who leads his fellow Gauls in a series of misadventures as they attempt to keep the invading Roman legionnaires at bay in the first century B.C. Rome is never defeated. But Asterix never gives up.

Much like Asterix, Bové has spent most of his adult life resisting modern-day incursions into the French heartland and way of life. In 1988, in Paris, he helped organize "Plowing the Champs Elysée," a mass protest against European agricultural policies which he contended discriminated against the small farmers who have long been the backbone of French peasant culture. A decade later, Bové led the French attack against genetically modified crops, which he believed would accelerate the corporate takeover of agriculture, drive family farmers out of business, and, by spreading into the wild, wreak havoc with the natural environment. Bové and two colleagues destroyed thousands of genetically modified rice plants at a Novartis research facility and hijacked some GM-grown corn. He did so, he told La Chaine Info television, because "GMOs are a necro-technology," a technology that kills. In other interviews he called his actions a "battle for the future."

Finally, in August 1999, in his most notorious exploit, Bové and nine of his fellow farm activists ransacked a half-built McDonald's restaurant in his hometown of Millau, in a region of south-central France known for its pungent Roquefort cheese. For Bové and his wrecking crew, the Golden Arches represented the industrialization of all food production, the worst of *malbouffé*, or bad food. But this was not simply a culinary protest. "There would have been no reason for the McDonald's protest if it hadn't been for the outrageous tariff placed on French cheese by the Americans because the French refused to let outlawed hormone-treated beef be imported from the States," Bové said in a 2001 interview. "The tariff meant that we lost our cheese market in the States. There was no political law against [the American tariff], nothing to stop it, so one solution was to attack McDonald's as a symbol of *malbouffé*."[1]

Bové became a folk hero in France, the leading crusader in the indigenous struggle against globalization. His subsequent trial drew thousands of anti-globalization protesters, environmentalists, trade unionists, and students. "This is a fight against free trade global capitalism," he said. The action was not, he contended, a symbolic attack on America. "It's about the logic of a certain economic system, not an American system. It can be a struggle against any country, this one or that one. It's not against those who have an American passport," he explained.

But such fine distinctions are disingenuous. Bové's very choice of McDonald's as his target underscored the fact that in the minds of many non-Americans, including some at the highest levels of European society, globalization and Americanization are one and the same phenomenon. "It would be in nobody's interests to allow one single power, albeit a respectable and friendly one, to rule undivided over the planet's food markets," said French president Jacques Chirac after Bové's action, in a thinly veiled attack on the American-led globalization of the food industry.[2]

In the twenty-first century, globalization—the rapid international-ization of economic, political, cultural, and personal life—has be-come what Thomas Friedman, in his bestselling book *The Lexus and the Olive Tree,* called "the dominant international system that re-placed the Cold War system after the fall of the Berlin Wall." America is now the symbol of all that is good and all that is feared about this new international order. It is American-style democracy that Wash-ington is attempting to plant and nurture in Iraq. It is American-style business practices that are being adapted in China, studied by bud-ding entrepreneurs in Africa, and reviled in Europe. And it is Ameri-can products that are on store shelves and desktops from Berlin to Beirut; American culture that dominates the silver screen in Paris and the bestseller list in Cape Town; and English that has become the common means of communication on the global Internet. Attitudes around the world toward globalization are tied up with public per-ceptions of America as an exceptional land that is both the beneficiary of and the proponent for a set of societal changes that are washing over people everywhere, from the favelas of São Paulo to the board-rooms in Tokyo.[3]

Americans for their part accept globalization and connect with the rest of the world technologically, but they have fewer personal con-nections with foreigners than many Europeans. They are supportive of the spread of U.S.-style business and culture, think the spread of American ideas and customs is good and good for other people, yet feel no compelling zeal to create a world in America's image and are largely unmindful of globalization's negatively perceived links to Amer-icanization. Like their foreign counterparts, Americans worry about globalization's impact on their traditional way of life. And, despite America's role as the avatar of globalization, Americans' attitudes to-ward globalization are, in general, not unlike everyone else's. It is only with regard to particular aspects of the new, interconnected world that Americans differ sharply from Europeans—they are far more protectionist, more disdainful of learning foreign languages, more accepting of immigrants, and less likely to blame globalization for their ills.

Such equivocation, however, suggests that even Americans—whom others see as the standard bearers of globalization—are far from exceptional when it comes to the global forces shaping today's world. In fact, when it comes to their attitudes toward globalization, what makes Americans exceptional is how unexceptional they are.

GLOBALIZATION AND AMERICANIZATION

Despite its widespread use, the term *globalization* has no precise definition. In the world of business and finance, it consists of "diverse forms of international integration," according to Jagdish Bhagwati, a professor of economics at Columbia University; these include foreign trade, multinational direct foreign investment, movements of capital to invest in stocks and bonds, technological diffusion, and cross-border migration. In the arts, it's the availability of Hollywood movies, English children's novels, and African music all over the world. To policymakers and government officials, contends Anne-Marie Slaughter, the dean of the Woodrow Wilson School at Princeton University, it's a horizontally networked world of judges, postal officials, policemen, bankers, environmentalists, and the like who share information and precedents across borders.[4]

Globalization's critics see a darker picture: multinational corporations exploiting child labor and impoverishing workers; the insatiable resource needs of the industrial world depleting the environments of Asia, Africa, and Latin America; and the cultural norms of Europe, Japan, and, especially, America overwhelming indigenous cultures.

Most non-Americans consider globalization and Americanization to be one and the same phenomenon, which explains why many anti-globalization demonstrations are almost indistinguishable from anti-American protests. "Globalization is nothing but Americaniza-tion," wrote University of Jordan Professor Ahmad Y. Majdoubeh in the *Jordan Times.* "Those who oppose globalization, or are skeptical of it, see it as an imposed, and thus unnatural, ideology or means (militaristic, political, and economic) by which the strong or the big dominate and manipulate the weak or the small. The anti-globalists have turned out to be absolutely correct in their argument."[5]

This morphing of globalization and Americanization is hardly new. In his book *Soft Power,* Joseph Nye notes that the United States has long symbolized modernity for people in other parts of the world. In the nineteenth century, for example, the European Roman-tics, as critics of industrialization, looked with scorn upon the United States, which was then in a headlong rush to build railroads and steel mills. And so it is again today, as American investment abroad, Amer-ican exports and imports, and American cultural hegemony fuel the pace of globalization.[6]

Nye argues that because of the multicultural nature of U.S. society—with large, vibrant populations of Asian, African, and His-panic Americans—the United States has become a laboratory for globalization. And, driven by modern communications technologies, including the Internet and satellite television, the pace of information that flows from this laboratory has accelerated, rapidly spreading American culture. Americans are well aware of their widening influ-ence. Fully 79 percent of Americans agreed that it is good that Ameri-can ideas and customs are spreading around the world, according to a Pew survey in 2002. At the same time, 57 percent of Americans be-lieved people in other parts of the world, rather than the American people, benefit most from such Americanization.

People in other countries disagree. The attractiveness of American culture combined with its capacity to overwhelm traditional ways of life in smaller countries generates a cognitive dissonance about globalization and Americanization. Such dissonance, more than any other concept, is useful in understanding the way the world judges

America's global reach. All too often, the contradiction between a people's core beliefs and the way they actually live their lives can intensify their anti-Americanism, as their conflicted sentiments are externalized and projected on the source of their confusion: the United States.

Europeans, for example, loudly lament Americans' anti-intellectualism and addiction to mindless television, but many of those same people have an avid appetite for imported products, including American music, movies, and television. The French, often the harshest of U.S. critics, love their American CDs and DVDs and rate them as good both for their families and for France. Yet they also complain that American cultural imports are threatening their traditional way of life.

Such schizophrenic sentiments are widespread, even among the British, the Canadians, and others who share with Americans both a cultural heritage and an economic stake in globalization. While various aspects of the international economy and modernization are viewed favorably, Europeans resent that America is setting the pace of change; they feel steamrollered into adopting American methods for everything from accounting to food labeling lest they fall further behind the United States. There are generational differences in these views—with the young more accepting of modernization than the old, as might be expected. And concerns about particular aspects of modernization vary among cultures. Each European nation has an individual historical identity and culture it wishes to preserve and protect, at least in part. But Americans, too, are wrestling with the consequences of globalization and harbor mixed feelings about the impact of modernization on their lives and traditions.

Americans' attitudes toward the internationalization of the economy and culture do not differ greatly from the views of Europeans and many others around the world. Nevertheless, the American stamp on globalization is driving a wedge between Americans and Europeans as well as others, which in turn aggravates anti-Americanism and appears to further isolate the United States in the world.

SUPPORT FOR GLOBALIZATION

For more than a decade, globalization has been a deeply divisive topic among social activists, scholars, workers, business leaders, policymakers, and politicians worldwide. But most of the public knows what they think about the subject. To varying degrees, people almost everywhere like globalization. The majority of 38,000 people in forty-four countries surveyed by the Pew Global Attitudes Project in 2002 reported that globalization is now a routine fact of their everyday lives. They experience it in many ways—through trade, finance, travel, communication, and culture. Majorities in every nation surveyed by Pew, including the United States, said growing business and trade ties are at least somewhat good for their country and themselves.

Americans are in no way exceptional in this regard. They were slightly more aware than many Europeans of increased trade and international business activity, and of international communications and increased international travel. But there is no real transatlantic difference in public awareness of the growing role of international culture and finance. Both Americans and Europeans overwhelmingly cited increased international trade and business ties and communication and travel as positive developments for their own countries. Europeans were even more likely than Americans to think such interconnectedness is *very* good—possibly reflecting their everyday experience as citizens of the European Union, where border barriers have largely been eliminated.

Solid majorities in North America and Western Europe also said increased trade has been good for them personally. But so did majorities in nearly every country that Pew surveyed. Unlike responses about interconnectedness in general, only about one in four Americans and Europeans felt the impact of increased trade has been very good for them personally. More broadly, most Americans and Europeans believed globalization in all its manifestations—trade, culture, travel, and communication—is a good thing.

TABLE 7.1

GLOBALIZATION A GOOD THING

	Globalization %	Global Trade and Business *Very* Good for . . .	
		Country %	Yourself %
North America			
United States	62	21	20
Canada	69	36	29
Western Europe			
Great Britain	68	32	28
France	60	32	24
Germany	67	37	23
Italy	51	19	15
Eastern Europe			
Bulgaria	33	41	22
Czech Republic	69	28	17
Poland	38	17	12
Russia	31	26	15
Slovak Republic	65	32	13
Ukraine	43	31	15

Among Europeans, the strongest support for globalization was found among the British, the descendants of Adam Smith, the Scottish economist whose book *The Wealth of Nations* trumpeted the virtues of open markets. On the other side of the coin, despite the publicity surrounding José Bové's activities and other anti-globalization protests, there was relatively little backlash against globalization among the European publics; only one-third of the French, a quarter of the Germans, and a fifth of the British said globalization is bad for their respective nations. (One-quarter of Americans felt the same way.)

It is hardly surprising that citizens of these rich industrial countries hold similar attitudes toward globalization. Their corporations dominate international trade and finance, and their music and films are on the cutting edge of commercially popular global culture. Yet such public enthusiasm for a more integrated world is not limited to the rich: it is almost universal. In fact, American and European support for globalization takes a backseat to that found in Africa, the world's poorest region. In many African countries, a third or more of the population not only said globalization is good, they said it is *very* good. Africans claimed the strongest support for globalization among the forty-four nations Pew surveyed.

Despite violent anti-globalization demonstrations, including those at the World Trade Organization meeting in Seattle in 1999 and at the G-7 Summit in Genoa, Italy, in 2001—in which black-masked young anarchists burned tires in the streets and stoned policemen as they raged against the putative inequities of the global economy and modern culture—younger people on both sides of the Atlantic are more supportive of globalization than their parents. Among people under

TABLE 7.2

GLOBALIZATION POPULAR AMONG THE YOUNG

Globalization Is a Good Thing . . .

	Age 18–29 %	Age 30–49 %	Age 50+ %	Spread between Older and Young
North America				
United States	64	66	59	+5
Canada	65	74	64	+1
Europe				
Poland	52	46	22	+30
Russia	41	34	21	+20
Germany	75	69	62	+13
France	72	57	59	+13
Great Britain	74	73	61	+13

age thirty, nearly three in four Britons, French, and Germans favor the emerging new global order, a support much stronger than that expressed by their elders. These young Europeans are slightly more likely to embrace globalization than their American counterparts.

More recent transatlantic polling reveals less overall support for globalization in all countries, but no significant gap growing between American and European attitudes. In a 2004 poll by the German Marshall Fund, about half of the Americans and the British surveyed, and more than two-fifths of the French and the Germans, favored globalization, with the English speakers somewhat more enthusiastic. At the same time, about one-fifth of the French were very negative.

That same poll also suggested that the average person distinguishes between globalization and international trade. People on both sides of the Atlantic were much more supportive of trade—eight in ten favored it—than they were of globalization per se, indicating that it is not trade driving anxiety about the interconnected world. There appears to be something about the new global society that is less tangible than international commerce but that, nevertheless, some people find threatening. Again, Americans were significantly more likely than the French to strongly favor trade. But the most enthusiastic supporters of such commerce were the British.

TABLE 7.3

UNITED STATES MORE FAVORABLE TO INTERNATIONAL TRADE

	Strongly Favor %	Somewhat Favor %	Oppose %	Don't Know %
United States	42	45	10	3
Great Britain	49	38	8	5
Germany	35	54	10	1
France	26	57	16	1

Source: German Marshall Fund, "Reconciling Trade and Poverty Reduction," 2004.

And while Americans generally support international commerce, they remain remarkably unmindful of the role the United States plays in the global marketplace and the benefits it derives from globalization. Although they consume more imports than any people on earth, Americans surveyed in 1999 by the Program on International Policy Attitudes believed that other nations benefit more from international trade than the United States does. And 2002 and 2005 Pew surveys confirmed the persistent perception among Americans that people in other parts of the world benefit more than they do from the global reach of American ideas and customs.[7]

THE PERSONAL AND THE PRACTICAL

Attitudes toward globalization and trade are not what set Americans apart from Europeans and peoples in the rest of the world. Some differences do exist, however, in how Americans live their lives, although even lifestyles are converging on a global norm. For example, Americans were more likely than the French, Germans, and Spanish to connect to the world through the Internet, a significant technological tool for the globalization of culture and commerce. Americans were also more likely than some Europeans to own or use a computer at home, at school, or in the workplace, and thus have a greater opportunity to go online. But these differences in use are rapidly shrinking. In fact, between 2002 and 2005 the gap in Internet use between Americans and Britons disappeared completely.

But Americans' technological interconnections with the world are deceiving. While both Americans and Europeans support globalization and believe it is good for their country and for their families, Americans are much less likely than Europeans to personally interact with the world community. Only one in five Americans traveled outside the United States between 1997 and 2002, and only one in four phoned, visited, or corresponded with people in another land during that period. Despite most Americans' strong perception that there is a

TABLE 7.4

COMPUTER AND ONLINE USERS, 2005

	Use Computer %	Computer Users Who Go Online %
United States	76	90
Netherlands	84	85
Great Britain	76	90
Germany	67	86
Spain	64	81
France	61	84
Poland	46	82
Russia	35	44

lot more communication and travel going on in the world today, they are not personally taking part in that aspect of globalization.

By comparison, three-quarters of the British and the Germans had traveled to another country in that same period, as had three-fifths of the French. More than twice as many British and nearly twice as many French and Germans had communicated with friends or relatives abroad. Even the Eastern Europeans, despite their relative poverty, were more likely than Americans to have had personal contact with people in other countries.

Geography certainly explains some of Americans' personal isolation. For a German, traveling abroad means going to France. A Pennsylvanian driving the same distance gets only as far as Ohio. America is a large continental country, separated from much of the rest of the world by two great oceans. So for many Americans, their relative lack of personal contact with foreigners and foreign locales may be unavoidable. Nonetheless, such isolation produces an inward-looking perspective, such as a distinct indifference to learning a foreign language, that has undeniable, real-world implications for the United States and for Americans as they attempt to understand and deal with other peoples.

When the debate turns to inequality and joblessness, Americans were less likely than many Europeans to blame globalization for many of the world's ills. Americans acknowledged that the gap between the rich and the poor is growing in their country, but less so than many Europeans who see the same trend on the continent. And Americans were less likely than the French or the Germans to attribute such inequity to globalization. Similarly, Americans agreed with their European counterparts that the availability of good-paying jobs is getting worse. But fewer Americans than French or Germans hold such views, and they less often blamed global commerce for their trouble finding work.

More broadly, many of the differences between Americans and Europeans reflect the internally inconsistent attitudes people everywhere hold about a range of issues relating to globalization and modernization. In this regard, Americans are hardly exceptional. And, as suggested earlier, these contradictory sentiments indicate a state of imbalance in people's views about the growing interconnectedness of the world, about America as both the purveyor and motivating force behind globalization, and about individual hopes and fears for the future.

For example, surveys have long shown that Americans are philosophically free traders but practically protectionists. This dissonance between principle and practice is, in some instances, even more evident among Americans than among Europeans. And this internal contradiction reflects a conditional exceptionalism—a difference that is dependent on the times, particularly the relative economic status of generations, neighbors, and countries, and the policies pursued by politicians—that may be at the root of much of the recent international tension over global trade issues.

Americans believe in free trade and have done so for some time. Roughly two in three people have said free trade with other countries is good for the United States, a consistent finding in polls by Pew and others over the last few years. Moreover, a plurality of Americans maintained that free-trade agreements, even the much-vilified North

American Free Trade Agreement with Mexico and Canada, have been good for the United States. And such positive attitudes toward trade are not a new thing. As far back as 1953, a majority of Americans favored "a policy of free trade."[8]

Nevertheless, Americans harbor many reservations about the practice of international commerce, with many people feeling they have been victims of such trade. More than half of those surveyed by the *Wall Street Journal*/NBC News in 2003, for instance, said they thought other nations benefited more from imports and exports than did the United States. Moreover, Americans are not sure such commerce is worth any resulting job losses when imports drive domestic producers out of business. Given the loss of manufacturing jobs in the United States in recent years, it may come as no surprise that two-thirds of blue-collar workers told the *Wall Street Journal* that they held negative views about trade. But nearly half of white-collar workers felt the same. Even information-technology workers, who once thought themselves immune from the vicissitudes of international competition, now worry that their jobs might be outsourced to India. Anti–free trade fears in the United States may thus be broadening.[9]

The contradiction between support for free trade in theory but concern about the human cost of open markets manifests itself in public support for protectionist practices. Three-fifths of Americans surveyed about trade in several polls over the last decade have consistently said they would favor tariffs to protect American jobs.[10]

Europeans also generally favor trade, but do not buy economists' arguments that it necessarily benefits them. A majority of the French, Germans, and British favored global commerce in a 2004 German Marshall Fund poll. But only one-fifth of the French, one-fourth of the Germans, and one-third of the British believed that people like themselves are the beneficiaries of greater trade. Who do people think benefit from international transactions? Multinational companies, answer nearly two-thirds of the French and the Germans and a plurality of the British.[11]

Yet Americans and Europeans differ about what to do to correct the injustices they believe are created by trade. Americans show far more protectionist instincts. They are much more likely than Europeans to favor raising tariffs on imported goods to protect local businesses. And they are also more supportive of providing subsidies to farmers, a practice that distorts trade and makes it harder for third world farmers to compete in the global market because their governments cannot afford such largess. When the Bush administration imposed tariffs on steel imports in 2002 and approved massive new agricultural subsidies that same year such moves had broad public support in the United States. The actions outraged Europeans. "At a time when all developed countries have accepted the direction of farm support away from trade- and production-distorting measures," said then European Union agriculture commissioner Franz Fischler, "the U.S. is doing an about-turn and heading in the opposite direction."[12]

Europeans are riled by a perceived American hypocrisy about trade—and this helps fuel their anti-Americanism. But hypocrisy cuts both ways. Europeans also strongly support their own farm subsidies—at least when they are linked with environmental protection for agricultural land—and the British and the French favor government aid for their businesses—such as the massive support the politicians in Berlin, London, and Paris have given to Airbus to build commercial aircraft, support that distorts free trade. On both sides of the Atlantic, what exists is not so much insincerity or duplicity about trade and globalization, but a cognitive dissonance, the capacity of both Americans and Europeans to hold mutually contradictory views at the same time. And, at least for Americans, these views show no likelihood of changing.

THE IMMIGRATION THREAT

The global economy is not just about the movement of goods around the world—it's also about people moving from one continent or society to another. Here again Americans claim contradictory, though hardly exceptional, sentiments, fearing migration but welcoming immigrants.

Americans and Europeans share concern about large-scale movements of people across borders. Seven in ten of those surveyed in the United States and Europe saw such migration as an international threat over the next decade, according to the 2005 German Marshall Fund poll. Further, both Americans and Europeans were xenophobic about who should get the jobs in the new global economy: native-born people, not immigrants, should be first in the employment line, according to polls in both the United States and Europe by the World Values Survey.

Despite such nativist sentiments, Americans are more tolerant of their most recently arrived countrymen than are most Europeans. Three in five Americans believed that Hispanics, the largest new

TABLE 7.5

VIEWS ON IMMIGRATION

	Good Thing %	Bad Thing %	Don't Know %
From Asia			
United States	62	27	12
From Mexico and Latin America			
United States	60	29	10
From the Middle East and North Africa			
Great Britain	61	30	10
France	53	45	2
Germany	34	57	9
Spain	67	26	7
Netherlands	46	49	5
From Eastern Europe			
Great Britain	62	28	10
France	52	47	1
Germany	31	60	9
Spain	72	22	6
Netherlands	50	47	3

immigrant group in the United States, have a good influence on the country, according to the 2005 Pew survey. Only a third of Germans take such a positive view of the Turkish and Eastern European immigrants in their midst, and only half the French look positively on recent arrivals from North Africa.

Europe has historically been a source of immigrants, rather than a recipient, which may help explain the unease many Europeans feel about strangers in their midst. But with the population in many European countries already shrinking and the pension burdens of caring for their aging populations skyrocketing, most economists believe Europe must open its borders to more foreign-born young people— who could become able and willing workers in European economies, if conditions are right. But what may make sense economically conflicts with what many Europeans are willing to do.

With its population largely composed of immigrants and their descendants, it is not surprising that the United States is more accepting of individuals from other lands. But this distinction is relative. American history has been punctuated by episodes of anti-German, anti-Irish, anti-Italian, and anti-Chinese sentiment. Nevertheless, this current embrace of the human side of globalization may give the United States an advantage in tapping in to the world's pool of human talent and skills, and thus make it better able to compete in the international marketplace.

THE CULTURAL THREAT

Frictions about the reach of a "globalized" lifestyle span the Atlantic, with deep concern among Americans and Europeans that their cultural traditions are getting lost in the emerging global society. American public opinion is typical in this regard: in 2005, two-thirds of Americans said their way of life was threatened by globalization, while less than one-third believed their traditions—broadly defined—remain strong. This sentiment—that something intangible is falling between the cracks in the rush toward a more modern world—was shared by American men and women.

Not too long ago, before global competition, before the Internet, cell phones, and jet travel, life was slower and, some believe, more enjoyable. People in most industrial societies resent the faster pace of modern life. Roughly half of all Americans, British, French, and Germans, and even more Italians, are critical of the more frenetic lifestyle of the new age. Such complaints are familiar. The English Romantic poets of the nineteenth century lamented the passing of pastoral life. Thoreau in America rhapsodized about a slower life at Walden Pond. Both were blessed with the time and resources to be so reflective. Today, globalization has made this concern a contemporaneous phenomenon around the world.

Disagreement over the quickened pace of modern life comes not between nations but between generations. In France and Great Britain, people age fifty and older were much less likely than those under thirty to be happy with the pace of life.

But other manifestations of the modern global lifestyle produce sharper contrasts between Americans and others. People in the United

TABLE 7.6

HOW WE LIKE THE PACE OF MODERN LIFE

	Ages 18–29 %	Ages 30–49 %	Age 50+ %	Spread between Older and Young
North America				
United States	64	46	41	+23
Canada	65	56	50	+15
Europe				
France	73	45	47	+26
Great Britain	68	58	36	+32
Germany	66	45	40	+26
Russia	58	41	15	+43
Italy	50	40	24	+26

States are divided over whether consumerism and commercialism—two targets of the anti-globalization critique—are a threat to American culture. Europeans are convinced such phenomena are a problem. In Pew's surveys, nearly two-thirds of the French and the Italians and nearly half the British and Germans, and many Eastern Europeans, thought consumerism and commercialism endanger their way of life. To Europeans, America is the epitome of this threatening culture.

José Bové's action against McDonald's reflected a widespread European antipathy toward the American fast-food ethic. More than half of Western Europeans feel that "a burger and fries to go" has ushered in a change for the worse in the modern world, a sentiment that has spurred the "slow food" movement, which advocates a return to traditional, leisurely meals at locally owned restaurants. Ironically, despite McDonald's having become an iconic symbol of the American way of life and of the United States, nearly half of all Americans rued the fact that their country has become "Fast Food Nation."

Nevertheless, Europeans like American movies, music, and television. Even the French, who have long looked down their noses at many American contributions to the arts—comic Jerry Lewis the notable exception—embrace foreign culture with a passion. Almost all the French think it is good that they and their families have the opportunity to watch such things as British movies and Dutch reality TV programs and listen to Italian music. And the proof is at the box office. In recent years, Hollywood films accounted for about two-thirds of movie receipts in France and nearly nine-tenths of the movie box office in other European countries. Not surprisingly, it is young people in both Europe and America who are most likely to think movies, music, and television from abroad are good for themselves and their families. On this score, Pew has found no significant transatlantic differences.[13]

But while watching *Harry Potter* films or listening to the American hip-hop group Outkast may be acceptable to most Europeans, the French draw the line when it comes to the growing dominance of

English as the lingua franca for international business and culture. They bemoan "Franglais," the inroads of English words into everyday French—*le drugstore, le hamburger, le T-shirt*. Yet nearly everyone in continental Europe understands that English is *the* language of the global economy. And to fully participate in that international market-place and to have a chance at succeeding there, even the French real-ize that their children need to learn English, which is rapidly becoming the second language of most people in the world. Witness that in the 2005 cabinet of the European Commission, twenty-four of twenty-five commissioners were fluent in English, while only twelve were fluent in French, which in the nineteenth century stood as the inter-national language of diplomacy.[14]

Most Americans acknowledge the importance of young people learning a language other than English—at least in theory. In this, American views differ very little from the attitudes of parents all over the world. However, three in ten Americans see no utility in learning a foreign language, such as Spanish or Chinese, which they say their children may never have to use. In contrast, despite their cultural chauvinism, only one in ten French would veto their children's op-portunity to learn English. Even fewer Germans, Japanese, Chinese, and Indians hold such ethnocentric views toward their native tongues. In fact, the greatest opposition to foreign language study is found in English-speaking countries. The American minority that insists on English-only education and signs in the United States has its counterparts in other English-speaking nations, particularly in Britain and Canada.

But while most Europeans accept English as a necessary tool to function in the modern world and enjoy American cultural exports, from sitcoms to rock and roll, they have grave doubts about the spread of American ideas and customs. They sense an implicit dan-ger: the supplanting of their European culture with an Americanized one. Americans fail to recognize such concerns about the long cul-tural shadow cast by their economic and political hegemony.

Four in five Americans surveyed believed the expanding American

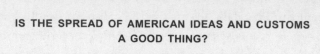

IS THE SPREAD OF AMERICAN IDEAS AND CUSTOMS
A GOOD THING?

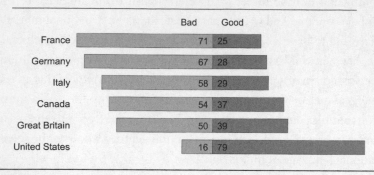

	Bad	Good
France	71	25
Germany	67	28
Italy	58	29
Canada	54	37
Great Britain	50	39
United States	16	79

footprint in the realm of culture and ideas is a good thing. No one else sees it that way. Only two in five people in Great Britain, where many Americans trace their cultural roots, thought Americanization is a good idea. On the continent, even fewer people agreed. Just a quarter of the French, and less than one-third of the Germans, Poles, and Italians, saw much good in the spread of American cultural norms.

THE GLOBALIZATION ENGINE

The driving forces behind globalization are science and technology. Advances in aeronautical engineering have shrunk the world. The Internet has enabled people all over the globe to communicate in real time. The ability to manipulate plant biology feeds millions in Asia. Cell phones open markets to entrepreneurs in Africa. Many of these technological and scientific accomplishments are American, and Americans' pride in those achievements mirrors the admiration of most of the world, including a strong majority of Europeans.

But there is a transatlantic rift over the utility and benefit of some scientific discoveries. Optimism about technology has long been an article of faith for many Americans, dating back to Jefferson's founding of the patent office. Today, Americans are more likely than Europeans to think that scientific advances will help rather than harm mankind, according to the 2000 World Values Survey. Among Europeans, only the Poles, heirs to Copernicus and Marie Curie, hold science in higher regard than Americans.

The relative lack of faith in science among Europeans has practical implications in the global economy. Although people on both sides of the Atlantic are critical of genetically modified foods, many more Europeans, like José Bové, have such fears. And though more than one-third of Americans thought scientifically altered fruits and vegetables are good, only one in ten of the French and less than one in five of the Italians and Germans agreed. Such differences fuel vexatious trade problems, including a long-running case before the World Trade Organization over a European Union ban on the import of genetically modified soybeans.

Such EU policy reflects the growing use by Europeans of the "precautionary principle," an approach to managing risk that can best be summed up as "better safe than sorry." On a range of issues, from the use of antibiotics in livestock to the assessment of the impact of chemicals in everyday products on human and environmental welfare, Europeans have responded to the uncertainty of the global economy by being more risk averse than Americans. Yet even within Europe, attitudes toward risk vary widely. Swedes are concerned about dangerous chemicals, contends Ragnar Lofstedt of the King's Centre for Risk Management in London, and Danes worry a lot about Sweden's nuclear power stations. Italians, although addicted to their mobile phones, are bothered about radiation.[15]

But as a useful reminder that things can change, European risk aversion and American risk tolerance are relatively recent attitudes. From the 1960s through the mid-1980s, the U.S. regulation of health, safety, and environmental risks was generally stricter than in Europe. The precautionary principle was the basis of the regulation of food safety and many U.S. environmental statutes developed just a few decades ago. For its part, Europe has only recently created an equivalent to the U.S. Food and Drug Administration, and this new body lacks any real power, despite the clamor among Europeans for tighter protections.[16]

THE GLOBAL FUTURE

It was once said of the British empire that "trade follows the flag"—and anti-British sentiment was not far behind. Globalization, Americanization, and anti-American sentiments are similarly linked today. Yet Americans and Europeans—the greatest beneficiaries of globalization—do not differ greatly in their attitudes toward the new interconnected world. In general they like it, and think it is good for their countries and for their families, but they worry about its impact on their way of life.

Where Americans differ is in their reaction to some of the particular manifestations of globalization—trade, immigration, the risks that may accompany modern life—and on the impact of American culture and economic might on others. On these issues, Americans stand apart. Their equivocal views suggest that U.S. relations with other nations concerning globalization may well depend on how the issues are framed and who does the framing. Americans believe that open markets are in their interest, but they also want some protection against unfettered global competition. They welcome immigrants but fear immigration. They love fast food and rock music but worry it may undermine their own traditions.

In the right economic circumstances, when the public feels flush and secure, Americans are likely to embrace globalization in all its manifestations; in hard times, more skeptical attitudes may prevail. The quarrels over globalization between the United States and the rest of the world depend on the times—and the country's leaders. With outward-looking leadership, Americans' global instincts can be expanded, resulting in more open borders, greater tolerance for immigrants, and a generally confident interaction with the rapidly changing world. But if American leaders are more preoccupied with domestic problems, Americans can expect less economic and cultural engagement with other nations and peoples, and more protests against globalization and America itself.

8

ACTING TOGETHER—OR ALONE

IN AUGUST 2005, weeks before the summit of world leaders to celebrate the sixtieth anniversary of the founding of the United Nations, the United States dropped an apparent bombshell. After months of tortuous negotiations involving scores of countries, Washington demanded 750 amendments to the resolution that had been proposed as a redefinition and restatement of the ideals of the international body. In particular, the Bush administration wanted to eliminate all specific reference to the U.N. Millennium Development Goals, a blueprint for shaping international development assistance that Washington had signed at the last major summit, in 2000. Another sticking point was global warming. The United States rejected the assertion in the proposed resolution that climate change is a long-term challenge that could potentially have global ramifications. The Bush administration also wanted any reference to the International Criminal Court deleted, and objected to any target being set for the amount of foreign aid rich countries would give to poor countries. It also refused to recommit itself to working toward nuclear disarmament. The mood at U.N. headquarters in New York was grim. John R. Bolton, the newly appointed U.S. ambassador to the United Nations, "seems intent on taking the U.N. by the collar and plainly saying to its face what America wants," David Usborne wrote at the time in *The Independent*, a British newspaper.[1]

As might be expected, Bolton disagreed. "The notion that . . . we have dumped a whole bunch of new changes out is simply not correct," Bolton argued. He claimed that the United States was not demanding "last-minute" alterations and asserted that over several months Washington had proposed four separate sets of changes that were only then becoming public. Whatever the timing, the proposed U.N. resolution—at twenty-nine pages—was so detailed that it was unlikely that Washington or any other government would have accepted it without some reservations. For example, the document asked the United States to pledge to enforce treaties—such as the Kyoto Protocol on climate change—that the U.S. Senate had never ratified.

Nevertheless, the United States appeared to demand far more changes than any other nation. And when its proposed alterations to the resolution were not accepted by its fellow U.N. members, the Bush administration refused to take no for an answer. It persisted in demanding rewording. In the end, both sides blinked and the world's leaders agreed on a watered-down text that urged countries to increase their foreign aid without committing them to a target; that recognized the need to live up to the Kyoto Protocol, but only for those countries that have ratified it; and that made no mention whatsoever of the International Criminal Court.

As it played in the foreign press, the episode read like a caricature of U.S. unilateralism, a "my way or the highway" approach to issues that many people around the world say they resent and that fuels foreigners' anti-Americanism. But whatever the merits of the U.S. position, the U.N. summit resolution incident was a stark example of the American people's long-standing ambivalence toward the United Nations and multilateralism in general. In principle, Americans believe in working with others to solve global problems. Indeed, Bolton's desire to amend the summit document rather than simply walk away from the process was testimony to that fact. But in practice, Americans are unwilling to cooperate on a range of issues—including the global environment and the International Criminal Court—if they think American self-interest might be compromised.

It was also significant that it was the Bush administration proposing these changes. American support for multilateralism has waxed and waned over the years, often depending on the attitudes of those in power. The current American leadership is less enamored of the United Nations than some of its predecessors and is thus more willing to be critical of multilateral initiatives and more assertive of U.S. unilateral interests. As unsatisfying as it was to many U.N. supporters around the world, the eleventh-hour compromise agreement still managed to reaffirm America's commitment to the U.N. Millennium Development Goals and to working cooperatively to reduce global poverty, though papering over substantial differences.

The episode is a prime example of how conditional American exceptionalism plays out in the world. Washington's demand to have its own way and its willingness, in the end, to accept a watered-down document that included some items it had at first rejected echo the ambivalence of the American people toward multilateralism. Yet the United States also persisted in pushing for its desired changes in the face of widespread international opposition and deep-seated resentment about the way U.S. leaders had treated international public opinion in the run-up to the Iraq war. Americans' love-hate affair with the United Nations, it seems, is likely to continue for the foreseeable future.

The complaint that the United States has turned unilateralist and has abandoned its commitment to working with allies and the United Nations—the hallmark of U.S. foreign policy since World War II—is probably the sharpest criticism leveled at the country over the last few years. From the very first days of George W. Bush's presidency, even before the September 11 attacks and the subsequent war on terrorism, Europeans considered Bush a cowboy president. In August 2001,

Bush's approval ratings among Europeans trailed those of Bill Clinton by very large margins: he came in 52 percentage points behind Clinton in France, 63 points behind in Germany, and 49 points behind in Great Britain. Europeans criticized Bush for his early foreign policy decisions on such issues as the environment and missile defense, according to a survey of the major nations of Europe by Pew and the *International Herald Tribune.*

In August 2001, overwhelming majorities of the French, Germans, Italians, and British complained that Washington made foreign policy decisions solely with American interests in mind and irrespective of European concerns. Attitudes toward Bush became even more negative after the United States went on the offensive in Afghanistan and Iraq. Such criticism led Francis Fukuyama to write that after Bush's denunciation of Iraq, Iran, and North Korea as an axis of evil, "it was not just European intellectuals but politicians and publics more generally who began to criticize the United States on a wide variety of fronts. What is going on here?" As Fukuyama pointed out, "An enormous gulf has opened up in American and European perceptions about the world, and the sense of shared values is increasingly frayed. Does the concept of 'the West' still make sense in the first decade of the twenty-first century? Is the fracture line over globalization actually a division not between the West and the Rest but between the United States and the Rest?"[2]

Foreign criticism of American foreign policy is not new. Even in the years of the Clinton administration there was considerable unease about how the world's sole superpower saw its relationship with the world. But at that time, Europeans and others did not worry about the American cowboy swashbuckling across the international stage. Quite the opposite: they fretted about the United States retreating from the global arena, ignoring its global responsibilities. They feared America was returning to its historic preference for isolationism. British prime minister Tony Blair voiced this anxiety in 1998, saying his "constant worry is that the forces of isolationism will gain the upper hand . . . in the United States." One year later, Martin Woollacott complained in the *Guardian* that "isolationism . . . undermines America's potential capacity to resolve the Serbian fight" in the Balkan wars.[3]

Prominent Americans gave foreigners reason for such concern. Republican senator Pete Domenici of New Mexico, for instance, stated the limits of American interests abroad. "We don't have an obligation to send our men and women of the military in every time there's a humanitarian problem in this world, or a civil strife, or a revolution in a country," he said, referring to the Balkans. Earlier, in justifying the hands-off approach toward the Balkans by the administration of President George H. W. Bush, Secretary of State James Baker, known to be a close confidant of the president, remarked, "We don't have a dog in that fight."[4]

Other voices argued for continued American engagement in the world and rebuked isolationist tendencies. President Bill Clinton, in a speech in San Francisco in February 1999, argued, "We must avoid the illusion that the proper response to [dangers] is to batten down the hatches and protect America against the world. The promise of our future lies in the world." And despite Baker's initial judgment, the United States did take part, and even led, the military campaign to end the ethnic slaughter in the Balkans—once, that is, the genocidal horror in Serbia and Kosovo finally outweighed Americans' disinclination to get involved.[5]

So, in less than a decade, U.S. foreign policy evolved from unilateral isolationism to multilateral engagement to unilateral international activism. At every step in this evolution strains of U.S. public opinion supported the move. American foreign policy sentiments reflected unfolding global conditions and changes in U.S. leadership.

NOT ISOLATIONIST, NOT INTERNATIONALIST

America's equivocation on its political relationship with other countries reflects the internally inconsistent and often contradictory cross-currents in American attitudes toward the world. Most Americans are to some extent both isolationist and internationalist. Until recently, domestic concerns dominated public priorities, at times almost to the exclusion of international issues. Yet a large majority of the American public also believes that national interest is linked to international order and friendly foreign relations. Over the past half-century, large percentages of the American public have said the United States should play an active role in the world to achieve those goals.[6]

The widespread perception that the United States prefers to go it alone is not new, nor is it confirmed by a more nuanced understanding of American history. Americans have usually defined their engagement with other countries through the narrow prism of domestic self-interest. At times, when domestic concerns have preoccupied the nation, the pursuit of that interest has taken the form of isolationism. At other times, the United States has pursued an internationally active course, sometimes alone and sometimes working closely with others.

Since the founding of the nation, Americans have certainly viewed the world with a jaundiced eye, their skepticism summed up in George Washington's 1796 farewell address. "It is our true policy," he established, "to steer clear of permanent alliances, with any portion of the foreign world." This attitude has been a recurring theme in U.S. foreign policy ever since, manifesting itself most prominently in the 1919 congressional fight over whether the United States should join the newly formed League of Nations. "If we join the League," said Senator William E. Borah, a Republican from Idaho and a staunch opponent of the League, "how can we protect and safeguard our own institutions and our own policies, as established by our systems? We cannot be entangled in European affairs and not be entangled at the same time."[7]

Such isolationist sentiments are often attributed to the selfishness of a nation spread over a full continent, blessed with an abundance of land and natural resources and the protection of great oceans. "Every time Europe looks across the Atlantic to see the American Eagle," complained the acerbic Englishman H. G. Wells in 1907, "it observes only the rear end of an ostrich." But this caricature of head-in-the-sand obliviousness does not give full justice to American actions or to a full understanding of American motivations—especially in the globalized modern world.

President Washington's advice must be examined in context. He was painfully aware of the costs of foreign entanglements. In his lifetime, the colonies had been dragged into Europe's Seven Years' War, known in North America as the French and Indian Wars. The United States had only recently revolted to free itself from Britain and that country's European adventures. Its independence was fragile. But neither Washington nor the infant Republic was isolationist in practice. Even as Washington warned against "entangling alliances," the American economy was prospering mightily as a result of an international trade boom spurred by yet more wars in Europe. Washington's rhetoric may have reflected prevalent public sentiments, but not commercial reality.[8]

Throughout much of the nineteenth century, the United States followed Washington's dictum and remained, according to historian Selig Adler, "neutral in foreign wars because their outcome had borne no relation to long-range American interests." But the young Republic actively pursued policies that were often internationalist in their orientation, such as establishing its influence throughout the Americas, constructing one of the world's largest navies, seizing Puerto Rico and the Philippines from Spain, and, in the early twentieth century, mediating a settlement of the Russo-Japanese War and joining in the Great War. In the 1920s and 1930s, however, the United States recoiled from its European internationalist venture, first by refusing to join the League of Nations and then by passing the protectionist Smoot-Hawley tariffs. It was World War II that reengaged the United States with the world. Afterward, America led the effort to create the United Nations, acquiring a postwar image as an ardent multilateralist. "The United States has to accept its full responsibility for leadership in international affairs," said Harry Truman in accepting the nomination for president in 1948, "so we can have everlasting peace in the world." America's history exhibits a country shifting between periods of isolationism and internationalism, depending on its national interest, circumstance, and the political sentiment of the day.[9]

U.S. UNILATERALISM DECRIED

Today, it is not American isolationism that concerns the world. The United States is now seen as too internationalist, in a sense, acting unilaterally in the sole pursuit of its own narrow interest. This perception of American unilateralism in international affairs is at the root of much of the anti-Americanism that has surfaced in nearly all parts of the globe over the last half-decade.

The global public is too diverse to agree on many things, but it is fairly united in its sense that America shows little regard for the interests of other countries in making international decisions. In 2005, more than eight in ten of the French said U.S. leaders do not take their interests into account in making policy, and substantial majorities in Britain, Germany, Spain, and Russia felt similarly that America ignores their concerns. Two-thirds of Americans, on the other hand, believed their government took into account the concerns of other nations, at least a fair amount.

The complaint about American unilateralism has been consistent in each of the Pew Global Attitude Project polls. In 2003, for example, majorities in sixteen of twenty nations surveyed said the United States paid little or no attention to the interests of their countries. When Pew resurveyed seven nations a year later, solid majorities said Washington ignored them in conducting foreign policy. By 2005, majorities in twelve of sixteen countries objected to American unilateralism. Even in Great Britain, historically America's closest ally and its steadfast supporter in the controversial invasion of Iraq, 66 percent of the public felt British interests were of no great concern to Americans. "For those of us who have never subscribed to British unilateralism," said British Liberal Democratic party leader Charles Kennedy in the run-up to the Iraq war, "we are not about to sign up to American unilateralism either."

TABLE 8.1

DOES U.S. FOREIGN POLICY CONSIDER OTHERS' INTERESTS?

| | Yes | | | 2003–2005 |
	2003 %	2004 %	2005 %	Change %
United States	73	70	67	–6
Canada	28	—	19	–9
Great Britain	44	36	32	–12
France	14	14	18	+4
Germany	32	29	38	+6
Spain	22	—	19	–3
Netherlands	—	—	20	—
Russia	22	20	21	–1
Poland	—	—	13	—
Turkey	9	14	14	+5
Pakistan	23	18	39	+16
Indonesia	25	—	59	+34
Lebanon	18	—	35	+17
Jordan	19	16	17	–2
India	—	—	63	—
China	—	—	53	—

Note: Respondents were asked whether the United States takes into account the interests of their country a great deal or a fair amount. U.S. respondents were asked if America takes into account the interest of other countries.

Frustration with American actions on the world stage is not new. The United States was widely criticized for the Vietnam War, and in the early 1980s Europeans were largely opposed to American emplacement on the continent of intermediate-range nuclear missiles to balance Soviet forces. But in the immediate aftermath of the September 11 attacks, there was an upwelling of sympathy for the United States. The leading Paris daily, *Le Monde,* long a critic of all things American, editorialized, "In this tragic moment . . . we are all Americans." The

European nations in the North Atlantic Treaty Organization offered the United States their full support in responding to the assaults.[10]

This sentiment proved short-lived. Just a few months after the attacks, a Pew survey of opinion leaders around the world found that outside of Western Europe there was a widespread sense that U.S. policies were a major cause of terrorism against America. Moreover, solid majorities in every region said that most people in their societies believed it was "good for Americans to know what it feels like to be vulnerable."

For many people around the world, the U.S.-led invasion of Iraq has become the pervasive emblem of the American unilateralism that they find so objectionable. One year after the fall of Baghdad,

TABLE 8.2

COUNTRY'S DECISION ON WAR IN IRAQ

	2003 %	2004 %	2005 %
Right Decision to Use Force			
United States	74	60	54
Great Britain	61	43	39
Spain	31	—	24
Netherlands	—	—	59
Poland	—	—	24
Right Decision *Not* to Use Force			
Canada	65	—	80
France	83	88	92
Germany	80	86	87
Russia	89	83	88
Turkey	—	72	81
Pakistan	73	68	63
Indonesia	78	—	70
Lebanon	86	—	85
Jordan	95	87	89
India	—	—	75

according to surveys by Pew, the German Marshall Fund, and Gallup International, huge majorities in France, Germany, and Russia thought that the invasion was a mistake. These opponents felt the war was not worth the costs, although a Pew poll found that Europeans believed Iraq will be better off without Saddam Hussein. Overall, of the thirty-eight countries polled by Gallup after the invasion, twenty of them in Europe, not a single one showed majority support for the war. By July 2005, a Pew survey found that vast majorities in France, Germany, and Russia thought the war was a mistake; two-thirds of the Poles and the Spanish, and half the British, all American allies in the war, concurred. Only the Dutch and the Americans thought invasion was the right decision, and that support in the United States was falling fast.[11]

THE CONSEQUENCES OF IRAQ

Such sentiment has had serious consequences. The failure to find weapons of mass destruction in Iraq, at one time the main justification for the invasion, has undermined American credibility around the world. Beyond that, the war has deepened the foreign policy rift between Americans and Western Europeans, further inflamed the Muslim world, softened global support for the war on terrorism, and significantly eroded public respect for the pillars of the post–World War II era, the United Nations and NATO.

Among any country's greatest assets on the world stage are its good name and the public's faith in its motivations. America's reputation was badly soiled by the Iraq war. At least half the respondents in eight countries Pew surveyed in March 2004 said the United States was less trustworthy as a consequence of the war. Moreover, large majorities in almost every one of those societies thought that American and British leaders lied when they claimed, before the war's start, that Saddam Hussein's regime had weapons of mass destruction. Washington's admission that such weapons never existed can only have heightened foreign distrust of American motives.

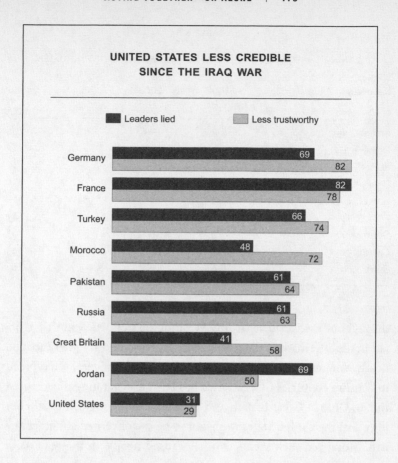

UNITED STATES LESS CREDIBLE
SINCE THE IRAQ WAR

■ Leaders lied   ▢ Less trustworthy

	Leaders lied	Less trustworthy
Germany	69	82
France	82	78
Turkey	66	74
Morocco	48	72
Pakistan	61	64
Russia	61	63
Great Britain	41	58
Jordan	69	50
United States	31	29

More significant is that international resentment toward America's perceived unilateralism in Iraq may undermine support in many societies for the United States' fight against terrorism, which is likely to be difficult and prolonged. These efforts were once widely viewed as a legitimate American response to the September 11 attacks, but no longer. While Europeans strongly supported the "war on terrorism" in the months following the attacks, most were fairly evenly divided by 2005. Outright opposition to the U.S. crackdown on terror doubled in France, Spain, Russia, and Poland, and nearly doubled in Britain and Germany, between 2002 and 2005.

One reason for the European pushback is the increasing skepticism

TABLE 8.3

WANING SUPPORT FOR THE UNITED STATES' WAR ON TERRORISM

Favoring in . . .	2002 %	2003 %	2004 %	2005 %
United States	89	—	81	76
Netherlands	—	—	—	71
Poland	81	—	—	61
Russia	73	51	73	55
Great Britain	69	63	63	51
France	75	60	50	51
Germany	70	60	55	50
Canada	68	68	—	45
Spain	—	63	—	26

throughout the world regarding Washington's efforts against terror-ists in the aftermath of the Iraq war. By 2004, a majority in France and nearly as many people in Germany agreed with the view widespread in Muslim countries that America has been exaggerating the terrorist threat. Only in Great Britain and Russia did large majorities still be-lieve that the United States was right to be so concerned about terror-ism. Moreover, such skepticism has caused people in many parts of the world to question not just U.S. antiterrorism actions, but Amer-ica's motives. In the March 2004 Pew survey, solid majorities in Ger-many and France—and even 41 percent of the British—said the United States was not sincere in its efforts to reduce terrorism.

Cynical about American motives and concerned about their effects on them, many foreigners have come to see the fight against terrorism as just another exercise of American power in pursuit of selfish U.S. interests. In seven of the nine nations surveyed, majorities of those who doubted American sincerity in this regard also said the United States was using the terrorist threat in an effort to control Middle Eastern oil. Nearly as many respondents believed America's ultimate aim is nothing less than world domination. Somewhat fewer people

WHAT ARE AMERICA'S MOTIVES?

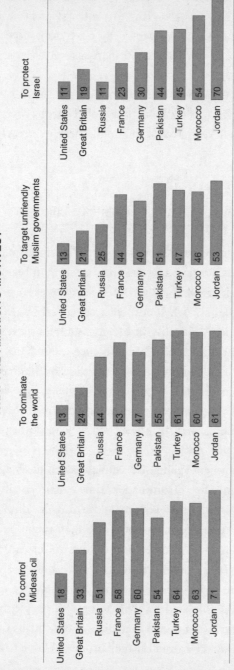

	To control Mideast oil	To dominate the world	To target unfriendly Muslim governments	To protect Israel
United States	18	13	13	11
Great Britain	33	24	21	19
Russia	51	44	25	11
France	58	53	44	23
Germany	60	47	40	30
Pakistan	54	55	51	44
Turkey	64	61	47	45
Morocco	63	60	46	54
Jordan	71	61	53	70

Note: Questions asked of those who believe the war on terrorism is not a sincere effort, or have mixed views. Percentages show the percent of the TOTAL POPULATION who believe each is an important reason the U.S. is conducting the war on terrorism.

suspected the United States of deliberately targeting Muslim nations and of using the war on terrorism to protect Israel. Nevertheless, those pejorative motives are accepted by nearly one-quarter of the French and nearly one-third of the Germans, as well as large segments in Muslim nations.

Americans, for their part, overwhelmingly see the war on terrorism as a sincere effort to respond to a global threat. Merely one in eight Americans believe that Washington has been overreacting to the terrorist danger.

AMERICAN LEADERSHIP, AMERICAN CONCERNS

Europeans increasingly fear America. In late 2004, large majorities of the French and the Germans surveyed by the German Marshall Fund thought it was undesirable for the United States to exert strong leadership in world affairs. Such sentiment was shared by people in all corners of the world. A plurality in fifteen countries surveyed by the BBC in January 2005 said that U.S. influence around the globe was mostly negative. In a dozen nations—including traditional and new U.S. allies such as France, Argentina, Germany, Russia, Turkey, Canada, and Mexico—majorities expressed negative concerns about the very existence of American power, military and other, as well as its use.[12]

Moreover, resentment against U.S. unilateralism has fed sentiment in Europe to distance itself from its longtime American ally. In 2004, among Europeans who believed that Washington does not take others' interests into account when making foreign policy, large majorities—nine in ten in France, three in four in Germany, and even seven in ten in Great Britain—thought Western Europe should take an approach more independent of America in security and diplomatic affairs. Going one step further, among all people, half of the British, nearly nine in ten of the French, and two-thirds of the Germans believed it would be good for the European Union to become as powerful as the United States. But few Europeans seem willing to spend money to that effect: only in France, Britain, and Turkey did small majorities say they would want the European Union to become a superpower "if this implies greater military expenditures," according to the German Marshall Fund. A "balanced" relationship between the world's major powers can only exist, said French president Jacques Chirac, "if the European Union itself becomes a major pole of international equilibrium, endowing itself with all the instruments of a true power."[13]

These attitudes extend beyond the vagueness of accepting undefined "international responsibilities" to public support for the creation of greater European military might. Three in five Europeans surveyed in 2004 agreed that "Europe must acquire more military power to be able to protect its interests separately from the United States." (Even though most Europeans balked at increasing defense spending to become more powerful militarily.) U.S. leaders have long prodded their counterparts in Europe to invest more in their own defense or, at least, become more efficient in how Europe uses its defense spending. But the implicit U.S. objective in pushing for such a European military buildup has been to better enable Europe to support U.S. security goals rather than for Europe to pursue its own distinct interests.[14]

In their newly blossomed desire for a separate, independent power, Europeans have the support of people around the world, undoubtedly the product of global frustration with American actions. Majorities in nine of the thirteen non-European countries surveyed by the Program on International Policy Attitudes (PIPA) in April 2005 said it would be mainly positive if Europe became more influential than the United States in world affairs. In five of those nine nations, people also believed that U.S. influence in the world was mainly negative.[15]

Foreign, and especially European, fears of American unilateralism can be traced to the rhetoric of U.S. leaders and U.S. actions in Iraq and elsewhere. But these fears also caricature Americans' attitudes, often confusing the actions of the U.S. government with the sentiments of the American public. In fact, on many questions of transatlantic concern, Americans, despite being generally less supportive of multilateralism than their European counterparts, favor working closely with other nations. As repeatedly demonstrated throughout U.S. history, Americans' attitudes are often highly nuanced, defying easy characterization as either unilateralist or multilateralist.

For example, take the transatlantic differences over the 1997 Kyoto Protocol, which aimed to regulate the emission of carbon dioxide as a means of controlling global warming. Both the Clinton and the Bush administrations refused to seek U.S. Senate approval of the treaty, decisions frequently cited by European commentators as glaring examples of American obduracy as well as an unwillingness to cooperate with other nations in addressing common global problems. Majorities in Denmark, Germany, Finland, Sweden, and the Netherlands surveyed in 2004 said they were worried about climate change and that global warming was among their greatest environmental concerns. Eight in ten Europeans criticized the Bush administration's decision to withdraw from the Kyoto agreement when it finally came into force in 2005.[16]

The promised efficacy of the Kyoto constraints has been disputed, as have such questions as whether the atmosphere is actually warming and what role human activity plays in that process. But despite their government's action, most Americans have long believed that the world's temperature is rising, that such warming is due to human activity, and that the effect represents a serious climatic problem. The American public's concern about this environmental issue and support for finding an equitable international solution have never been in doubt.

For example, in 2004 four out of five Americans said that dealing with global warming should be given at least some priority and that the U.S. government should develop a plan to reduce the emission of gases that trap heat in the earth's environment. To do so, a plurality of Americans—42 percent—believed that the United States should agree to abide by the Kyoto Protocol, and a similar plurality—47 percent—disapproved of the United States' decision to withdraw from the agreement. It may have been poll numbers like these that convinced the Bush administration to back down on excluding any reference to the Kyoto Protocol from the 2005 U.N. summit document.[17]

But Americans' support was qualified. A strong majority of Americans believed that poorer countries should bear as much of the burden in dealing with global warming as richer nations; the Kyoto Protocol does not provide for such sharing. And American concern about climate change is relatively weak. Only two in five Americans stated that global warming will be an extremely important threat over the next decade, while half of Europeans were extremely worried. One reason for the difference may be that most Americans admit they have not followed the issue very closely. It is uncertain what the public might feel about the Kyoto agreement after a full debate.[18]

Similarly, Americans are of two minds on the International Criminal Court, a body established in The Hague to try suspected war criminals. President Bush opposed the court from the start, calling it "a foreign court . . . where unaccountable judges [could] put our troops and officials at an unacceptable risk of politically motivated prosecutions," and his U.N. ambassador succeeded in keeping any mention of the ICC out of the 2005 U.N. resolution. Even the editors of *The Economist,* who often support Washington on similar international issues, disagreed. "America has little need to fear the court," they wrote. "Its statutes already contain ample safeguards to protect every country against frivolous prosecutions."[19]

Europeans frequently cite the antagonism toward the ICC as yet another example of American unilateralism. But such characterizations misrepresent the American public's views. In principle, Americans embrace the idea of international punishment for war criminals, whoever they may be. In early 2005, a strong majority of Americans favored U.S. participation in an ICC that would try individuals for war crimes, genocide, or crimes against humanity when their own country would not prosecute. An even larger majority favored trials for terrorists at the ICC. When asked if they preferred a temporary international tribunal to try those accused of crimes against humanity in Darfur, Sudan—the question had been formulated expressly to avoid implicitly legitimizing the permanent ICC—three in five Americans still preferred referring such cases to The Hague. Americans see it differently, however, if American GIs are in the dock. Half of Americans would not allow U.S. soldiers to be tried by the ICC, and only one-third would permit such a venue. In contrast, half the British and about two-thirds of the Germans and the French were willing to see their military men and women tried by the ICC.[20]

In case after case, Americans are multilateralists in principle and unilateralists in practice. Since the mid-1960s, Gallup surveys have documented this public dichotomy. For most of the past forty years, more than six in ten Americans have consistently rejected the notion that the United States should mind its own business and let other countries get on the best they can. At the same time, the surveys have shown equally large majorities saying that America should not be so concerned about international issues and should concentrate more on domestic concerns. When these conflicting attitudes are analyzed more closely, one-third of Americans are found to hold consistently internationalist opinions and another third consistently isolationist views. The remaining third of Americans are conflicted. The isolationist-internationalist divide in America runs along class, gender, and racial lines as well as generations.

AMERICANS AND THE UNITED NATIONS

Americans' two-mindedness about global engagement is exemplified by their attitudes—and the actions of U.S. leaders—toward the United Nations. Support for the United Nations among Americans is rather fragile and highly vulnerable to daily news events. In 1994, 76 percent of Americans said they were favorably disposed toward the international body; less than a year later, that majority had slipped to

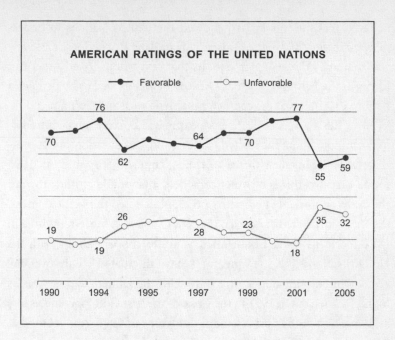

AMERICAN RATINGS OF THE UNITED NATIONS

●— Favorable   —○— Unfavorable

76

77

70

64

70

62

55   59

26

19   23   35   32

19   28   18

1990   1994   1995   1997   1999   2001   2005

62 percent. Immediately before September 11, the U.N.'s favorability ratings in the United States had climbed back up to 77 percent; by October 2005, support had fallen to 48 percent.

The reputation of the United Nations in the United States was, it appears, wounded by the Iraq war. In March 2003, immediately before the U.S.-led invasion, more than half of Americans felt that the United Nations had an important role to play in dealing with international conflicts. Immediately after the fall of Baghdad, probably reflecting international refusal to sanction the war, only one-third of Americans thought the international body still had an important role to play.

Americans were not alone in their disillusionment with the United Nations, although presumably non-Americans were critical of the U.N.'s failure to stop rather than approve the war. Positive ratings for the world body tumbled in nearly every country for which benchmark measures are available. Majorities or pluralities in most countries believed that the war in Iraq showed the United Nations to be less relevant in view of America's essentially unilateralist actions. This view was shared by the people in nations that sent troops to aid American forces in the fighting—such as Great Britain—as well as by people in nations that opposed the conflict, notably France and Germany.

Over the years, Americans have expressed quixotic and contradictory opinions about the United Nations and, by extension, about multilateral engagement with the world. A Times Mirror study in 1995 found that two-thirds of Americans held a favorable attitude toward the body, appreciably higher than the public rated the U.S. Congress, the U.S. court system, and even the NATO alliance. Moreover, three in five Americans wanted the United States to cooperate fully with the United Nations. But such measures have fluctuated wildly over the years. Opinion on cooperating fully with the United Nations was as high as 77 percent in 1991 in the wake of the first Gulf War, and as low as 46 percent in the post-Vietnam doldrums of 1976. And it stood at 54 percent in the fall of 2005.[21]

Americans see the United Nations as a means of sharing the burden of global leadership. Those who favor the world organization applaud it primarily for relatively vague reasons: bringing nations together to talk; aiding countries in need; helping to combat disease; and improving health care around the world. It has been most harshly criticized for its poor record of solid accomplishments, mainly in the peacekeeping field. Seeing the United Nations as ineffective is not new. Surveys by Gallup and the Roper Organization in 1971 and 1989, respectively, found the public similarly judgmental of U.N. performance at those times. Only during the 1990 Gulf War crisis, when an international coalition of forces drove Iraq out of Kuwait, did Americans view the United Nations as effective.[22]

It is little wonder that Americans have relatively limited expectations for the United Nations. Only one in four Americans strongly support the organization for what might be called a multilateralist reason: because it was better than any single country at managing global problems, according to a 2005 German Marshall Fund poll. By comparison one in three Europeans strongly hold such views.

OUT OF TOUCH

Whether Americans want to unilaterally impose their foreign policies on a reluctant world or whether they harbor both unilateralist and multilateral sentiments which shift depending on the international issue at hand will continue to be the subject of intense debate. What is indisputable, however, is that Americans don't see the world and the U.S. role in global affairs the same way foreigners see it. This difference in perspective, especially between the United States and Europe, could stand as a recurrent obstacle to dealing with joint challenges around the world.

This disconnect is quite evident with respect to views on America's place in the world. In 2005, the German Marshall Fund survey, which found that a majority of the French and the Germans opposed a stronger U.S. role in the world, also discovered that an overwhelming majority of Americans supported such American global leadership. A BBC poll taken at about the same time came up with a similar disjuncture: seven in ten Americans thought the United States was having a positive influence in the world, while most people in sixteen of twenty other countries saw American influence as negative.[23]

The self-perception of being the world's leader weighs heavily on American shoulders. Even after the September 11 attacks, a plurality of Americans believed that the United States spent too much time and effort dealing with international problems. Contrast this with how others characterize America's efforts. When Pew asked people around the world in 2002 about American efforts to solve world problems, majorities in thirty-five out of forty-two nations said the United States was either doing too much or too little in the international scene. Analysis of their answers showed both responses were meant as criticism.

Some might dismiss Americans' strong sense of self-worth and attendant world-weariness as harmless hubris coupled with normal human carping. This would be easy enough, except that Americans and Europeans hold contrasting views on key international issues—such as relations with Iran and China, the Israel-Palestinian conflict, and responsibility for global poverty. These issues, and Americans' distinct approach to handling them, are likely to dominate international relations for years to come.

Both Europeans and Americans have supported existence of the state of Israel since its founding. But the intensity of that support and the balance struck between Palestinian and Israeli interests have long divided the West. In 2004, a plurality of Americans sympathized more with Israel than with the Palestinians. Europeans, in comparison, were more likely to empathize with both or neither of these Middle Eastern protagonists. Among those Europeans who take sides, both the British and the French were most likely to sympathize with the Palestinians.

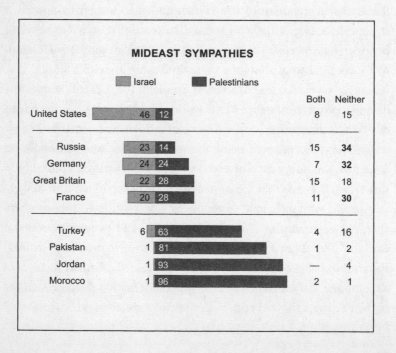

MIDEAST SYMPATHIES

Israel   Palestinians

	Israel	Palestinians	Both	Neither
United States	46	12	8	15
Russia	23	14	15	**34**
Germany	24	24	7	**32**
Great Britain	22	28	15	18
France	20	28	11	**30**
Turkey	6	63	4	16
Pakistan	1	81	1	2
Jordan	1	93	—	4
Morocco	1	96	2	1

Similarly, large majorities of Europeans said in 2005 that the West should continue negotiating with the Iranians and provide them with economic incentives to keep Tehran from acquiring nuclear weapons, while only a slim majority of Americans agreed. More strikingly, nearly one in seven Americans struck a more bellicose pose, believing that the West should threaten Iran with military action to curb its nuclear program. Only one in twenty Europeans agreed. In a telling reflection of the stubborn transatlantic animosity that exists, a 2003 German Marshall Fund poll found that a majority of Americans and an overwhelming majority of the French and Germans said they would not change their minds on Iran, even if it would help gain the support of their erstwhile allies.[24]

These attitudinal differences extend to views on poverty. In 2002, a plurality of Americans believed U.S. actions either lessened the gap between the rich and the poor around the world or had no effect on the global wealth divide. In contrast, majorities in twenty-four of forty-three other countries surveyed thought U.S. actions actually worsened income disparities. Such sentiments were widely held in Europe, where most governments contribute more of their national income to foreign aid than Washington, but also surfaced in Japan and most of Latin America.[25]

It may be that, as with the Kyoto Protocol, the inattention of many Americans to global affairs may be at least in part the reason why Americans' views on major international challenges often conflict with the views of others. Despite the tumult of recent years, the American public is not generally more interested in foreign news than a decade ago.

The terrorist attacks of September 11 and the war in Iraq slowed the overall decline in attentiveness to news, and there was even a notable upturn in the percentage of Americans who said they followed international news closely most of the time, not just when important developments occurred. This represents a significant change from the period before September 11, when most Americans said they focused on overseas news only during times of crisis. But not surprisingly, nearly all of this increased interest is attributable to the Iraq war and the threat of terrorism. International news stories that did not directly affect Americans or the United States—the humanitarian crisis in Sudan, turmoil in Haiti, political instability in Venezuela—drew little public attention. When the fighting in Iraq abates and terrorism declines, the previous trend in foreign news interest is likely to reassert itself.

Americans fared poorly compared to Europeans in following the news and also in understanding it, according to a 1994 Times Mirror survey, the only survey of its kind. Although the differences were not great, Americans were less likely than the Germans or the British to have read a newspaper the day before the survey, and they were less likely than the Germans, Italians, and British to have watched television news. When given a five-question current events test based on items then in the news, Americans ranked next to last among the eight transatlantic nations polled, trailed only by the Spanish. More important, young Americans trailed British, Spanish, Italian, and German members of their generation in reading a newspaper and were the least likely to comprehend the international news that they had read.[26]

This relative disinterest in anything more than headline-grabbing foreign news may in part explain why many Americans differ with many foreigners on the United States' role in the world and specific global issues. Americans are likely to be wrong on the facts about current foreign events, and the views they then express on international matters are, at best, difficult to interpret. But this blindered knowledge of current events, focused on those issues that directly affect Americans or the United States, may explain why Americans often have an inflated view of America's burdens in the world and why they resent them.[27]

Even when Americans express an inherent commitment to multilateralism, as with their principled support for efforts to slow global warming and for the International Criminal Court, it is not clear if they are agreeing with others or are simply out of touch with the world. It could be a bit of both. Most Americans did not know that the Kyoto Protocol deals with the global environment, according to a Pew survey. Another poll found that two out of three Bush supporters in September 2004 believed—incorrectly—that President Bush favored U.S. participation in the ICC. One month later, after the president described his opposition to the court in the presidential debates, half of the Republicans surveyed still believed he supported it. (Support for U.S. participation in the ICC among Bush voters was 61 percent in October of the election year, down from 71 percent the previous July.)[28]

There are even starker examples of this phenomenon, which is either widely held misinformation on international issues or selective inattention to the news by partisan Americans. In July 2004, half of strong and highly likely Bush voters surveyed by Pew believed the United States to be as respected or even more respected abroad than in the past, despite two years of steady and widely publicized international polling results showing just the opposite. Similarly, surveys done by PIPA in mid-2004 found that a large majority of Bush supporters believed that Iraq did possess weapons of mass destruction or a major program for building them before the U.S.-led invasion, and further, that this had been verified by numerous postwar government inquiries. Even in January 2005, four in five Republicans still thought Iraq probably had WMD, though the Bush administration had acknowledged that no WMD program was ever found. In addition, a large majority of Bush supporters said Iraq had provided substantial support to Al Qaeda and that clear evidence of this support had been found; moreover, they believed that the widely respected and independent 9/11 Commission had made that same judgment. They were wrong on all counts.[29]

In the same fashion, before the 2004 election, only three in ten Bush supporters believed that the majority of people in the world opposed the Iraq war, at a time when Gallup and Pew were both reporting widespread global condemnation of the conflict. A slim majority of Bush supporters also thought that most people in the Islamic world favored U.S.-led efforts to fight terrorism, despite extensive press coverage of opposition to such American antiterrorism efforts in most Islamic societies.

Foreign critics often cite American attitudes toward foreign aid and the United Nations as further expressions of unilateralist sentiments, but these attitudes may be more a product of ignorance than any inherent animus toward multilateralism. Many Americans of all stripes grossly overestimate how much of their tax dollars are spent on foreign aid. Eight in ten claimed that more than 3 percent of the federal budget is spent on economic and humanitarian assistance, for example, when in fact foreign aid accounted for less than 1 percent of the 2005 federal budget of the United States.[30]

Similarly, many Americans are under the impression that Washington allocates a disproportionate amount of money to the United Nations. When asked how much the United States should spend on the United Nations, a majority of Americans favored an amount that is substantially higher than the amount appropriated. Informed of the actual U.S. contribution, most Americans confirmed that it is both less than they expected and less than the amount they support.

Given that Americans consistently overestimate the extent of U.S. help for other countries, it is perhaps not surprising that foreign aid has long been unpopular with the American public. But this parsimony is not simply the product of faulty information, as demonstrated many years ago in an elaborate Times Mirror survey that tried to disentangle misinformation about foreign aid from public attitudes toward such assistance. The thesis was that Americans typically called for cuts in foreign aid because they were mistaken about how much the United States actually spent helping others. In a unique experiment, participants were given a coin to represent each percentage of the federal budget at the time. They were given twenty-seven coins to reflect defense spending, twenty-six coins for Social Security, and so on—and just two coins for the conduct of foreign policy, including foreign aid. Respondents were then instructed to cut the budget by 5 percent, or five coins. Surprisingly, fully knowing how little the government spent on foreign aid, respondents elected to cut that category by nearly 60 percent, effectively wiping it out completely.[31]

ENGAGED WITH THE WORLD

Several years after the searing terrorist attacks on the United States, Americans see their country as more engaged with the world. But they are not totally happy about it. In 2004, nearly half of the American people said the United States plays a more important and powerful role as world leader than it did a decade earlier, which is the largest proportion expressing that view since the question was first asked in the 1970s. Yet two-thirds also believed that the United States is less respected by other countries than in the past. The recent prevalence of this sentiment surpasses the level expressed in May 1987, during the Iran-Contra hearings, and is nearly double that of January 1984 when the Iran hostage crisis was fresh in the public's minds. Furthermore, four in ten Americans considered the declining respect for the United States to be a major problem, twice the number of those who saw it as either a minor problem or no problem at all.[32]

While Americans reject the role of single world leader for the United States, as discussed in chapter 4, they also resist the pull of isolationism. Only 11 percent of Americans said the United States should be the single world leader, though only 9 percent said the United States should play no leadership role at all. Roughly three-quarters believe the United States should play a shared leadership role in the world.

This broad consensus that America must work with others has remained fairly stable for more than a decade. But public opinion has been volatile over whether the United States should be the most active among leading nations or merely about as active globally as other nations. After September 11, there was a notable increase in American support for the United States to take the lead around the world, rising from 25 percent in early September 2001 to 33 percent in mid-October. This was the highest percentage of the population expressing that sentiment in the eleven years Pew has asked the question. When combined with the 12 percent who believed the United States should be the "single world leader," nearly half of Americans favored a decidedly assertive leadership position in the world.

The American public, however, still wants their government to cooperate with America's allies. Overall, a majority rated improving relations with U.S. friends abroad to be a top foreign policy priority. In a pre–September 11 survey, 48 percent of Americans also said that the nation's foreign policy should strongly take into account the interests of U.S. allies; only 38 percent believed it should be based mostly on the national interests of the United States. One month later, after the terrorist attacks, this feeling was even stronger: 59 percent said Washington should take allied interests into account. Within a year, however, opinion shifted dramatically in favor of basing policy mostly on U.S. national interests. In August 2002, a plurality of 45 percent said national interests should predominate with respect to the war on terrorism. Views have remained largely the same since then. Nevertheless, and despite the strains in transatlantic relations over Iraq, the American public has remained supportive of continued close ties with Western Europe. In 2005, two-thirds believed the partnership between the United States and its traditional allies should remain as close as it has been in the past.

The riddle of whether Americans are multilateralist or unilateralist by inclination can also be addressed by looking at their current foreign policy priorities. In the post-9/11 world, many of those priorities tend to unilateralism.

It is true that most Americans support international efforts to prosecute crimes against humanity and to help slow global warming. But such concerns are not high on the international agenda of most Americans today. Only 36 percent believed in mid-2004 that global warming should be a major U.S. foreign priority, down greatly from 56 percent who felt that way in 1993. Fewer than half of Americans said that protecting groups threatened with genocide should be a top priority of the United States.[33]

International issues that strike close to home are Americans' priority. Even before September 11, self-defense was the public's leading concern. Eight in ten Americans said taking measures to protect the United States from terrorist attacks should be one of the nation's top foreign policy priorities. That preoccupation remains. Similarly, the public attaches great importance to protecting the jobs of American workers: 84 percent gave it a top foreign—not just domestic—policy priority in mid-2004, up from 74 percent in 2001, a level of concern about joblessness comparable to the anxiety expressed in September 1993, when jobs and the plight of the domestic economy were foremost in Americans' minds. Faced with rising gas prices and political instability in the Middle East, strong majorities of Americans indicated in 2004 that ensuring adequate energy supplies and reducing dependence on foreign oil were major concerns. Americans focus on immediate problems.

In theory, even these priorities could be pursued in a multilateral fashion by the U.S. government. Washington routinely cooperates with other nations to track terrorists' financial support and to limit their ability to travel or to ship the tools of their trade. The United States works with other nations through the World Trade Organization to open markets, stimulate economic growth, and create new jobs. In the 1970s, when faced with parallel energy challenges, the United States led the effort to create an International Energy Agency.

But in practice, in the eyes of many Americans accountability and responsibility for acting on these issues rests with their own government. When terrorists struck, Americans did not look to others for their defense. They demanded action by their own elected officials, protection from their own forces. Countless surveys have shown that Americans prefer unilaterally taxing imports to protect jobs rather than relying on multilateral trade liberalization to create new employment opportunities. Public cries for action on the energy issue have been for American "energy independence," not for international cooperation or burden sharing.

Thus Americans are best categorized neither as multilateralists nor unilateralists. They are pragmatists, whose views about whether to go it alone or cooperate with others on the world stage very much depend on the issue and the context. In recent years, in the wake of September 11 and the war in Iraq, their assessment of America's interests has led them in a primarily unilateralist direction. But history teaches that this unilateralism is conditional. In a few years, with different international circumstances, and with new U.S. leadership, Americans might once again be more willing to work closely with others.

9

USE OF FORCE

AS U.S. FORCES made last-minute preparations for their fast-fire march to Baghdad in March 2003, French foreign minister Dominique de Villepin made a last-ditch pitch for allowing U.N. weapons inspectors to complete their search for Iraqi weapons of mass destruction. "The choice before us is between two visions of the world," de Villepin said. "To those who choose to use force and think that they can resolve the world's complexity through swift, preventive action, we offer in contrast resolute action and a long-term approach." Citing de Villepin's comment, foreign policy analyst Robert Kagan later observed that "the differences over Iraq were not only about policy. They were also about first principles."[1]

No difference in attitudes looms larger between Americans and Europeans than their respective approaches to international conflicts. How, when, and by what authority a country employs force are questions that lie at the heart of many transatlantic disputes. They are also central to the growing concerns about U.S. unilateralism discussed in the preceding chapter. These diverging views existed before President George W. Bush took office and before the U.S.-led invasion of Iraq, but the man and the war, Kagan said, "have deepened and hardened the transatlantic rift into an enduring feature of the international landscape." To Kagan, these differences on the use of force are especially important because they are indicative of a much broader transatlantic values divide.

Interestingly, on at least one issue—whether their own government should obtain U.N. approval before using force to deal with an international threat—Americans are much closer to the opinions of Russians and people in Muslim countries than to the European point of view. Indeed, the gulf between European and American perspectives on the use of force is profound. Most Americans believed that war is sometimes necessary to obtain justice, while less than half of Europeans felt the same way, according to a 2005 German Marshall Fund survey. Americans are much more willing than Europeans to resort to military power on their own, in their own defense, or in defense of others, an attitude that supports the Bush administration doctrine asserting the right of the United States to strike on its own at any perceived threat to its security.[2]

There is no global consensus on which international body, if any, could sanction a war. U.N. secretary general Kofi Annan publicly complained that the U.S.-led war on Iraq was illegal because the U.N. Security Council did not approve it, and indeed, much of the world seemed prepared to accept the propriety of the war if the United Nations had sanctioned it, as it had the Gulf War a decade earlier. Yet the United Nations did not approve the U.S.-led attacks on Serbia to end ethnic cleansing in Kosovo and Bosnia either. And Annan did not see fit to pronounce on the legitimacy of that war, probably because NATO approved and participated in it. In coming years, Europeans may feel that their European Union holds the authority to judge the legitimacy of war, as Kagan suggests. "Europeans, as French president Jacques Chirac explained, want international crises to be addressed by the international community, not 'by one nation acting alone on the basis of its own interests and judgments,'" he writes in his book, *Of Paradise and Power*.[3]

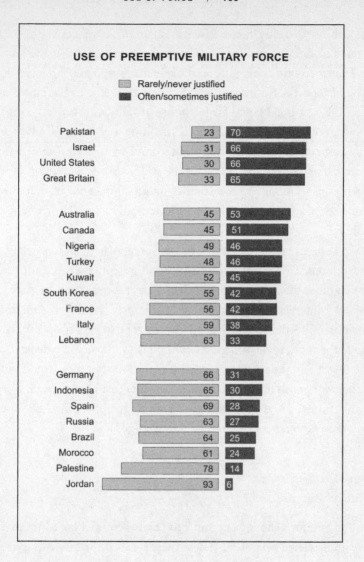

USE OF PREEMPTIVE MILITARY FORCE

Rarely/never justified
Often/sometimes justified

	Rarely/never justified	Often/sometimes justified
Pakistan	23	70
Israel	31	66
United States	30	66
Great Britain	33	65
Australia	45	53
Canada	45	51
Nigeria	49	46
Turkey	48	46
Kuwait	52	45
South Korea	55	42
France	56	42
Italy	59	38
Lebanon	63	33
Germany	66	31
Indonesia	65	30
Spain	69	28
Russia	63	27
Brazil	64	25
Morocco	61	24
Palestine	78	14
Jordan	93	6

The differing experience with war in the twentieth century has undoubtedly shaped views on each side of the Atlantic about the best way to deal with international conflict. The two major wars that Europeans fought in a hundred years on their own soil have largely bled them of their militarism, perhaps, for some, to the point of pacifism. The Germans, and especially Eastern Germans, express the strongest opposition to using force. Because so many conflicts begin as attempts to retrieve ancient lands, it is also significant that the French and Germans are among the least likely in Europe to believe territory now beyond their borders really belongs to them. In the larger picture, the new bond being forged between European nations with the creation of the European Union is instilling a greater and often sincere respect for the legitimacy that comes from multilateral agreements. For Americans, Vietnam is still a bitter reminder of the horrors of war. But it was a conflict fought thousands of miles away from home and one that directly affected only a small portion of the public.[4]

In their attitudes toward the use of force, Americans are relatively exceptional. This is not a misunderstood exceptionalism; Europeans are right in their fear that Americans are more willing to resort to military intervention to defend U.S. interests. However, Americans are not quite the trigger-happy gunslingers some European critics make them out to be. Americans' willingness to use force depends on the threat and the costs, and when it comes to war, they would much rather work with others if possible. For the most part, though, American attitudes toward the use of force set them apart from Europeans, and these differences are not likely to change.

GOING TO WAR

Public opinions about using force to resolve conflict are connected to two interrelated sets of attitudes: the overall disposition to exercise the military option and beliefs about what justifies a nation's taking up arms.

International surveys find Americans are among the people most inclined to favor military force as a way of dealing with global conflict. In its 2005 transatlantic opinion survey, the German Marshall Fund found that 42 percent of Americans strongly agreed that "under some conditions, war is necessary to obtain justice." In contrast, only 11 percent of Europeans held such strong sentiments. Another 36 percent of Americans, compared to 25 percent of Europeans, agreed "somewhat." European support for resorting to war would have been even lower if only the opinions of continental Europeans were considered: Britons were three times as likely as the French, Germans, or Spanish to strongly believe that war is sometimes necessary.[5]

Similarly, the Pew Research Center's 2003 survey of twenty-one nations found Americans much more supportive of the concept of preemptive war than the peoples of other countries. Fully two-thirds of Americans said that taking military action against countries that have not attacked the United States could sometimes or often be justified. Again with the notable exception of the British, fewer Europeans agreed. But this survey, which polled beyond Europe and America, found that mainland Europeans are the outliers; majorities of Pakistanis, Israelis, Australians, and Canadians also said they could sometimes justify preemptive wars.

It is noteworthy that in most of these surveys, the British and other English-speaking publics were usually closer to the American point of view, while the Germans and the Mediterranean publics were among those least inclined to favor military force. In this regard, much has been made of the Spanish public's demand that its troops be brought home from Iraq in the wake of the Madrid terrorist bombings in 2004. The withdrawal was less surprising than the initial commitment of troops, since more than 80 percent of Spaniards were opposed to their country's participation in "the coalition of the willing" both before and after the war began. More than 80 percent of Italians were also against the war, yet Italy, too, sent troops to Iraq, one reason Italy's participation in the war has been an ongoing domestic political problem.[6]

The disagreement between Americans and Europeans about the use of force, even the deployment of troops, is not new. In the 1980s, European publics opposed the Reagan administration's military buildup and its hard-line rhetoric against the Soviet Union. The U.S. plan to increase the number of intermediate-range Pershing missiles in Europe in response to the modernization of Soviet weapons created a transatlantic divide among the publics of NATO countries. A January 1983 Gallup Organization poll found pluralities of Americans and Britons in favor of missile deployment, while the French and Germans were split on the issue and a clear majority of Dutch opposed the action. Furthermore, fewer than 40 percent of Europeans in the survey considered U.S. president Ronald Reagan more credible on arms control matters than Soviet premier Yuri Andropov, who was a former head of the KGB secret police. American leadership was no more trusted then than it is now.[7]

Even as the Cold War was ending and the United States successfully led a true international coalition to fight the first Gulf War, substantial differences about the use of force remained. In the spring of 1991, many more Americans than Europeans believed that a strong military was the best way to ensure peace. When the survey was repeated by Pew in 2002, similar gaps were found on this issue, and in 2004, the German Marshall Fund reported that almost twice as many Americans as Europeans agreed that military strength was the best

TABLE 9.1

PEACE BEST ENSURED THROUGH
MILITARY STRENGTH

	1991 %	2002 %
United States	52	58
Great Britain	41	35
France	43	65
Germany	29	40
Russia	23	78

Source: Times Mirror Center for the People & the Press, 1991; Pew Global Attitudes Project, 2002.

insurance against war. The most striking difference between these polls conducted over the span of a decade was that Russians had become far more militant in the new century than they were in the fading days of the Soviet Union, presumably as a result of the terrorist threat from the breakaway Chechen republic.[8]

While the September 11 attacks on the United States vaulted national security interests to the top of Americans' concerns, the differences between Americans and Europeans about the use of force changed rather little. The threat of terrorism has merely brought front and center the disposition of Americans to use force against its enemies. Not that Americans are always spoiling for a fight. The first Gulf War, for example, was brought on not by public desire for a confrontation but by the Iraqi invasion of Kuwait. Neither President Reagan nor President George H. W. Bush took action in response to reports that Iraq had used chemical weapons against the Kurds during its war with Iran. It was only when President Bush became concerned that Saddam Hussein might seize the Saudi oil fields that the United States felt it had to act. That same administration, when faced with the war in the Balkans and the destabilizing dissolution of Yugoslavia, refused to intervene.

This reluctance to act reflected public sentiment. Surveys at the time about the use of force concluded that the public had little appetite for intervention in the Gulf, Somalia, or the Balkans—unless the president demonstrated that significant national interests were at stake or that America had a clear moral responsibility to act. It was difficult to convince Americans of a national security threat during the 1990s. The Soviet Union had collapsed and the Cold War had ended. The public preferred to look past horrible events in faraway places. Further, Pew analyses during the period concluded that even when the public felt the United States had a responsibility to itself or to humanity to act, a president was still required to overcome the public's preference for diplomatic or economic sanctions before using force. Only after mounting evidence of the genocidal ethnic cleansing by Serbs in the Balkans did the Clinton administration garner the modest public support necessary to intervene, and even then, force was used in conjunction with NATO and without the deployment of U.S. ground troops.[9]

Americans' attitudes about the use of force during the last decade of the twentieth century had some parallels to the U.S. reluctance to take up arms on the eve of World War II. Much as the attack on Pearl Harbor in 1941 transformed public sentiment overnight, the September 11 attacks dramatically brought home the message to Americans that the world had changed and that the danger to the United States was clear and present. As it had sixty years earlier, Americans adopted a war stance. A Pew poll conducted in conjunction with the Council on Foreign Relations in October 2001 found that half the public supported increased U.S. military spending, far surpassing levels dating back a quarter-century. There was also a "collateral increase" in support for building a missile defense system. As the Council's Kenneth Pollack wrote in commenting on the poll, "The Bush administration's own approach toward the crisis, and its subsequent restructuring of priorities, has produced a foreign policy that appears perfectly in accord with public attitudes." Another Pew poll, conducted in January 2002, found the American public in a bellicose frame of mind, perhaps more so than at any time since World War II. Solid majorities expressed support for taking action not only against Iraq, but also Somalia and Sudan, as part of the struggle against terrorism. That desire for forceful action, however, was not unilateralist in impulse.[10]

The American public clearly preferred to proceed against Iraq on a multilateral basis if possible. Pew polls at the start of 2002 found 53 percent willing to go to war to remove Saddam Hussein provided that long-standing U.S. allies joined in the effort. With the increasing prospect that the United States would largely go it alone, without most of its allies and without U.N. approval, public outcries against the war increased through 2002 and the months before the war began in 2003. Still, when the decision was made, most Americans rallied to it. Nearly 75 percent supported the war in the spring of 2003. Strong majorities continued that support after the quick and impressive march on Baghdad, despite the failure to find weapons of mass destruction and despite signs that the occupation would be long and difficult. Significant disapproval of the war came only after the bloody Iraqi insurrection began in earnest in the spring of 2004.

LEGITIMACY AND SELF-DEFENSE

The war in Iraq rejuvenated the fundamental issue of what constitutes "legitimate" reasons for a nation to go to war. The question has been debated by philosophers and theologians as well as mere politicians for centuries, without the discovery of a universally accepted answer. New attempts are likely to be made. In 2005, U.N. secretary general Kofi Annan proposed that the Security Council adopt principles by which to determine when war was justified, using among the possible criteria whether the force used was proportional to the threat.

There are other issues to be considered as well. If a nation looks to others to sanction its use of force, should it also rely on others for its defense? Put another way, should any multinational entity be given veto power over a nation acting on behalf of its perceived vital interests? Here the public opinion gap between the United States and its European allies is broad, and broader than that between those Americans who supported and those who opposed the Iraq war.

The American public looks primarily to its own military for its defense. Europeans, in sharp contrast, do not believe their own nation-states are best able to defend them. Only 4 percent of people in member states of the European Union believe that their own country would be most capable of fighting terrorism, according to a Gallup poll from January 2005. Europeans' favored instrument for their own defense in this regard was the United Nations: 30 percent said the United Nations was most capable, 26 percent looked to the United States, 15 percent to NATO, and 14 percent to the European Union. The survey did not ask this question of Americans, but it is inconceivable that it would have yielded a result in which Americans believed their country was least able to defend them against terrorist attacks.[11]

Americans simply do not feel that responsibility for their defense can rest elsewhere. The idea of the United States asking permission of an international organization to allow it to take up arms on its own behalf is unpopular in America. In contrast, a Pew survey in 2004 found large majorities of Europeans—as many as 80 percent of Germans and more than 60 percent of the French and British—believed their own government should obtain U.N. approval before using force to deal with an international threat. A plurality of Americans rejected this idea. And, it should be noted, so did the Russians.

TABLE 9.2

THE GAP OVER USING FORCE

	Country Needs United Nations' Approval First?		
	Yes %	No, Too Difficult %	Don't Know/ Refused %
United States	41	48	10
Great Britain	64	30	6
France	63	35	2
Germany	80	15	6
Russia	37	41	21
Turkey	45	44	11
Pakistan	38	34	28
Jordan	47	38	15
Morocco	42	42	16

The transatlantic self-defense gap identified by Pew was also apparent in a German Marshall Fund poll in 2005. In that survey, 62 percent of Americans said it is justifiable to bypass the United Nations when vital interests of the nation are at stake. Only 49 percent of Europeans agreed with that position. But once again, a continental divide appeared within Europe. A 51 percent majority of Britons agreed with Americans that ignoring the United Nations was sometimes justified, compared to 44 percent of Germans and 43 percent of Italians and Spaniards.[12]

As mentioned earlier, it is understandable that Europeans, whose countries have recently joined together into a twenty-five-nation union, have a more multilateral orientation than Americans. But there is a good deal of ambiguity among peoples on both sides of the Atlantic about the right way to deal with international threats. Many Americans (although not most) come close to the European point of view on this issue in the wake of the divisive debates about the ongoing war in Iraq. Still, the center of American public opinion is some distance from the center of European opinion. Moreover, there is some suggestion that Europeans are, like Americans, often inattentive to international issues that do not affect them directly. A majority of Europeans agreed that they are "too preoccupied with their own affairs and are unwilling to take responsibility for dealing with world problems."[13]

Americans in the secure 1990s were reluctant to exercise military power and not particularly inclined to support huge military budgets. Their views about their global might are now quite different. In 2005, a wide majority of the American public believed that U.S. policy should aim to preserve American global military dominance. Fully 63 percent of Americans said the United States should try to remain the only military superpower in the world. Even among the deeply partisan divides of George W. Bush's second administration, Republicans and Democrats were largely in agreement about the desirability of military hegemony. This public outlook, translated into national security policy, has tremendous implications when applied to any other potential U.S. rival, particularly China.[14]

In the view of J. Stapleton Roy, a former U.S. ambassador to China, the American public's desire to maintain American military hegemony will have a fundamental impact on the shape of the U.S. relationship to the world in the new century. Roy sees this desire as being at odds with traditional American values. "The American system of checks and balances is predicated on the notion that power is corrupting," he observed. "And the same principle is viable in the international community. Being the sole superpower is a dangerous position for the United States to be in." The apparent lack of international restraint on its policies makes the United States suspect to lesser nations.[15]

TABLE 9.3

SHOULD THE UNITED STATES REMAIN THE ONLY MILITARY SUPERPOWER?

		Party ID		
	Total %	Republican %	Democrat %	Independent %
U.S. policies should keep America the sole superpower	63	73	56	60
Okay if other countries became as powerful	26	19	31	30
Don't know	11	8	13	10

Source: Pew Research Center for the People & the Press, 2005.

The issue of U.S. global military hegemony has not been seriously debated yet. The public's desire to retain that position may be instinctive, without recognizing the significant expenditures it would require to maintain it into the indefinite future. But even as Americans say they want to remain the sole military superpower, they continue to reject the idea that the country should be the sole leader of the world. In every Pew survey since 1993, no more than 13 percent of Americans have wanted the country to be the "single world leader."

Thus, much as they refuse to acknowledge the imperial implications of their country's might, Americans are ambivalent about the very idea of power. As Council on Foreign Relations senior fellow

Walter Russell Mead observed, "Americans want their power expressed in law and order, but see law and order as an expression of power." As a consequence, they are reluctant to embrace the responsibilities of being a superpower, even if they are not resistant to using the power when deemed necessary. For them, the use of force is driven by the exigencies of the times.[16]

10

TWO AMERICAS, ONE AMERICAN

NOW THAT WE have explored the various qualities that make America distinct, the question remains as to whether the picture we have drawn of America, a nation exceptional in its optimism, individualism, patriotism, religiosity, and faith in technology, is a fair representation of the opinions and values of a large, very heterogeneous country. Is there another America of substantial size and importance ignored in this depiction? Perhaps one peopled by cadres of closet Europhiles?

Quite so, contends the British academic and columnist Timothy Garton Ash. In his recent book, *Free World,* Garton Ash argues that there are "two Americas," whose borders track the "red-blue" divide now familiar from election-night TV maps. Moreover, he maintains that "blue" America—the more liberal states, primarily on the two coasts—often turn out to be a "quite European shade of pink." Contrary to Robert Kagan's dichotomy in which Americans are from Mars and Europeans from Venus, Garton Ash claims that Democrats are from Europe and Republicans are from America—or at least, Democrats are more similar to Europeans in outlook than they are to

Republicans in the largely conservative central and southern "red" states.[1]

In a similar vein, political scientists Ronald Asmus, Phillip P. Everts, and Pierangelo Isernia assert that "the real gap across the Atlantic is between American conservatives and the European mainstream." Analyzing findings from a 2004 survey sponsored by the German Marshall Fund, they observe that "for all substantive issues in the survey, the difference between EU and U.S. is 16 percentage points, while the difference between Democrats and Republicans is 24 percentage points." They trace the source of this gap between the two American political parties to different attitudes on the key international issues discussed in the previous two chapters: the importance of NATO and the United Nations; the use of force as a foreign policy tool; and the impact of the invasion of Iraq on the terrorism threat.[2]

What happens if the American public is deconstructed? Is there really more than one distinctive American point of view, which may call into question, if not undermine, the notion of a unique American exceptionalism? No doubt, political divisions between Americans have sharpened in recent years, with national security issues emerging as a major focal point of partisan differences. Pew Research Center polls have demonstrated the rapid dissipation of the spirit of unity that prevailed in the country—and indeed across much of the world—in the wake of the September 11 attacks. By some measures, the gaps between American political parties on issues such as the war on terrorism and the use of military force are greater than in any earlier period covered by systematic polling. Despite this, however, the data simply do not support the notion that members of the Democratic Party or residents of the coastal regions of the country would feel more at home on the other side of the Atlantic.

The most that can be concluded from the Pew data is that the views of Democrats, and to a lesser degree Independents, are somewhat closer to those of the French, Germans, Italians, and especially the British than they are to those of Republicans with respect to most national security issues. Partisan divisions are also clear with regard to the efficacy of government and the breadth and depth of the social safety net. Still, when a wide range of American values are assessed, not simply foreign and military policy concerns of interest to international relations scholars, Americans of all political and cultural stripes are more like one another than they are like Western Europeans.

CORE VALUES

After American opinions are sliced and diced and compared to European views, Alan Wolfe had it right, by and large, when he concluded that Americans are *One Nation, After All,* as he titled his 1998 book. The well-known sociologist spent two years conducting lengthy interviews with two hundred middle-class Americans in eight communities spread across every region of the country. His sample was small but his findings are remarkably in tune with those that emerge from Pew's larger surveys.[3]

Yes, there are value differences, Wolfe found, between policemen and firemen in Massachusetts, retirees in a gated West Coast retirement community, African-Americans in Georgia, Latinos and Asians in California, and southern whites in the Bible Belt. Views on family structures, women in the workplace, immigration, race, and welfare do vary, but the differences are more of degree than of kind, and are further from the cultural elites of the Left or the Right than they are from each other. The same is true in comparing these diverse Americans to Europeans.

Among the most striking findings is Americans' bipartisan consensus on personal optimism: Americans virtually lead the world as the most satisfied wealthy people. On this measure, there is no significant difference between Republicans and Democrats in their contentment with their lives. On an index of progress keyed to per capita income, in which respondents rated their lives five years in the past, at the present, and five years into the future, Americans lead all the

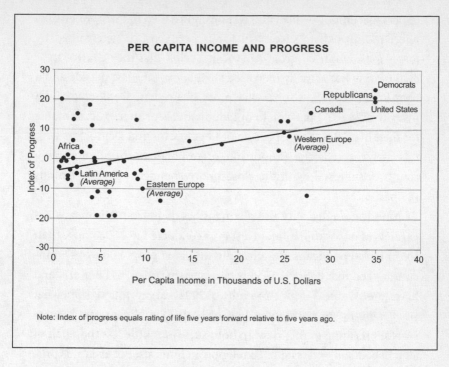

PER CAPITA INCOME AND PROGRESS

Note: Index of progress equals rating of life five years forward relative to five years ago.

peoples of the developed world by a wide margin. In this case, Democrats are even more optimistic than Republicans.

Americans from both political parties are also strongly individualistic. Personal independence has long been the cornerstone of the American character. In the early nineteenth century, Alexis de Tocqueville noted in a trenchant and enduring observation that Americans' "complete independence, which they constantly enjoy in regard to their equals and in the intercourse of private life, tends to make them look upon all authority with a jealous eye, and speedily suggests to them the notion and the love of political freedom." True to these sentiments, Americans consider themselves among the freest people in the world. Fully 24 percent say that they have a great deal of freedom, according to the World Values Survey. By contrast, only 13 percent of Germans, 12 percent of Britons, and 9 percent of Spaniards and Italians consider themselves that free.[4]

With this sense of independence comes a uniquely American sense of personal empowerment and responsibility. Two in three Americans reject the idea that "success in life is pretty much determined by forces outside our control." Americans' belief that they control their own destiny has actually increased slightly over the last decade and a half. Republicans are somewhat more likely than Democrats, by a margin of 78 to 61 percent, to hold individuals primarily accountable for their lives. But the proportion of Republicans and Democrats with this view exceeds the proportion of respondents in all European countries surveyed, with the closest correspondence among Britons (48 percent).

Americans' religiosity also distinguishes them from Europeans, regardless of party affiliation. In a survey conducted in 2002, more than six in ten Republicans and virtually the same proportion of Democrats agreed that belief in God is necessary in order "to be moral and have good values." More recently, a 2004 survey found somewhat smaller numbers, with about half of both Republicans and Democrats subscribing to this view. In both surveys, a little less than half of all independent voters equated religion and morals. But even this proportion was far higher than in much of Europe, where in 2002 only one in three Germans and a mere one in eight of the French said they saw belief in God and morality as inextricably linked. The Americans who thought most like these secular Europeans were highly educated Democrats and Independents with a college degree or better. Only three in ten among these groups saw a necessary tie between religious faith and morals.[5]

On the question of the importance of religion "in your own life," Republicans were, by and large, more religious than Democrats, while Independents were the most secular. However, all three groups scored well above the European averages, with 66 percent of Republicans, 55 percent of Democrats, and 48 percent of Independents saying that religion is very important in their lives. The numbers of Europeans rating religion of high personal importance in the same 2002 survey ranged downward from 33 percent of the British to 11 percent of the French. Within the U.S. political parties, the only important regional variation in religiosity is among Southern Democrats, 71 percent of whom believe religion is very important. The relatively large numbers of African-Americans remaining in the Democratic Party in the South may explain this figure.[6]

Views on homosexuality reflect a considerable partisan divide among Americans, but also a substantial disagreement with Europe. Democrats and Independents were significantly more likely than Republicans (59 and 52 percent, versus 38 percent) to agree that "homosexuality is a way of life that should be accepted by society." But these rates are still well below European acceptance levels, which ranged from 72 percent in Italy to a high of 83 percent in Germany.

Some regional variance in Americans' attitudes toward homosexuality exists along the "red-blue" divide. Two-thirds of Democrats in the Northeast, and slightly more in the West, believed society should accept homosexuality, levels that approached European views. In the Midwest and South, fewer Democrats agreed (60 and 42 percent, respectively). Education is also a factor influencing Democrats' attitudes: 83 percent of those with a postgraduate degree took a tolerant

SHOULD HOMOSEXUALITY BE ACCEPTED BY SOCIETY?

	No	Yes
United States Total	42	51
Republican	54	41
Democrat	40	54
Independent	34	58
Canada	26	69
Great Britain	22	74
France	21	77
Italy	20	72
Germany	15	83

view of homosexuality, which was quite near the rate of acceptance among highly educated French and Germans. Republicans, on the other hand, whatever their educational level, differed little in their views about homosexuality.[7]

TABLE 10.1

HOMOSEXUALITY SHOULD BE
ACCEPTED BY SOCIETY

	Republican %	Democrat %
By Education		
Post-college	44	83
College graduates	41	76
Some college	37	67
High school graduates	33	45
Less than high school	30	37
Total, all levels	36	58

Source: Pew Research Center for the People & the Press, 2004.

VIEWS ON GOVERNMENT AND THE SOCIAL SAFETY NET

In the United States, rugged individualism is a much prized and storied virtue, bound up with both Americans' self-image and foreigners' perception of the American character. With such a go-it-alone heritage, it should come as no surprise that eight in ten Americans believe that if people don't succeed in life it is because of their own individual failures.

On this issue, the views of Democrats and Independents are indeed much closer to those of Europeans than they are to those of Republicans. In 2002, barely one in ten Republicans blamed society for the plight of poor people, compared with nearly three in ten Democrats

TABLE 10.2

INDIVIDUAL VS. GOVERNMENT RESPONSIBILITY

	Total United States %	U.S. Rep. %	U.S. Dem. %	U.S. Indep. %	Europe Avg. %
To provide food, clothes, and housing for their children under age 18					
Individual entirely responsible	82	89	79	82	57
Expects government to help	11	6	14	12	29
Depends	6	3	5	6	10
Don't know/refused	1	1	2	—	3
To save enough money to meet at least their basic expenses in retirement					
Individual entirely responsible	59	69	54	59	42
Expects government to help	33	25	37	33	45
Depends	6	5	7	6	9
Don't know/refused	2	1	2	2	3

Note: Question was worded, "Now I'm going to read you a list of issues facing people in our society today. For each, please tell me if it is something you think people like you should feel entirely responsible for, or if it is something people like you should expect the government to help with."
Source: Americans Discuss Social Security, Princeton Survey Research Associates, 1997.

and one in four Independents who put the primary onus on society. The French agreed with the Democrats, as did one in five Germans and Britons. Among Americans, there is little variation on this question by region, indicating that it does not fall into the shorthand of the red-blue divide. However, 45 percent of Democrats with a college degree or more said society is at fault for people's poverty—in this case a much greater tendency to blame society than prevails in Europe.[8]

Other "quasi-European" tendencies among Democrats were identified in an exploration of intergenerational attitudes toward Social Security and the safety net, conducted by Princeton Survey Research

Associates in 1997. Democrats stood on a middle ground between Republicans and Europeans on certain issues surrounding whether the individual or the government carries responsibility, such as help for poor children, saving money for retirement, and ensuring that retired people maintain their standard of living. They were somewhat closer to Europeans in assigning government the responsibility for seeing that individuals save enough to maintain their standard of living in retirement, for ensuring that old people do not retire into poverty, and especially for ensuring that "no one lives in poverty." But when respondents were asked whether "people like you" should feel "entirely responsible" for providing food, clothing, and housing for their children under age eighteen, Democrats were far closer to Republicans on average (79 and 89 percent agreed, respectively) than to Europeans (57 percent agreed). The level at which Independents agreed was precisely the average for Americans as a whole: 82 percent. A more recent poll in 2005 backed these findings. Eight in ten Americans agreed that it is the government's responsibility to see that the elderly have a decent standard of living, with Democrats much more likely to agree than Republicans. Again, Independents agreed at the same rate as the national average.[9]

Such European leanings among Democrats do not, however, support the broader contention that Democrats and "blue state" residents are more like Europeans than they are like Republicans and "red state" citizens. With one sole exception, their views on national security issues, Democrats and Republicans stand to the right of Europeans. Moreover, it is noteworthy that on nearly every question regarding social issues, Independents—who are the controlling center of American politics—again stand squarely between the two parties and thus also to the right of Europeans.

THE NATIONAL SECURITY DIVIDE

As mentioned earlier, a number of commentators see a widening gap on national security between "red state" Republicans and "blue state"

Democrats. For example, the political scientists Asmus, Everts, and Isernia identify a strong tendency among Democrats to hold views more similar to Europeans than their Republican fellow citizens. "The United States stands out from the European mainstream," they note, "in large part because of the existence of a strong 'hawk' minority centered in the Republican Party that believes that military power is more important than economic power and that war is, at times, necessary to obtain justice." Asmus, Everts, and Isernia argue further that Democrats and Independents "are more 'hawkish' than the European norm." But these Americans' attitudes align "more closely with countries like the United Kingdom and the Netherlands as opposed to more dovish countries on the continent like France, Germany, or Spain. . . . The real gap across the Atlantic is between American conservatives and the European mainstream." Leaving aside the question of whether some of the "dovish countries" in Europe have a meaningful military capacity, Pew's data support this analysis to a large degree. Americans are certainly more willing to use force than most Europeans, and significant differences are found among the opinions of Republicans, Independents, and Democrats on these issues.[10]

In 2004, almost nine out of ten Republicans agreed that "the U.S.-led war on terrorism is a sincere effort to reduce international terrorism." Independents were more skeptical, with two-thirds agreeing. Democrats, however, were doubtful, with barely more than half accepting the war as sincere. In Europe, British views were very close to those of Democrats, but the Continent was more dubious, with only one-third of the French and three in ten Germans agreeing. Most striking was that the gap between Republicans and Democrats was double that between Democrats and French: a 36-percentage-point "red-blue" spread versus a 17-percentage-point transatlantic difference.[11]

Republicans also took a far dimmer view of the United Nations than did Democrats. Merely 21 percent agreed that the United States "should have UN approval before it uses military forces to deal with an international threat" compared to 57 percent of Democrats,

64 percent of the British, 63 percent of the French, and 80 percent of Germans. Again, the gap between the American partisans is much greater than that between Democrats and Europeans. Republicans also held a less favorable view of the United Nations overall than did Democrats, with the Democrats supporting the international body at virtually the same rate as the Germans and the French. But at the same time, 53 percent of American Independents held a favorable view of the United Nations, support closer to that expressed by Republicans.

Republicans were also more inclined than Democrats to use military force "to deal with threats to world peace." In this case, however, the partisan gap was not nearly so great. In a 2002 survey, 92 percent of Republicans said they completely or mostly agreed to military intervention in such situations, compared with 77 percent of Democrats. Here Democratic views were closest to those in Great Britain, where 81 percent of the public supported the use of military force, but far more bellicose than those in Germany, where 64 percent of those surveyed supported military force. Little regional variation was found within the American political parties in this regard. Even among Democrats in the Northeast, the putative hotbed of liberal pacifism, support for military action against threats to world peace was 72 percent.[12]

On the Middle East, a sensitive issue in American politics, Democrats fell midway between Republicans and Europeans on sympathy for Israel. Six in ten Republicans, compared to slightly more than four in ten Democrats and Independents, said they sympathize more with Israelis than with Palestinians. Only two in ten Europeans agreed.

Republicans, once the major isolationist party in the United States, have in general become more internationally minded and activist since September 11. However, relatively few members of either party believe that the nation should be "the single world leader." The proportion of Republicans holding that view actually declined slightly in the past few years, from 19 percent in pre-September 2001 attack to 14 percent in 2004. But Republicans were more likely to agree in 2004 that the United States should be the "most active of the leading nations" in the world: 40 percent supported this role for the country, compared

TABLE 10.3

U.S. GLOBAL LEADERSHIP ROLE?

		Party		
	Total %	Republican %	Democrat %	Independent %
Single world leader	11	14	8	13
Shared world leadership	74	76	76	72
No leadership role	9	5	10	11
Don't know	6	5	6	4

Source: Pew Research Center for the People & the Press, 2004.

with 26 percent three years earlier. (By contrast only 22 percent of both Democrats and Independents subscribed to that view in 2004, down from 28 percent among Democrats in 2001; the view among Independents was unchanged between those years.)

Along the same lines, Republicans are now *less* likely than Democrats to believe that America "should not think so much in international terms but concentrate more on our own national problems and building up our strength and prosperity here at home." Fully 55 percent of Republicans in 2004 still favored focusing more on the home front, but that response level was markedly lower than the 76 percent of Democrats who favored a domestic focus. Significant differences on this question were found within both parties according to educational level. The internationalist outlook was supported by fewer than three in ten Republicans with a high school education or less compared with more than half of both Republicans and Democrats with college or postgraduate degrees.

Republicans were also far more inclined, by a 29 percentage point margin, than Democrats to believe the United States "takes into account the interests of other countries around the world" (85 versus 56 percent in 2004). But even here, where the partisan division was sharp, the American outlook was significantly different from the viewpoint in Europe, where few respondents believed that the United States is mindful of other national interests. Only Democrats with postgraduate degrees were as dubious as Europeans about American concerns for other countries.[13]

Still, it is easy to overstate the durability of the "red-blue" divide even on the international issues that have become so contentious in recent political debates. Foreign policy differences between American political parties have often been influenced by perceptions of the man in the White House. During Bill Clinton's tenure, Republicans were inclined to criticize American interventions in Bosnia, Kosovo, and Somalia. With Republicans in firm control of both the presidency and Congress, the U.S. government took a tougher line on foreign policy even before the September 11 attacks. Whether it will endure if there is a change in Republican political fortunes is not certain.

Moreover, there are many other international issues on which partisan differences are slight. On the matter of "promoting democracy in other nations," one of the building blocks of Bush administration foreign policy, Republicans were only slightly more likely to rate it as a top priority than were Democrats or Independents in a July 2004 Pew survey.

Another issue of agreement between American political partisans deals with a united Europe. Most Democrats and Republicans did not believe it would be "a good thing . . . if the European Union becomes as powerful as the U.S." By comparison, support for a stronger Europe was overwhelming in European countries. And little separates Republicans and Democrats on the question of whether "the U.S. and Europe should remain as close" as in the past on diplomatic and security affairs: 51 percent of Republicans and 61 percent of Democrats agreed. In comparison, only 40 percent of Britons, 36 percent of Germans, and a mere 21 percent of the French favored remaining as closely tied to America.[14]

So even as partisan differences have escalated in the United States in recent years, the divisions among Americans are not great enough to contend that there is no coherent American point of view on many issues. Certainly with respect to core personal values, the differences in the United States are minimal across partisan, regional, and class lines when compared to European views. Democrats, as members of America's left-of-center party, stand closer than Republicans to the publics of the social democracies of Western Europe when it comes to the role of government in society and the extent of the social safety net. Nevertheless, Democrats as a whole are more conservative than Europeans. The same is true with respect to the national security issues that have been so polarizing in the United States during the Bush II years.

The gap between parties on America's leadership role in the world is not huge. And despite their extraordinary loyalty to President Bush, Republicans endorse his call for promoting democracy around the world only marginally more than Democrats do. Members of both parties agree that it would be a nice thing to spread democracy, but both give it very low priority relative to other international objectives for the United States.

These attitudes reflect the skepticism and pragmatic realism that are important qualities in the American character. The United States is, at heart, a nation of realistic centrists, with the important caveat that the middle of the American national road runs considerably to the right of the European mainstream. Most Americans are wary of ideologues of the left or of the right, and are rarely inclined to impose their moral and religious beliefs upon others even when those beliefs are strongly held. In the end, Americans are far more alike than different from one another, and still exceptional in being distinct from Europeans by most measures.

CONCLUSION: WHAT WE ARE,
WHAT WE ARE NOT

WE HAVE DEMONSTRATED with data that Americans do indeed hold patterns of thought and values that distinguish them from Europeans and other people in the world. We have also demonstrated that while Americans are exceptional, they are not alone. Virtually all peoples are exceptional in some ways. But American exceptionalism is important because U.S. power and influence are exceptional in this unipolar world. Globalization has extended America's reach so broadly that American values and beliefs are uniquely exposed and prone to criticism.

We have also shown that these differences in outlook and values have real consequences for the way Americans look at the world. Yet not all of the aspects of exceptionalism we have reviewed here are of equal importance. Some of the many criticisms of Americans arise from simple misunderstanding: the charge of out-of-control U.S. nationalism is the most easily refuted. Americans are more nationalistic than most Western European publics, but they do not stand out in this respect compared to non-European publics. More important, despite the rhetoric of many of their leaders, there are no indications, recent or otherwise, that the U.S. public seeks to export American ideals. The default disposition of the average American is to ignore the rest of the world, not to try to convert or conquer it.

Americans are also devoutly religious, a fact that has engendered great concern, especially in Europe, about the impact of religious values on U.S. foreign and domestic policy. But in their faith and practice, Americans are no more religious than many Muslims in the Middle East or Catholics in Latin America. On religious matters, it is secular Europeans who are out of step. And while American religiosity has a big influence on such issues as abortion and a modest influence on public attitudes toward Israel, there is little evidence that faith drives support for the unilateralist U.S. foreign policy that has fueled anti-Americanism in recent years.

America's exceptional attitudes fall in a different category and are responsive to the course of events and to leadership. Public opinion, especially in the United States, does set limits on U.S. policymakers, but at pivotal moments in the nation's history, American presidents have moved beyond those bounds and taken the public with them. So it has been with George W. Bush. The threat of terrorism in the aftermath of the September 11 attacks enabled him—at least for a time—to shape opinion in ways almost inconceivable for his predecessor, Bill Clinton, who served in far less momentous times. However, the constraints that public opinion put on Bush are not the same as those faced by Western European leaders. The center of American public opinion on many important issues such as multilateralism and the use of force is usually to the right of that in Western European nations such as Germany, France, and Britain. Many of the qualities that Americans have exhibited in the war on terrorism so far reflect Walter Russell Mead's "Jacksonian" approach to the world. Despite their general disposition to ignore the world, Americans, when challenged, have demonstrated a willingness to strike back strongly—even if it requires bypassing niceties of international conventions. Yet, after striking back, Americans often revert to form: disengagement.

In other respects, some aspects of American exceptionalism are clearly problematic. Certain basic American values do not dispose Americans to be exemplary global citizens. Relative lack of interest in foreign countries and events results in little awareness of the new phenomenon of global interconnectedness. Aversion to government means only soft support for international organizations. Individualism inclines Americans to believe that they do not need the rest of the world. Optimism fosters a tendency to postpone tackling large problems in the belief that technology, and Americans, can fix anything.

Looking ahead, America's greatest strengths—its individualism and self-confidence—pose its greatest potential for problems with the world. These qualities have nourished Americans' extraordinary expectations almost to a national sense of entitlement. The risk going forward is that Americans will ignore the lessons of history, which teach that hubris, and the inattentiveness to others that so often accompanies it, can lead to trouble.

Maximum danger may arise when American exceptionalism tends toward unilateralism, when the United States chooses to ignore international, environmental, human rights, and International Criminal Court conventions that may well affect both its own future and its leadership role. By disregarding the importance of international cooperation and the implications of economic, energy, and environmental interdependence, Americans may limit their ability to solve or even address problems ranging from terrorism to pandemics to longer-range geopolitical challenges. American self-reliance and optimism could meet its limits.

Americans underestimate their interdependence with the rest of the world. Yet, while they are not disposed to play especially well with others, Americans' indifference toward many foreign policy questions does have the effect of giving U.S. leaders far greater leeway in shaping foreign policy than in shaping its domestic counterparts. But in times of crisis, America's best leaders—from Washington to Roosevelt to Reagan—have been able to find ways to get the public to share their view of America's place in the world.

The rest of the world can also take comfort in the values Americans do not hold. The U.S. brand of nationalism is a good deal more benign than British imperialism was in the nineteenth century, let alone the many other forms in which nationalism has manifested itself over the course of history. In short, Americans do not want to rule the world. Religiosity is one of the defining characteristics of the American character, but Americans are tolerant of religious diversity and most have no interest in converting the world to their faith. Americans are strongly individualistic and quick to move unilaterally in their own defense, but they are not against working with others when need be. So it is both what Americans are and what they are not that make them truly exceptional. This is not the exceptionalism that Alexis de Tocqueville described, but perhaps it is not too different from the directions he would have prophesied had he been able to foresee the developments of the last two centuries.

As to anti-Americanism in the twenty-first century, the American public's exceptional values and basic attitudes have undoubtedly contributed to discontent with the United States. Experiencing unparalleled feelings of vulnerability after September 11, Americans endorsed foreign policies that were resented as unilateral by much of the world. They were also willing to use military force twice: in Afghanistan and Iraq, creating concerns in Europe and, particularly, in the Muslim world about Washington's long-term intentions. The underlying American predispositions that initially supported these military ventures, and then turned ambivalent, are unlikely to change. The intervention in Iraq became an unpopular war not because it was seen as the wrong course of action, but because it did not work out well.

Some commentators have contended that the citizens of Democratic, "blue state" America do not differ much from the publics of Western Europe, and that it is the Republican, "red state" America of today that sets the United States apart politically. True, there is somewhat greater harmony of social goals and attitudes between Democrats and Europeans, compared with Republicans and Europeans, but the degree of resemblance is overstated. Democrats are distinctly American, but even if they were not, it is the Independents whose views not only bridge the gap between Republicans and Democrats but also swing elections and the tight questions in public opinion.

While overseas critics fret that America wants to control the world and promulgate its ideology, there is just no evidence that the American public has imperial aspirations or really cares that much about spreading democratic ideals. Yes, the public did reelect a president who is both a Wilsonian and a Jacksonian. But the public mostly voted for Bush's tough Jacksonian approach, not his Wilsonian idealism. Should the current administration or a future one overplay idealism or imperialism, public support probably will not be there. U.S. hegemony in Latin America notwithstanding, not even a popular Reagan administration dared consider overt military solutions to problems in Central America. Public disapproval of Reagan's policies in that area were in fact a clear indication of the limits the American public set at that time in that part of the world. The same constraint may have also prompted Reagan to pull U.S. forces out of Lebanon following the bombing of the U.S. Marine barracks in Beirut.

Americans do bear some responsibility for global complaints that the United States does not do enough to deal with world problems and is a soft supporter of international organizations and aid efforts. Individualism, self-reliance, and unflagging optimism are great American strengths, but they do not encourage internationalism. More broadly, these traits sometimes result in little pressure being brought on American leaders to deal with important, but not seemingly pressing problems. One of the things that the National Commission on Terrorist Attacks upon the United States, the 9/11 Commission, got wrong was its assertion that the American public did not recognize and give priority to the risks of international terrorism. Nothing could be further from the truth.

Throughout the 1990s and into the new century, terrorism ranked near or at the top of the public's foreign policy agenda. But acknowledgment of the problem had no relationship to a commitment to dealing with it. Americans remain a silent majority on many issues that confront their country and concern the world.

In the end, American exceptionalism, all that it is and all that it isn't, is what shapes attitudes toward the United States around the world. Much of what fuels current anti-American sentiment around the world—perceptions of American nationalism and religiosity—is misinformed. A better understanding of the American people could change that. Many American attitudes that frustrate foreigners, particularly a propensity to act unilaterally, are dependent on the times and leadership. They too can change. But much of what makes Americans distinctive—their individualism—will not change.

Thus, in conclusion, American exceptionalism and anti-Americanism are inextricably related. And if Americans are to find some *modus vivendi* with their critics, both the world and Americans will have to adapt.

APPENDIX

Pew Global Attitudes Polling
in Fifty Nations and the
Palestinian Authority, 2002–2005

The Americas	Sample Size	Europe	Sample Size
Argentina	814	Bulgaria	514
Bolivia	782	Czech Republic	500
Brazil	1,000	France	507
May 2003	1,000	November 2002	1,007
Canada	500	March 2003	485
May 2003	500	May 2003	504
May 2005	500	March 2004	504
Guatemala	500	May 2005	751
Honduras	506	Germany	1,000
Mexico	996	November 2002	1,022
Peru	711	March 2003	524
United States	1,501	May 2003	500
November 2002	1,000	March 2004	500
January 2003	1,000	May 2005	750
March 2003	1,032	Great Britain	501
May 2003	1,201	November 2002	1,000
March 2004	1,000	March 2003	962
May 2005	1,001	May 2003	499
Venezuela	700	March 2004	500
Total Americas	**16,244**	May 2005	750

Note: Results from Summer–Fall 2002 survey unless otherwise noted.

Italy	508		March 2003	513
March 2003	500		May 2003	1,000
May 2003	500		March 2004	1,017
Netherlands (May 2005)	754		May 2005	1,003
Poland	500		Uzbekistan	700
March 2003	500		**Total Mideast**	**23,981**
May 2005	1,024			
Russia	1,002		**Africa**	
November 2002	1,000		Angola	780
March 2003	501		Ivory Coast	708
May 2003	501		Ghana	702
March 2004	1,002		Kenya	658
May 2005	1,002		Mali	697
Slovak Republic	500		Nigeria	1,000
Spain (March 2003)	503		May 2003	1,000
May 2003	503		Senegal	710
May 2005	751		South Africa	700
Ukraine	500		Tanzania	720
Total Europe	**25,331**		Uganda	1,008
			Total Africa	**8,683**
Middle East/Conflict Area				
Egypt	1,013		**Asia**	
Israel (May 2003)	903		Bangladesh	689
Jordan	1,000		China	3,000
May 2003	1,000		May 2005	2,191
March 2004	1,000		India	2,189
May 2005	1,000		May 2005	2,042
Kuwait (May 2003)	500		Indonesia	1,017
Lebanon	1,000		May 2003	1,011
May 2003	1,000		May 2005	1,022
May 2005	1,000		Japan	702
Morocco (May 2003)	1,001		South Korea	719
March 2004	1,000		May 2003	525
Pakistan	2,032		Philippines	700
May 2003	999		Vietnam	772
March 2004	1,242		**Total Asia**	**16,579**
May 2005	1,225			
Palestinian Authority			**Pacific**	
May 2003	800		Australia (May 2003)	501
Turkey	1,006			
November 2002	1,027		**TOTAL INTERVIEWS**	**91,319**

NOTES

INTRODUCTION

For additional information on Pew Research Center survey data pertaining to the introduction, see: http://pewglobal.org/aatw/introduction/.

1. Pew Research Center and the *International Herald Tribune*, survey: "Little Support for Expanding War on Terrorism: America Admired, Yet Its New Vulnerability Seen as Good Thing, Say Opinion Leaders," December 19, 2001.

2. Pew Global Attitudes Project, survey: "Views of a Changing World," June 3, 2003.

1. AMERICA UNDER THE MICROSCOPE

For additional information on Pew Research Center survey data pertaining to chapter 1, see: http://pewglobal.org/aatw/chapter1/.

1. Pew Research Center and the *International Herald Tribune*, survey: "Little Support for Expanding War on Terrorism: America Admired, Yet Its New Vulnerability Seen as Good Thing, Say Opinion Leaders," December 19, 2001.

2. "A Nation Apart," *The Economist*, November 6, 2003.

3. Ibid.

4. Ibid.

5. Tony Judt, "Europe vs. America," *New York Review of Books,* February 10, 2005, p. 37.

6. Ron Brownstein, "Court of Public Opinion Becomes Key Battleground," *Los Angeles Times,* March 13, 2003.

7. Thomas J. McNulty, "Television's Impact on Executive Decisionmaking and Diplomacy," *The Fletcher Forum of World Affairs,* vol. 17 (Winter 1993), p. 82.

8. Gallup International Association, press release, September 19, 2001. Pew Global Attitudes Project, survey: "Views of a Changing World," June 3, 2003.

9. World Values Survey, 1999–2000; see: http://wvs.isr.umich.edu/index.shtml.

10. Wikipedia, cited November 10, 2005, http://en.wikipedia.org/wiki/Ameri can_exceptionalism.

11. Seymour Martin Lipset, *American Exceptionalism: A Double-edged Sword* (New York: W. W. Norton & Co., 1996), p. 1.

12. Data drawn from Lexis Nexis search; source: U.S. Newspapers & Wires; terms: "U.S. exceptionalism."

13. Data drawn from Lexis Nexis search; source: U.S. Newspapers & Wires; terms: "American empire."

14. Joseph S. Nye, Jr., *Soft Power: The Means to Success in World Politics* (New York: Public Affairs, 2004).

15. Clyde Prestowitz, *Rogue Nation: American Unilateralism and the Failure of Good Intentions* (New York: Basic Books, 2003), pp. 35–36.

16. Minxin Pei, "The Paradoxes of American Nationalism," *Foreign Policy,* May–June 2003.

17. Jeremy Rifkin, "The European Dream," *Utne,* September–October 2004; Anatol Lieven, *America Right or Wrong: An Anatomy of American Nationalism* (New York: Oxford University Press, 2004), p. 4.

18. Harold Evans with Gail Buckland and David Lefer, *They Made America: From the Steam Engine to the Search Engine* (New York: Little, Brown and Co., 2004); Evans is quoted in Jeff Madrick, "The Producers," *New York Review of Books,* March 10, 2005.

19. Lieven, *America Right or Wrong.* Originally cited by Ernest Lee Tuveson, *Redeemer Nation: The Idea of America's Millennial Role* (Chicago: University of Chicago Press, 1968), p. 212.

20. Michael Ignatieff, ed., *American Exceptionalism and Human Rights* (Princeton, N.J.: Princeton University Press, 2005); Stephen Sestanovich, "Not Much Kinder and Gentler," *New York Times,* February 3, 2005.

21. Robert Cooper, "Mapping Out Europe's Strategy," *The Globalist,* April 13, 2005. Available online at http://www.theglobalist.com/dbweb/storyid.aspx?storyid=3852.

22. President George W. Bush quoted in "A Nation Apart," *The Economist,* November 6, 2003. The quote comes from a speech made in Daytona, Florida, January 30, 2002.

23. President George W. Bush, Second Inaugural Address, Washington, D.C., January 20, 2005.

24. David Brooks, "Ideas and Reality," *New York Times,* January 22, 2005. President

George W. Bush, speech at the National Defense University, Washington, D.C., March 7, 2005.

25. Walter Russell Mead quoted in "A Nation Apart," *The Economist*; Sestanovich, "Not Much Kinder and Gentler," *New York Times*; Claus Christian Malsahn, "Could George W. Bush Be Right?" *Der Spiegel* online, February 23, 2005, http://service.spiegel.de/cache/international/0,1518,343378,00.html.

26. Robert Kagan, "Power and Weakness," *Policy Review*, no. 113, June 2, 2002.

27. Robert Cooper, *The Breaking of Nations: Order and Chaos in the Twenty-First Century* (New York: Atlantic Monthly Press, 2004), p. 165.

28. Walter Russell Mead, *Special Providence: American Foreign Policy and How It Changed the World* (New York: Routledge, 2002).

2. THE RISE OF ANTI-AMERICANISM

For additional information on Pew Research Center survey data pertaining to chapter 2, see http://pewglobal.org/aatw/chapter2/.

1. Tina Barney, "An Ocean Apart, a World of Difference," *New York Times*, August 21, 2004; Charles Dickens, *American Notes for General Circulation* (London: Chapman and Hall, 1842).

2. Jerry Adler, "What the World Thinks of America," *Newsweek*, July 11, 1983, p. 44.

3. Ibid.

4. Pew Global Attitudes Project, survey: "What the World Thinks in 2002," December 4, 2002; survey: "Views of a Changing World," June 3, 2003.

5. Eurobarometer survey published November 2003, based on interviews with 500 people in each of fifteen EU nations.

6. Pew Research Center for the People & the Press, survey: "Foreign Policy Attitudes Now Driven by 9/11 and Iraq," August 18, 2004.

7. Michael Ignatieff, "Who Are Americans to Think That Freedom Is Theirs to Spread?" *The New York Times Magazine*, June 26, 2005, p. 42.

3. THE AMERICAN WAY

For additional information on Pew Research Center survey data pertaining to chapter 3, see http://pewglobal.org/aatw/chapter3/.

1. Alexis de Tocqueville, *Democracy in America* (New York: Signet Books, 2001). Text originally published in 1835, vol. 1, and 1840, vol. 2.

2. Despite its connotations, nationalism is more neutrally considered to be "the

expression of the intense need for affirmation of national or communal identity as
the anchor of individual identity." See William Pfaff, *New York Review of Books,* July
14, 2005, p. 27.

3. World Values Survey, 1999–2000. Question wording: "How proud are you to
be (NATIONALITY)?"

4. Times Mirror Center for the People & the Press, survey: "The People, Press
and Politics Survey III," May 1988. Pew Research Center for the People & the Press,
survey: "Foreign Policy Attitudes Now Driven by 9/11 and Iraq," August 18, 2004.

5. This question has been asked numerous times in Pew surveys. Pew Research
Center for the People & the Press, survey: "9/11 Commission Has Bipartisan Support," July 20, 2004. Pew Research Center, "Foreign Policy and Party Images
Survey—9/11 Commission Has Bipartisan Support; Democratic Party Image Improvement; Foreign Policy Attitudes Now Driven by 9/11 and Iraq," July 8–18, 2004,
based on interviews with a national sample of 2,009 adults. Times Mirror Center,
survey: "America's Place in the World," November 1993.

6. Gallup Organization, survey: "Hopes and Fears," October 1964, based on personal interviews with a national sample of 1,564 adults. Gallup, survey: "State of the
Nation," May 1972, based on personal interviews with a national sample of 524 adults.

7. Attitudes toward the work ethic among Americans, as discussed later, may
contribute to their view of the safety net.

8. "Living with a Superpower," *The Economist,* January 2, 2003. For additional
information on the history of Hadley Cantril and Lloyd Free's development of the
"ladder of life" questions, see Everett Carll Ladd, "Bowling with Tocqueville"
(Washington, D.C.: American Enterprise Institute, 2000). Available at http://
www.aei.org/publications/pubID.16054,filter.all/pub_detail.asp.

9. Charles F. Kettering Foundation and Gallup International Research Insti-
tutes, "Human Needs and Satisfactions: A Global Survey," June 1977. The poll was
conducted during the fall and winter of 1974–75.

10. Jeff Madrick, "The Producers," *New York Review of Books,* March 10, 2005, p. 26.

11. Pew Research Center for the People & the Press, survey: "Optimism Reigns,
Technology Plays Key Role," October 24, 1999. World Values Survey, 1999–2000.

12. Pew Research Center, Poll Watch: "Reading the Polls on Evolution and
Creationism," September 28, 2005.

13. De Tocqueville, *Democracy in America,* vol. 1, chap. 28.

14. "Living with a Superpower," *The Economist,* http://www.aei.org/publications/
pubID.16054,filter.all/pub_detail.asp.

15. De Tocqueville, *Democracy in America,* vol. 2, chap. 12.

4. THE PROBLEM OF AMERICAN EXCEPTIONALISM

For additional information on Pew Research Center survey data pertaining to
chapter 4, see http://pewglobal.org/aatw/chapter4/.

1. Minxin Pei, "The Paradoxes of American Nationalism," *Foreign Policy*, May–June 2003.

2. "God and American Diplomacy," *The Economist*, February 6, 2003.

3. Gallup survey, February 7–10, 2005, based on telephone interviews with a national adult sample of 1,008. The Chicago Council on Foreign Relations and the Program on International Policy Attitudes, September 15–21, 2005, based on a nationwide sample of 808 Americans (margin of error was +/– 3.5–4.0%) is available at http://www.ccfr.org/publications/opinion/main.html.

4. Polls from 1993 through 1995 were conducted by the Times Mirror Center for the People & the Press; polls from 1995 through 2005 were conducted by the Pew Research Center for the People & the Press.

5. Robert Kagan and William Kristol, "The Bush Doctrine Unfolds," *Weekly Standard*, March 4, 2002.

6. Pew Research Center for the People & the Press and the Council on Foreign Relations, survey: "Foreign Policy Attitudes Now Driven by 9/11 and Iraq," August 18, 2004.

7. John Lewis Gaddis, *Surprise, Security, and the American Experience* (Washington, D.C.: Council on Foreign Relations, 2004), p. 38.

8. Ibid., p. 50.

9. Ibid., p. 52.

10. Pew Global Attitudes Project, survey: "American Character Gets Mixed Reviews," June 23, 2005.

11. Pew Research Center for the People & the Press, survey: "Optimism Reigns, Technology Plays Key Role," October 24, 1999.

12. Pew Research Center, survey: "Bush Unpopular in Europe, Seen as Unilateralist," August 15, 2001.

13. Pew Research Center, survey: "Economic Pessimism Grows, Gas Prices Pinch," September 15, 2005.

14. *Newsweek*/Princeton Survey Research Associates, November 8–9, 2001, based on telephone interviews with a national sample of 1,001 adults.

5. A BLESSED PEOPLE

For additional information on Pew Research Center survey data pertaining to chapter 5, see http://pewglobal.org/aatw/chapter5/.

1. *NBC Nightly News*, October 15, 2003. William Arkin, "The Pentagon Unleashes a Holy Warrior," *Los Angeles Times*, October 16, 2003.

2. Janadas Devan, "Why State and Religion Should Not Mix," *Korea Herald*, October 30, 2003; editorial, "Mr. Bush and the Almighty," *Japan Times*, November 30, 2003; Sonya Ross, "For Bush, an Unwanted Mixing of Religion and the War on Terror," *Turkish Daily News*, October 26, 2003; Dennis C. Sasso, "The Faith Factor:

Religion and the Political Process," *National Jewish Post & Opinion,* October 27, 2004; Tom Plate, "Rein in Your Own Radical Preachers, America," *South China Morning Post,* August 30, 2005.

3. CNN/*USA Today,* survey, conducted by the Gallup Organization, November 19–21, 2004, based on telephone interviews with a national sample of 1,015 adults. Question wording: "Do you think the church or organized religion currently has too much or too little political influence in America?"

4. Pew Research Center for the People & the Press, survey of religion, July 7–17, 2005, based on a national sample of 2,000 adults.

5. Josef Braml, "Religious Right in the United States" (Berlin, Germany: SWP, September 2004).

6. Many scholars distinguish between fundamentalist and evangelical Christians, categorizing the former as those who focus on doctrine and the literal, unerringness of the scripture and the latter as those who emphasize preaching the gospel at home and abroad and who focus on personal conversion experiences. Referring to these categories, it can be argued that while religiosity is rising in the United States, fundamentalism may be declining in a backlash against violent fundamentalism of any faith. These scholars also maintain that most of the Christian Right in the United States are evangelicals rather than fundamentalists. "More Religion, But Not the Old-Time Kind," *New York Times,* January 9, 2005.

7. In the National Election Pool, a cooperative venture by the Associated Press and the major U.S. television networks, voters were presented with a list of seven issues raised in the campaign and asked to choose the one that was most important to them: terrorism, Iraq, the economy and jobs, taxes, health care, the environment, and moral values. Two out of five voters chose "moral values." Moral values are clearly important to Americans, but their relative importance depends greatly on how the issues are posed. In a post-election survey by the Pew Research Center replicating the exit poll, a plurality of voters did choose moral values as most important to their presidential vote. (See www.people-press.org/reports/display.php3?ReportID=233.) But in a separate survey, when another group of voters were asked to name, in their own words, the most important factor in their vote, only half as many mentioned moral values; and equally important, those who did offered varying interpretations of the concept. Less than half said the term related to specific concerns over social issues, such as abortion and gay marriage. Others pointed to factors like the candidates' personal qualities or made general allusions to religion and values. Nonetheless, it is significant that Bush voters most frequently cited moral values while Kerry voters seldom did. The issue resonated with and benefited Bush far more than his opponent. But it was not the single most important reason for Bush's victory.

8. Personal communication, S. Scott Rohrer, author of *Hope's Promise: Religion and Acculturation in the Southern Backcountry* (Tuscaloosa: University of Alabama Press, 2005). Alexis de Tocqueville, *Democracy in America* (New York: Signet Books, 2001). Text originally published in 1835, vol. 1, and 1840, vol. 2.

9. Robert Fogel quoted in Nicholas Kristof, "God, Satan and the Media," *New York Times,* March 4, 2003.

10. Ronald Reagan, remarks to the Spirit of America Rally, Atlanta, Ga., January 26, 1984. Richard Land, president, Ethics and Religious Liberties Commission, Southern Baptist Convention, speaking at the Council on Foreign Relations, September 22, 2005.

11. Pew Research Center for the People & the Press, religion and public life survey, February 25–March 10, 2002, based on interviews with a national sample of 2,002 adults.

12. Arthur M. Schlesinger, Jr., "Forgetting Reinhold Niebuhr," *New York Times,* September 18, 2005.

13. "Therapy of the Masses," *The Economist,* November 6, 2003.

14. Dale Hurd, "Is Europe the New 'Dark Continent'?" Christian Broadcasting Network, www.cbn.com/CBNNews/News/040301a.asp. James Q. Wilson quoted in *What's God Got to Do with the American Experiment?: Essays on Religion and Politics* (Washington, D.C.: Brookings Institution Press, 2000).

15. George W. Bush, remarks by the President at the 2002 Graduation Exercise of the United States Military Academy, West Point, N.Y. , June 1, 2002.

16. Elizabeth Bryant, "Faith's Influence on U.S. Politics Alienates Secular Europe," *Washington Post,* November 6, 2004.

17. Peter Singer, *The President of Good and Evil* (New York: E. P. Dutton, 2004).

18. Daniel Webster, *The Writings and Speeches of Daniel Webster* (Boston: Little, Brown, 1903), p. 220.

19. *Catholic Digest,* survey, conducted by the Gallup Organization, November 1965, based on personal interviews with a national sample of 2,783 adults; President George W. Bush quoted in *Washington Times,* January 11, 2005; Noah Feldman, "A Church-State Solution," *New York Times Magazine,* July 3, 2005, p. 28.

20. World Values Survey, 1999–2000, see www.worldvaluessurvey.org.

21. Frank Bruni, "Faith Fades Where It Once Burned Strong," *New York Times,* October 13, 2003.

22. Religion & Ethics NewsWeekly, *U.S. News & World Report,* survey conducted by Greenberg Quinlan Rosner Research, March 16–April 4, 2004, based on telephone interviews with a national sample of 1,610 adults. The survey included oversamples of white evangelicals, African-Americans, and Hispanics. Results were weighted to be representative of the national adult population and are available from the Roper Center.

23. Eduardo Porter, "Values Gap: Where Playboy and 'Will and Grace' Reign," *New York Times,* November 21, 2004. Pippa Norris and Ronald Inglehart, *Sacred and Secular: Religion and Politics Worldwide* (New York: Cambridge University Press, 2004).

24. Religion & Ethics NewsWeekly, *U.S. News & World Report,* survey, March 16–April 4, 2004.

25. BBC, conducted by ICM, poll: "What the World Thinks of Religion," January 2004.

26. World Values Survey, 1999–2000. 1990 data include citizens of the former West Germany before unification.

27. Pew Global Attitudes Project, survey: "Views of a Changing World," June 3, 2003.

28. Ibid.

29. Gallup Organization, survey, January 3–5, 2005, based on telephone interviews with a national sample of 1,005 adults. NBC/*Wall Street Journal,* survey, May 12–16, 2005, based on telephone interviews with a national sample of 1,005 adults. Pew Research Center for the People & the Press, survey: "Abortion and Rights of Terror Suspects Top Court Issues," August 3, 2005.

30. Cherie Booth, book review: "Death Penalty: A Lawyer Sees the Light," *The Tablet,* July 2, 2004. Harold Hongju Koh, "Paying 'Decent Respect' to World Opinion on the Death Penalty," *U.C. Davis Law Review,* vol. 35, no. 5 (June 2002), p. 1086.

31. Pew Research Center, survey of religion, July 7–17, 2005.

32. *Time* magazine, poll: "The Faith Factor," June 2–4, 2004, based on telephone interviews with 1,280 American adults.

33. Pew Research Center, Survey of Foreign Policy, July 8–18, 2004, based on a national sample of 2,009.

34. President George W. Bush, "International Campaign against Terror Grows," speech at the Colonnade, Washington, D.C., September 25, 2001. The second quotation comes from remarks by President Bush to State Department employees on October 4, 2001. The third quote comes from Howard Fineman et al., "Bush and God," *Newsweek,* March 10, 2003.

35. Singer, *President of Good and Evil.*

36. Pew Research Center, survey, July 2005.

37. Tracy Wilkinson, "Arab World Sees the Conflict in Religious Terms," *Los Angeles Times,* March 18, 2003.

38. Braml, "Religious Right in the United States."

6. DOING BUSINESS, PRACTICING DEMOCRACY

For additional information on Pew Research Center survey data pertaining to chapter 6, see: http://pewglobal.org/aatw/chapter6/.

1. President George W. Bush speaking at a televised press conference, January 30, 2005, quoted in Robin Wright, "President Hails Election as a Success and a Signal," *Washington Post,* January 31, 2005.

2. Bruce Stokes, *The National Journal,* June 4, 2004.

3. In polls, these phrases were not defined. *U.S.-style democracy* likely refers to its literal features—a balance of power or system of checks and balances between the legislative, judicial, and executive branches; a presidential system of elections and

governance—as well as its social components, such as an emphasis on individualism and a thin social safety net. *U.S.-style business practices* include the free enterprise system, minimal government regulation, and low taxes, but respondents may also have had in mind excesses committed by U.S. companies, from illegal accounting practices at home (e.g., Enron), to disregard of environmental constraints abroad (e.g., Bhopal, India).

4. The assertion that Americans work harder comes from international studies showing that the number of hours Americans work per year are much higher than their European counterparts. See http://money.cnn.com/2003/10/06/pf/work_less/.

5. Seth Schiesel with John Tagliabue, "Shake-up at Vivendi," *New York Times,* July 2, 2002.

6. According to the International Institute for Democracy and Electoral Assistance.

7. Alexis de Tocqueville, *Democracy in America* (New York: Signet Books, 2001). Text originally published in 1835, vol. 1, and 1840, vol. 2. President Calvin Coolidge, speech to the American Society of Newspaper Editors, January 17, 1925.

8. World Values Survey, 1999–2000.

9. "Love of Leisure and Europe's Reasons," *International Herald Tribune,* July 29, 2004.

7. GLOBALIZATION AND AMERICANIZATION

For additional information on Pew Research Center survey data pertaining to chapter 7, see http://pewglobal.org/aatw/chapter7/.

1. Lynn Jeffress, "A World Struggle Is Under Way: An Interview with José Bové," *Z Magazine,* June 2001.

2. "Chirac Slams US Food Domination," BBC News, September 16, 1999. See http://news.bbc.co.uk/1/hi/world/europe/449715.stm.

3. Thomas Friedman, *The Lexus and the Olive Tree: Understanding Globalization* (New York: Anchor Books, 2000).

4. Jagdish Bhagwati, *In Defense of Globalization* (New York: Oxford University Press, 2004). For a complementary argument, see Anne-Marie Slaughter's *A New World Order* (Princeton, N.J.: Princeton University Press, 2004).

5. Ahmad Y. Majdoubeh, *Jordan Times,* November 28, 2003.

6. Joseph Nye, Jr., *Soft Power: The Means to Success in World Politics* (New York: Public Affairs Press, 2004).

7. Program on International Policy Attitudes (PIPA), University of Maryland, survey: "International Trade." See the "Americans & the World" Web site (http://www.americans-world.org/digest/global_issues/intertrade/poorcountries.cfm). Pew Global Attitudes Project, 2002 and 2005.

8. First surveyed by the Gallup Organization, March 28–April 2, 1953, based on personal interviews with a national sample of 1,602 adults.

9. *Wall Street Journal*/NBC News poll conducted by Hart and Teeter Research Companies, September 20–22, 2003, based on telephone interviews with a national sample of 1,004 adults. Results released September 26, 2003.

10. WIIT poll conducted by EPIC-MRA, October 7–11, 2001, surveyed 850 U.S. adults. Results released October 26, 2001.

11. German Marshall Fund, Transatlantic Trends Survey. See http://www.transatlantictrends.org.

12. Franz Fischler, quoted in Paul Blustein and Dan Morgan, "Showdown on Subsidies," *Washington Post*, May 2, 2002.

13. Alan Riding, "A Global Culture War Pits Protectionists against Free Traders," *New York Times*, February 5, 2005.

14. Personal interviews tieh EU officials by Bruce Stokes, January 2005.

15. "The Price of Prudence," *The Economist*, January 22, 2004.

16. David Vogel, "Ships Passing in the Night: GMOs and the Politics of Risk Regulation in Europe and the United States," European University Institute, Florence, Italy. Working Paper no. 2001/16.

8. ACTING TOGETHER—OR ALONE

For additional information on Pew Research Center survey data pertaining to chapter 8, see http://pewglobal.org/aatw/chapter8/.

1. David Usborne, "The U.S. vs. the U.N.," *The Independent*, August 26, 2005.

2. Francis Fukuyama, "The West May Be Cracking," *International Herald Tribune*, August 9, 2002.

3. Martin Kettle, "Why We Can Make a Difference," *Guardian*, May 15, 1998; Martin Woollacott, "Muddling Along Gives Way to Muddled Nationalism," *Guardian*, March 14, 1999.

4. Pete Domenici, quoted in Robert Kagan, "Kosovo and the Echoes of Isolationism," *New York Times*, March 24, 1999. James Baker, quoted in Barton Gellman, "Slaughter in Racak Changed Kosovo Policy," *Washington Post*, April 18, 1999.

5. Bill Clinton, *Remarks by the President on Foreign Policy*, Grand Hyatt Hotel, San Francisco, Calif., February 26, 1999.

6. Polls from the Gallup Organization, the Times Mirror Center for the People & the Press, and the Pew Research Center for the People & the Press.

7. William E. Borah, speech to the League of Nations, November 19, 1919.

8. Jeremy Atack, Peter Passell, and Susan Lee, *A New Economic View of American History: From Colonial Times to 1940* (New York: W. W. Norton and Company, 1979).

9. Selig Adler, *The Isolationist Impulse* (New York: Collier Books, 1961). Harry S. Truman, speech at the Democratic National Convention, Philadelphia, Penn., July 15, 1948.

10. Jean-Marie Colombani, *Le Monde*, September 12, 2001.

11. Gallup-International, poll, January 2003, based on polling in thirty-eight countries.

12. German Marshall Fund, Transatlantic Trends Survey, 2004. See question 2, www.transatlantictrends.org, BBC poll, January 2005. The countries included were Argentina, Australia, Brazil, Canada, Chile, France, Germany, Great Britain, Italy, India, Indonesia, Japan, Lebanon, Mexico, the Philippines, Poland, Russia, South Africa, South Korea, Spain, Turkey, and the United States.

13. Pew Global Attitudes Project, 2005. German Marshall Fund, Transatlantic Trends Survey, 2004. See question 4b: www.transatlantictrends.org. Jacques Chirac, speech at IFRI conference, Paris, France, November 4, 1999.

14. German Marshall Fund, Transatlantic Trends Survey, 2004. See question 26f. Pew Research Center data have shown similar results in surveys conducted from 2002 through 2005.

15. Program on International Policy Attitudes, University of Maryland, survey: "Evaluating the World Powers," April 6, 2005. For full results, see http://www .pipa.org/OnlineReports/europe/040605/Qnnaire04_06_05.pdf.

16. Eurobarometer Survey No. 217, "Attitudes of Europeans toward Environment," October 27–November 29, 2004. Pew Research Center for the People & the Press, survey: "America's New Internationalist Point of View," October 24, 2001.

17. Pew Research Center for the People & the Press and the Chicago Council on Foreign Relations, survey conducted by Princeton Survey Research Associates International, July 8–18, 2004, based on telephone interviews with a national sample of 2,009 adults. *Time*/CNN, survey conducted by Harris Interactive, March 21–22, 2001, based on telephone interviews with a national sample of 1,025 adults. Gallup Organization, survey, March 7–10, 2005, based on telephone interviews with a national sample of 1,004 adults.

18. German Marshall Fund, Transatlantic Trends Survey, May 2005. See question 7a.

19. "Justice in Darfur," *The Economist*, February 5, 2005.

20. Chicago Council on Foreign Affairs, survey conducted by PIPA/Knowledge Networks, "Americans on the Darfur Crisis and the International Criminal Court," February 18–25, 2005. See http://www.pipa.org/onlinereports/africa/darfurICC_ mar05_quaire.pdf. Pew Global Attitudes Project, six-country survey, November 4–10, 2002.

21. Gallup Organization and the Pew Research Center for the People & the Press surveys. Trend found in Pew Research Center, "Beyond Red vs. Blue," May 10, 2005. Pew Research Center, survey: "Public Opinion of the U.N.: Strong Support, Strong Criticism," June 25, 1995. Gallup Organization, survey, June 1976, based on personal interviews with a national sample of 1,071 adults. Princeton Survey Research Associates, survey, October 21–24, 1993, based on telephone interviews with a national sample of 1,200 adults.

22. Gallup Organization, survey, October 29–November 2, 1971, based on

personal interviews with a national sample of 1,558 adults. United Nations Association, survey conducted by Roper Organization, March 11–18, 1989, based on personal interviews with a national sample of 1,978 adults.

23. German Marshall Fund, Transatlantic Trends Survey, May 2005. See question 9. BBC poll, January 2005, conducted by GlobeScan, November 15, 2004–January 5, 2005, and conducted in twenty-two countries. Poll released January 20, 2005.

24. German Marshall Fund, Transatlantic Trends Survey, 2003.

25. Pew Global Attitudes Project, survey: "What the World Thinks in 2002," December 4, 2002.

26. Times Mirror Center for the People & the Press, survey: "Mixed Message about Press Freedom on Both Sides of the Atlantic: Eight Nation People & The Press Survey," March 16, 1994.

27. Pew Research Center for the People & the Press, survey: "America's New Internationalist Point of View," October 24, 2001. PIPA/Knowledge Networks, survey: "Public Perceptions of the Foreign Policy Positions of the Presidential Candidates," September 29, 2004. PIPA/Knowledge Networks, survey: "The Separate Realities of Bush and Kerry Supporters," October 21, 2004.

28. Program on International Policy Attitudes, University of Maryland, survey conducted by Knowledge Networks, September 8–12, 2004, based on interviews with a national sample of 959 adults. The margin of error was plus or minus 3.2–4.0 percent, depending on whether the question was administered to two-thirds or the entire sample. The poll was fielded using a randomly selected nationwide panel drawn from the entire adult population; respondents are subsequently provided Internet access. For more information about this methodology, see www.knowledgenetworks.com/ganp. Conducted by CBS News/New York Times, January 14–18, 2005, based on telephone interviews with a national sample of 1,118 adults.

29. PIPA/Knowledge Networks, survey: "The Federal Budget: The Public's Priorities," March 7, 2005. Program on International Policy Attitudes, University of Maryland, April 19–23, 1995, based on telephone interviews with a national sample of 1,204 adults.

30. Times Mirror Center for the People & the Press, survey conducted by Princeton Survey Research Associates, August 19–25, 1990, based on telephone interviews with a national sample of 1,000 adults.

31. Times Mirror Center, survey: "The People, the Press & Politics: Public Opinion about Economic Issues," conducted by the Gallup Organization, January 27–February 5, 1989, based on face-to-face interviews with 2,048 adults. Results released March 1989. Pew Research Center for the People & the Press, survey: "Foreign Policy Attitudes Now Driven by 9/11 and Iraq," August 18, 2004.

32. Pew Research Center, survey: "Foreign Policy Attitudes Now Driven by 9/11 and Iraq," August 18, 2004.

33. Ibid.

9. USE OF FORCE

For additional information on Pew Research Center survey data pertaining to chapter 9, see http://pewglobal.org/aatw/chapter 9/.

1. Robert Kagan, "America's Crisis of Legitimacy," *Foreign Affairs,* March–April 2004.

2. German Marshall Fund, Transatlantic Trends Survey, 2005. See www .transatlantictrends.org.

3. Robert Kagan, *Of Paradise and Power: America and Europe in the New World Order* (New York: Random House, 2003), p. 119.

4. Pew Global Attitudes Project, survey: "Views of a Changing World," June 3, 2003.

5. German Marshall Fund, Transatlantic Trends Survey, 2005.

6. Pew Global Attitudes Project, survey: "Views of a Changing World," June 3, 2003.

7. *Newsweek,* survey conducted in five countries by Gallup International, January 17–19, 1983.

8. Times Mirror Center for the People & the Press, survey: "The Pulse of Europe: A Survey of Political and Social Values and Attitudes," September 16, 1991. According to the German Marshall Fund, 54 percent of Americans versus 29 percent of Europeans thought military strength was the best insurance against war.

9. Andrew Kohut and Robert C. Toth, "Arms and the People," *Foreign Affairs,* November–December 1994.

10. Andrew Kohut, "Post–Cold War Attitudes toward the Use of Force," speech prepared for the George H. W. Bush School of Government and Public Service Dedication Conference, September 9, 1997. Pew Research Center for the People & the Press, survey: "America's New Internationalist Point of View," October 24, 2001. Pew Research Center for the People & the Press, survey: "Americans Favor Force in Iraq, Somalia, Sudan and . . . ," January 22, 2002. Pew Research Center for the People & the Press, Iraq War tracking surveys, March–April 2003.

11. Gallup International, Europe Poll, January 2005.

12. German Marshall Fund, Transatlantic Trends Survey, 2005.

13. German Marshall Fund, Transatlantic Trends Survey, 2003.

14. Andrew Kohut and Robert C. Toth, "The People, the Press, and the Use of Force," in Aspen Strategy Group, *The United States and the Use of Force* (The Aspen Institute: Queenstown, Md., 1995), pp. 133–69.

15. Conversation with Andrew Kohut, March 19, 2005.

16. Ibid., March 23, 2005.

10. TWO AMERICAS, ONE AMERICAN

For additional information on Pew Research Center survey data pertaining to chapter 10, see: http://pewglobal.org/aatw/chapter 10/.

1. Timothy Garton Ash, *Free World: America, Europe, and the Surprising Future of the West* (New York: Random House, 2004), p. 77.

2. Ronald Asmus, Philip P. Everts, and Pierangelo Isernia, "Across the Atlantic and the Political Aisle: The Double Divide in U.S.-European Relations," Transatlantic Trends Report (German Marshall Fund, 2004).

3. Alan Wolfe, *One Nation, After All: What Americans Really Think about God, Country, Family, Racism, Welfare, Immigration, Homosexuality, Work, the Right, the Left, and Each Other* (New York: Penguin Books, 1999).

4. Alexis de Tocqueville, *Democracy in America* (New York: Signet Books, 2001). Text originally published in 1835, vol. 1 and 1840, vol. 2. World Values Surveys, 1995–2000.

5. Pew Research Center for the People & the Press, "Religious Beliefs Underpin Opposition to Homosexuality," November 18, 2003. Pew Global Attitudes Project, survey: "Views of a Changing World," June 3, 2003.

6. Pew Research Center for the People & the Press, political typology: "Beyond Red vs. Blue," May 10, 2005. Pew Global Attitudes Project, survey, "Views of a Changing World," June 3, 2003.

7. Pew Research Center, "Beyond Red vs. Blue," May 10, 2005.

8. Pew Research Center Forum on Religion & Public Life, survey: "Public Makes Distinctions on Genetic Research," April 9, 2002. European data come from "What the World Thinks in 2002," December 4, 2002.

9. Princeton Survey Research Associates, survey: "Americans Discuss Social Security," 1997; CBS/*New York Times*, poll, February 24–28, 2005, based on telephone interviews with a national sample of 1,111 adults.

10. Asmus, Everts, and Isernia, "Across the Atlantic and the Political Aisle."

11. Pew Global Attitudes Project, survey: "A Year after Iraq War: Mistrust of America in Europe Ever Higher, Muslim Anger Persists," March 16, 2004.

12. Pew Global Attitudes Project, survey of six nations, November 2–10, 2002.

13. Pew Research Center for the People & the Press, survey: "Foreign Policy Attitudes Now Driven by 9/11 and Iraq: Eroding Respect for America Seen as Major Problem," August 18, 2004.

14. Pew Global Attitudes Project, survey: "A Year after Iraq War."

ACKNOWLEDGMENTS

IN A WORK of this magnitude—assessing Americans' values and attitudes toward a range of issues from individualism to religion to the use of force over decades of U.S. history and then comparing and contrasting those views to the attitudes toward America and Americans held by tens of thousands of people from all over the world— our debts, both intellectual and practical, are profound and ultimately unpayable. But in the end, *America Against the World* owes the most to the Pew Global Attitudes Project, which provided the data and intellectual resources to write this book.

Robert Toth and Jodie Allen, former and current editors, respectively, at the Pew Research Center provided substantial editorial support throughout the project. Their substantive contributions, their years of experience, and their editing sharpened our analysis and leavened our prose.

Nicole Speulda, project director of the Pew Global Attitudes Project, worked tirelessly, researching survey results, annotating findings, digging out obscure references. Her intimate understanding of the Global Attitudes data made her the go-to person when a fact had to be checked or a graphic designed. She kept the whole project on track. This book would have been impossible without her. Pew's Kaitlyn DeLuca ably assisted at every turn.

Elizabeth Mueller Gross, Pew's director of administration, was the first to urge us to write this book. She shepherded the process and provided key editorial advice in structuring the final manuscript.

The Pew Research Center gang—Paul Taylor, Michael Dimock, Scott Keeter, Carroll Doherty, Nilanthi Samaranayake, Peyton Craighill, Cary Funk, and Courtney Kennedy—provided ideas, inspiration, and moral and logistical support. Matthew Kohut and Michael Robinson, friends of the Pew Research Center, gave us helpful advice over the course of writing the book.

Former U.S. secretary of state Madeleine K. Albright, who co-chairs the Pew Global Attitudes Project, encouraged this project from the beginning. Her insights, based on her extensive experience as an academic and a high-ranking government official, were invaluable, especially in understanding how people's reaction to American exceptionalism affects America's place in the world.

Mary McIntosh, president of Princeton Survey Research Associates International, was involved from the beginning with the design of the Global Attitudes survey and the analysis of its results. She and her team, working under impossible deadlines, orchestrated the polling in fifty countries around the world and the Palestinian Authority.

The bulk of the data used in this book comes from the Pew Global Attitudes Project's unprecedented multicountry, multiyear set of public opinion surveys. Our analysis also benefited immeasurably from other international polling done by the Gallup Organization, the World Values Survey at the University of Michigan, the German Marshall Fund of the United States, and the Program on International Policy Attitudes at the University of Maryland, among others.

We owe much to the Pew Charitable Trusts that have long supported the work of the Pew Research Center, including generously funding the Pew Global Attitudes Project. Rebecca Rimel, president and CEO of the Pew Charitable Trusts, and Donald Kimelman, director of information initiatives for the Trusts, deserve particular thanks for originally encouraging and then backing over a six-year period a global survey project of this magnitude.

We are also indebted to Robert F. Erburu, former CEO of Times Mirror and Donald S. Kellermann, founding director of the Times Mirror Center for the People & the Press. They initiated the first round of multinational polling in 1989 that served as a prototype for the Pew Global Attitudes Project.

Paul Golob and Robin Dennis of Times Books gave us good counsel at the beginning of the project and then worked tirelessly with us to shape the final product and to highlight the book's most arresting conclusions.

The editors of the *National Journal* were supportive of this project from the beginning. Their flexibility with regard to Bruce Stokes's schedule and their support for public policy research and writing are a model of quality journalism.

Our wives, Diane Colasanto and Wendy Sherman, encouraged and supported our efforts from the beginning. Their professional expertise, in survey methodology and foreign affairs, respectively, has been of invaluable help in designing the Pew Global Attitudes Project and in conceptualizing this book. They are both real pros and loving spouses.

Finally, we would like to thank those 90,000 people around the world who took time out of their busy lives to talk about their hopes and fears, what they value and what they disparage, their judgments about their own lives and the world around them, and how they view America, Americans, and the American way of life. Without them, neither *America Against the World* nor the Pew Global Attitudes Project could have been possible. We will be forever in their debt.

INDEX

ABOUT THE AUTHORS

ANDREW KOHUT is one of America's foremost pollsters and commentators on how public opinion is shaping the national and international agendas. He is currently the director of the Pew Research Center for the People & the Press (formerly the Times Mirror Center for the People & the Press) in Washington, D.C. Kohut was president of the Gallup Organization from 1979 to 1989, and founded Princeton Survey Research Associates, an attitude and opinion research firm specializing in media, politics, and public policy studies, in 1989. He served as founding director of surveys for the Times Mirror Center from 1990 through 1992 and was named its director in 1993. He has also served as president of the American Association of Public Opinion Research and the National Council on Public Polls.

Kohut has written widely about public opinion for leading newspapers, magazines, and scholarly journals, and has coauthored three reports, *The Diminishing Divide; The People, the Press and Politics;* and *Estranged Friends? The Transatlantic Consequences of Societal Change.* He lives in Washington, D.C.

BRUCE STOKES is the international economics columnist for the public policy magazine *National Journal,* a consultant to the Pew Global Attitudes Project, and a journalism fellow at the German Marshall Fund. A former senior fellow at the Council on Foreign Relations, Stokes is the coauthor of three Council on Foreign Relations reports, *Democratizing U.S. Trade Policy; A New Beginning: Recasting the U.S.-Japan Economic Relationship;* and *The Tests of War and the Strains of Peace.* He edited the books *Partners or Competitors, Future Visions for U.S. Trade Policy, Trade Strategies for a New Era,* and *Open for Business.* He authored the book *Helping Ourselves.* Stokes was also a member of President Bill Clinton's Commission on United States–Pacific Trade and Investment Policy, and he wrote the commission's final report, *Building American Prosperity in the 21st Century.* He lives in Maryland.